Third-Millennium Legal and Administrative Texts in the Iraq Museum, Baghdad

Mesopotamian Civilizations

1. *The Lamentation over the Destruction of Sumer and Ur*
   Piotr Michalowski

2. *Schlaf, Kindchen, schlaf! Mesopotamische Baby-Beschwörungen und -Rituale*
   Walter Farber

3. *Adoption in Old Babylonian Nippur and the Archive of Mannum-mešu-liṣṣur*
   Elizabeth C. Stone and David I. Owen

4. *Third-Millennium Legal and Administrative Texts in the Iraq Museum, Baghdad*
   Piotr Steinkeller and J. N. Postgate

Third-Millennium Legal and Administrative Texts in the Iraq Museum, Baghdad

Piotr Steinkeller

with Hand Copies by J. N. Postgate

Eisenbrauns
Winona Lake, Indiana
1992

Library of Congress Cataloging-in-Publication Data

Third-millennium legal and administrative texts in the Iraq Museum, Baghdad / Piotr Steinkeller, with hand copies by J. N. Postgate.
p. cm. — (Mesopotamian civilizations ; 4)
Texts transliteration and translation into English from Sumerian and Akkadian.
Includes indexes.
ISBN 0-931464-60-9
1. Law, Assyro-Babylonian—Sources. 2. Cuneiform inscriptions, Sumerian. 3. Cuneiform inscriptions, Akkadian. I. Steinkeller, Piotr. II. Postgate, J. N. III. Matḥaf al-ʿIrāqī. IV. Series.
KL708.T48 1992
499′.95—dc20 91-27938

In Memory of
Ignace J. Gelb

Contents

Acknowledgments

We wish to express our heartfelt gratitude to Dr. Muayad Saeed, President of the State Organization of Antiquities and Heritage, and to Dr. Behija Khalil, Director of the Iraq Museum, for placing the texts at our disposal and for making our work at the Iraq Museum both pleasant and profitable.

We are also deeply indebted to Jeremy A. Black for his efforts in locating and collating several tablets, and for the permission to include his hand copies of nos. 38, 42, and 68 in this volume.

Postgate, Miguel Civil, Dietz O. Edzard, and Johannes Renger were kind enough to read various parts of the preliminary version of the manuscript and offered many valuable suggestions. M. A. Powell read the final version, contributing some very important improvements and ideas. It goes without saying that responsibility for the final product rests with Steinkeller alone.

We thank William W. Hallo, Curator of the Yale Babylonian Collection, for his permission to cite a number of unpublished tablets in his care.

Our special thanks go to Jerrold S. Cooper for agreeing to publish this book in the Mesopotamian Civilizations series.

Most of all, however, we are indebted to the late Ignace J. Gelb, who made available to us all his previous work and enthusiastically supported this project until his untimely death. Clearly, it is he who made this volume possible, and in many respects this is his own book. It is in the recognition of that contribution, and in the reflection of our profound gratitude, that we affectionately dedicate these pages to his memory.

For his part, Steinkeller offers his sincere thanks to the American Council of Learned Societies for a travel grant which enabled him to collate the tablets in August 1984; to Robert A. DiVito for his expert editorial assistance; and to David P. Aiken for the superb job he has done in seeing this volume to print.

Abbreviations

Abbreviations according to the *Assyrian Dictionary of the Oriental Institute of the University of Chicago* (Chicago, 1956–), with the following exceptions and additions.

Alster, *Death*
B. Alster (ed.), *Death in Mesopotamia* (CRRA 26; Mesopotamia 8; Copenhagen, 1980)

Alster, *Instructions*
B. Alster, *The Instructions of Suruppak: A Sumerian Proverb Collection* (Mesopotamia 2; Copenhagen, 1974)

ARET Archivi reali di Ebla, Testi (Rome)

ASJ *Acta Sumerologica* (Japan)

BAL R. Borger, *Babylonisch-assyrische Lesestücke*, vol. 2 (AnOr 54; Rome, 1963)

Bridges, *Mesag Archive*
S. J. Bridges, *The Mesag Archive: A Study of Sargonic Society and Economy* (Ph.D. diss., Yale University, 1981)

BSA *Bulletin on Sumerian Agriculture*

Buchanan, *Ashmolean*
B. Buchanan, *Catalogue of Ancient Near Eastern Seals in the Ashmolean Museum*, vol. 1: *Cylinder Seals* (Oxford, 1966)

Cagni, *Bilinguismo*
L. Cagni (ed.), *Il Bilinguismo a Ebla* (Istituto Universitario Orientale, Dipartimento di Studi Asiatici, Series Minor 22; Naples, 1984)

Cagni, *Ebla 1975–1985*
L. Cagni (ed.), *Ebla 1975–1985: Dieci Anni di Studi Linguistici e Filologici* (Istituto Universitario Orientale, Dipartimento di Studi Asiatici, Series Minor 27; Naples, 1987)

Cagni, *Lingua*
L. Cagni (ed.), *La Lingua di Ebla* (Istituto Universitario Orientale, Seminario di Studi Asiatici, Series Minor 14; Naples, 1981)

Cooper, *Agade*
J. S. Cooper, *The Curse of Agade* (Baltimore, 1983)

Diakonoff, *Šumer*
I. M. Diakonoff, *Obščestvenny i gosudarstvenny stroy Drevnego Dvurečya: Šumer* (Moscow, 1959)

ECTJ A. Westenholz, *Early Cuneiform Texts in Jena* (Det Kongelige Danske Videnskabernes Selskab, Historisk-Filosofiske Skrifter 7/3; Copenhagen, 1975)

ELTS I. J. Gelb, P. Steinkeller, and R. M. Whiting, *Earliest Land Tenure Systems in the Near East: Ancient Kudurrus* (OIP 104; Chicago, 1991)

FAOS Freiburger altorientalische Studien (Stuttgart)

Foster, *Institutional Land*
B. R. Foster, *Administration and Use of Institutional Land in Sargonic Sumer* (Mesopotamia 9; Copenhagen, 1982)

gsg gur-sag-gál

JANES Journal of the Ancient Near Eastern Society of Columbia University

Klein, *Hymns*
J. Klein, *Three Šulgi Hymns: Sumerian Royal Hymns Glorifying King Šulgi of Ur* (Ramat-Gan, 1981)

Kraus, *Sumerer und Akkader*
F. R. Kraus, *Sumerer und Akkader: Ein Problem der altmesopotamischen Geschichte* (Mededelingen der Koninklijke Nederlandse Akademie van Wetenschappen, Afd. Letterkunde 33/8; Amsterdam, 1970)

Kraus, *Verfügungen*
F. R. Kraus, *Königliche Verfügungen in altbabylonischer Zeit* (Studia et Documenta 11; Leiden, 1984)

Krebernik, *Beschwörungen*
M. Krebernik, *Die Beschwörungen aus Fara und Ebla: Untersuchungen zur ältesten keilschriftlichen Beschwörungsliteratur* (Texte und Studien zur Orientalistik 2; Hildesheim, 1984)

L. siglum for tablets excavated at Lagaš, in the collections of the Archaeological Museum of Istanbul

LAK A. Deimel, *Liste der archaischen Keilschriftzeichen* (= *Die Inschriften von Fara*, vol. 1; WVDOG 40; Leipzig, 1922)

Lambert Tablet
M. Lambert, "Grand document juridique de Nippur du temps de Ur-zag-è, roi d'Uruk," *RA* 73 (1979) 1–22

MEE Materiali Epigrafici di Ebla (Naples)

Michalowski, *Lamentation*
P. Michalowski, *The Lamentation over the Destruction of Sumer and Ur* (Mesopotamian Civilizations 1; Winona Lake, Ind., 1989)

NATN D. I. Owen, *Neo-Sumerian Archival Texts Primarily from Nippur in the University Museum, the Oriental Institute, and the Iraq Museum* (Winona Lake, Ind., 1982)

OA *Oriens Antiquus*

Pomponio, *Prosopografia*
F. Pomponio, *La prosopografia dei testi presargonici di Fara* (Studi semitici, n.s. 3; Rome, 1987)

PSD Å. W. Sjöberg et al., *The Sumerian Dictionary of the University Museum of the University of Pennsylvania* (Philadelphia, 1984–)

Rasheed, *Himrin*
F. Rasheed, *The Ancient Inscriptions in Himrin Area* (Himrin 4; Baghdad, 1981)

RÉC F. Thureau-Dangin, *Recherches sur l'origine de l'écriture cuneiforme* (Paris, 1898)

Reiner AV
Language, Literature, and History: Philological and Historical Studies Presented to Erica Reiner (ed. F. Rochberg-Halton; AOS 67; New Haven, 1987)

RGTC Répertoire géographique des textes cunéiformes (Wiesbaden)

Rosengarten, *Répertoire*
Y. Rosengarten, *Répertoire commenté des signes présargoniques sumériens de Lagaš* (Paris, 1967)

SANE Sources from the Ancient Near East (Malibu, Calif.)

SE Sillabario di Ebla. Pp. 196–200 in G. Pettinato, *Testi lessicali monolingui della biblioteca L. 2769* (MEE 3; Naples, 1981)

SEb *Studi Eblaiti*

SEL *Studi epigrafici e linguistici*

SF A. Deimel, *Schultexte aus Fara* (= *Die Inschriften von Fara*, vol. 2; WVDOG 43; Leipzig, 1923)

Sigrist, *Syracuse*
M. Sigrist, *Textes économiques néo-sumériens de l'Université de Syracuse* (Études assyriologiques, Mémoire 29; Paris, 1983)

Snell, *Ledgers*
D. C. Snell, *Ledgers and Prices: Early Mesopotamian Merchant Accounts* (Yale Near Eastern Researches 8; New Haven, 1982)

SRU D. O. Edzard, *Sumerische Rechtsurkunden des III. Jahrtausends aus der Zeit vor der III. Dynastie von Ur* (ABAW, Philosophisch-historische Klasse, n.F. 67; Munich, 1968)

Steinkeller, *Sale Documents*
P. Steinkeller, *Sale Documents of the Ur III Period* (FAOS 17; Stuttgart, 1989)

STTI V. Donbaz and B. R. Foster, *Sargonic Texts from Telloh in the Istanbul Archaeological Museums* (Occasional Publications of the Babylonian Fund 5, and American Research Institute in Turkey, Monographs 2; Philadelphia, 1982)

SVS G. Pettinato and H. Waetzoldt, *Studi per il vocabolario sumerico*, vol. 1: G. Reisner, *Tempelurkunden aus Telloh* (Rome, 1985)

Thomsen, *Sumerian*
M.-L. Thomsen, *The Sumerian Language: An Introduction to Its History and Grammatical Structure* (Mesopotamia 10; Copenhagen, 1984)

USP B. R. Foster, *Umma in the Sargonic Period* (Memoirs of the Connecticut Academy of Arts and Sciences 20; Hamden, Conn., 1982)

VE Vocabolario di Ebla. Pp. 197–381 in G. Pettinato, *Testi lessicali bilingui della biblioteca L. 2769* (MEE 4; Naples, 1982)

Westenholz, *OSP*
A. Westenholz, *Old Sumerian and Old Akkadian Texts in Philadelphia Chiefly from Nippur*, vol. 1 (BiMes 1; Malibu, Calif., 1975); vol. 2 (The Carsten Niebuhr Institute Publications 3; Copenhagen, 1987)

WF A. Deimel, *Wirtschaftstexte aus Fara* (= *Die Inschriften von Fara*, vol. 3; WVDOG 45; Leipzig, 1924)

Plates

Plate	*Text*	*IM*
1	1	14182
2	2	14073
3	3	10629
4–5	4	11053/156
6	7	10598
	8	11053/61
7	9	43418
8	10	43693
	11	43749
	12	44013
9	13	13369
	14	13372
	15	13381
10	16	13709
	17	13711
	18	13383
	19	13384
	20	13710
11	21	13377
	22	5592/4a
	23	5592/4b
12	24	5592/7
	25	5592/16
13	26	5592/9
14	27	5592/ . . .
15	28	5592/8
16	29	5592/17
	30	5592/11
17	31	5592/6
	33	11053/118
18	35	10630
	36	11053/25
19	37	11053/44
	38	11053/106

Plate	*Text*	*IM*
20	40	11053/21
	41	11053/333
21	42	11053/337
	43	11053/41
22	44	11053/23
	45	10628
23	46	10599
	47	26175
	48	43612
24	49	43613
	50	2886/D
	51	11053/277
25	52	10604
	53	10613
	54	23457/21
	55	23459
26	56	30350
	57	43431
27	58	43451
	59	43741
	60	43759
28	61	43453
	63	43702
29	64	43706
	65	44026
	66	43726
30	67	43765
	68	44018
	69	44019
31	70	44021
	71	44025
	72	43381
32	73	43488
	74	43490

Introduction

History of the Project

This volume presents the administrative and legal texts in the collection of the Iraq Museum, Baghdad, which date to the Fara, Pre-Sargonic, and Sargonic periods, and which stem from illicit excavations. The seventy-four texts offered here represent virtually all such material identified at present in that institution. Of this group, sixty-eight texts are published for the first time.

The overwhelming majority of these tablets were transliterated in the summer of 1947 by Ignace J. Gelb, with the permission of Dr. Naji al-Asil, Director-General of Antiquities. The tablets written in Old Akkadian were subsequently cited (under the siglum "Iraq Mus.") by Gelb in his *Old Akkadian Writing and Grammar* and *Glossary of Old Akkadian*,[1] in anticipation of the planned publication of the whole group in one of the Materials for the Assyrian Dictionary volumes.

In the early 1970s Gelb made available to Benjamin R. Foster his transliterations of the Iraq Museum "mu-iti" texts. Some of these documents were subsequently cited by Foster in his *Umma in the Sargonic Period*.[2]

In 1975 J. N. Postgate, at that time Director of the British Archaeological Expedition to Iraq, obtained Gelb's permission to copy the tablets for use in Gelb's eventual edition. The sixty-five copies from his hand in this volume were prepared over the following two years.

Unable to proceed with the publication of the texts, due to various prior commitments, in 1983 Gelb generously ceded the publication rights to Postgate and Piotr Steinkeller, also putting his transliterations at their disposal. At that time it was decided that Postgate and Steinkeller would publish the tablets jointly: Postgate would contribute the copies, and Steinkeller, the transliterations, translations, commentaries, and indexes.

During the spring of 1984 Steinkeller prepared new transliterations of the tablets, on the basis of Gelb's original transliterations and Postgate's copies. In August of the same year he spent a week in the Iraq Museum collating the tablets. Thanks to the enthusiastic cooperation of Dr. Behija Khalil and her staff, he was able to collate virtually all of the tablets copied by Postgate.

[1] I. J. Gelb, *Old Akkadian Writing and Grammar* (MAD 2; Chicago, 1952; 2d ed. in 1961); idem, *Glossary of Old Akkadian* (MAD 3; Chicago, 1957).

[2] B. R. Foster, *Umma in the Sargonic Period* (Memoirs of the Connecticut Academy of Arts and Sciences 20; Hamden, Connecticut, 1982).

During the first half of 1985 Steinkeller wrote the translations and commentaries. He and Postgate then met in the fall to discuss and to incorporate Steinkeller's collations.

In 1986 Jeremy A. Black, then Director of the British Archaeological Expedition to Iraq, succeeded in collating several of the tablets Steinkeller had failed to locate in 1984. In addition, he located and subsequently copied three tablets (nos. 38, 42, and 68) that had originally been transliterated by Gelb, but could not be found by Postgate.

Text 39 was on display in the Museum, and thus could not be copied. It is published here in Gelb's transliteration, which has been checked against the original (fully visible in the display case) by Black.

In spite of repeated searches, two of the tablets (nos. 32 and 34) studied by Gelb could not be found. For both of them, however, Gelb's transliterations are available.

The only tablet studied by Gelb that is not published here is IM 43433. This tablet is on display in the Museum and could neither be copied nor transliterated. Gelb identifies it in his notes as "Pre-Sargonic, Umma, 4 cols, [dealing with] še." He also notes the occurrences, in cols. i and iii respectively, of the personal names Puzur$_4$-^{d}Aš$_7$-gi$_4$ and Ur-dun IM^{ki}-kam.

Six of the tablets treated in this volume (nos. 2, 5, 6, 10, 61, and 62) were previously published by J. van Dijk in TIM 9.[3] Three of them (nos. 2, 10, and 61) were recopied by Postgate.

The Texts

The seventy-four texts comprising this volume are divided chronologically into (1) Fara, (2) Pre-Sargonic, and (3) Sargonic periods. Within these chronological groups, the texts are further subdivided according to the place of origin. In the case of the Sargonic Umma material, a still further subdivision into earlier and later texts has been made.

Most of the texts date to the Sargonic period. Of these, the largest number (twenty) stem from Umma (nos. 13–32). Second in number (thirteen) are the tablets associated with the official Mesag (nos. 33–45); though apparently discovered at Umma, these documents seem to have originated in the town of Sagub. Smaller groups come from Mukdan (three; nos. 47–49), the Diyala Region (two; nos. 50–51), and Isin (one; no. 46). The provenience of twenty-three Sargonic tablets (nos. 52–74) is either unknown or uncertain.

There are eleven Pre-Sargonic tablets in this collection. Three of them come from Isin (nos. 4–6), one from Lagaš (no. 2), and one from Umma (no. 3). The origin of six tablets (nos. 7–12) cannot be determined.

The Fara material is represented by only one tablet (no. 1).

The language of the overwhelming majority of the texts is Sumerian. Of the seventy-four tablets studied here only eight (nos. 47–51, 72–74) are written in Akkadian. In addition, it is possible that the "Sagub" tablets (nos. 33–45),

[3] J. van Dijk, *Cuneiform Texts: Texts of Varying Content* (TIM 9; Leiden, 1976).

which are written in a curious mixture of Sumerian and Akkadian, were actually read in Akkadian.

Fara Texts (no. 1)

The only Fara-type text in the present collection is no. 1, a record of the purchase of a house. At present the number of published Fara sale documents stands at thirty-seven (twenty-four field/orchard sales and thirteen house sales). Of these, twenty-one were edited and discussed extensively by D. O. Edzard.[4] Eight additional Fara sale documents were subsequently treated by J. Krecher, in an article designed to supplement and to update Edzard's book.[5] Since the appearance of Krecher's study eight other sale documents have become available.[6]

To be added to this list is our no. 1, plus two other unpublished texts: A 33676 (house sale) and YBC 12305 (object of sale not preserved). All of the Fara sale documents cited here, including the unpublished ones, are tabulated and discussed in I. J. Gelb, P. Steinkeller, and R. M. Whiting, *Earliest Land Tenure Systems in the Near East: Ancient Kudurrus*.[7] Copies of the two unpublished tablets will be published by Steinkeller elsewhere.

Regarding their form and content, the Fara-type sale documents constitute a remarkably homogeneous group of texts. As shown by numerous prosopographic links between individual tablets and the mention of the same bala officials throughout the whole corpus, these texts undoubtedly come from the same place and date roughly to the same period.[8] Since at least seven of them were definitely excavated at Šuruppak, in private houses securely dated to the ED IIIa period,[9] it follows that the other tablets stem from Šuruppak too. The only uncertainty here pertains to the origin of one tablet, reportedly excavated at Uruk, together with literary texts of an OB date.[10] However, given the

[4] Edzard, *SRU*, nos. 1-13, 22–29.

[5] J. Krecher, "Neue sumerische Rechtsurkunden des 3. Jahrtausends," *ZA* 63 (1974) 194–212 (nos. 1-4, 4a, 5), 224–31 (nos. 11–12).

[6] A. Westenholz, *Or.* 44 (1975) 436 no. 1; G. Farber and W. Farber, *WO* 8 (1976) 180; J.-P. Grégoire, MVN 10 82–86; L. Milano, *SEL* 3 (1986) 11-12. A photograph of the obverse of MVN 10 85 had previously been published in an auction announcement in *L'Oeil* 221–22 (Déc. 1973–74) 78. When the photograph was taken, a small fragment recording the beginning of col. iii was still attached (upside down) to the tablet. This fragment must have been subsequently removed and discarded, since it does not appear on Grégoire's copy. Based on the original print of the photograph, kindly supplied to me by J. Vinchon, whose firm had handled the tablet, the now missing beginning of col. iii can be read as follows: (1) [8 ⸢PAB⸣ ḪI×DIŠ], (2) 8 PAB [LAGAB×ḪA], (3) 3 ì si[la_3], (4) [. . .] ⸢x⸣ [. . .].

[7] I. J. Gelb, P. Steinkeller, and R. M. Whiting, *Earliest Land Tenure Systems in the Near East: Ancient Kudurrus* (OIP 104; Chicago, 1991).

[8] The only exception here appears to be the text published by L. Matouš in *ArOr* 39 (1971) 14 (= Krecher, *ZA* 63 [1974] 212–13, no. 5), which, because of various textual peculiarities, may actually be slightly younger than the other Fara sale documents. Cf. Krecher, ibid., 213–14.

[9] See H. P. Martin, in *Le temple et le culte* (CRRA 20; Leiden, 1975) 173–82.

[10] A. Falkenstein, UVB 10, p. 19 and pl. 26b (W 17258); Krecher, *ZA* 63 (1974) 209–12, no. 4a.

context of its discovery, this tablet evidently represents a collector's item, whose ultimate origin, we have every reason to believe, was Šuruppak.[11]

Legal aspects of the Fara sale documents are treated in detail by Edzard and Krecher.[12] Among the newly published texts, of special interest for the legal historian are MVN 10 82–83, which concern the sale of two adjoining(?) houses by the same sellers (Ur-kinnir, Ur-Inanna, and GAN-Gula) to the same buyer (Nammaḫni, gardener of Ninsig). Since both texts involve the same witnesses[13] and name the same bala official (Inimanizi), the two transactions must have taken place simultaneously. The unique feature of MVN 10 82–83 is that each contains an additional clause, endowing the sellers' parents with a section of the sold house: ½ sar é, é rig$_9$(DU.TUKU), Abzu-ir-nun, an-na-sum, '½ sar of (that) house, a donated house,[14] was given to A. (by the main seller)' (MVN 10 82 vii 7-10); ½ sar sar é, Abzu-ir-nun, ad-da-ni, ama-ni, ì-na-ba, é rig$_9$(DU.TUKU), inim-ba šu nu-bala, '½ sar of (that) house he (i.e., the main seller) gave/allotted to A., his father, (and) to his mother; this is a donated house; (with respect) to the (concluded sale) transaction, he (i.e., the buyer) will not violate (its status)' (MVN 10 83 vii 2–8). I assume that the donor of the two "houses" (apparently single rooms) was Ur-kinnir, who acted on behalf of Ur-Inanna and GAN-Gula, probably his younger siblings. As far as we can reconstruct the background of these two texts, it appears that the houses in question had originally been occupied by Ur-kinnir, his two siblings, and his parents. The children later subdivided the houses, selling the larger sections to an outside party, and giving the smaller ones to their parents. It is noteworthy that prior to the division of the houses the parents had no proprietary rights to them, apparently being totally dependent on the children for their upkeep. Also of interest is the fact that, when the children later sold the houses and moved out, the parents did not follow them, but stayed behind in the old residence.

Pre-Sargonic Texts (nos. 2-12)

The Pre-Sargonic texts represented in our corpus come from Lagaš, Umma, and Isin. In a number of cases the provenience of texts is either unknown or uncertain.

[11] A. Westenholz, *OSP* 1, pp. 1–2, has speculated that at least some of the Fara-type tablets brought to Philadelphia by the Nippur Expedition could have been excavated at Nippur. Since, however, Hilprecht did some exploratory work at Šuruppak in 1900, a more likely possibility seems to be that the tablets in question were dug up at Šuruppak at that time. In any case, whether they were brought to Nippur in antiquity or in 1900, there is no doubt that the ultimate provenience of these texts was Šuruppak.

[12] Edzard, *SRU*, pp. 18–42, 52–65; Krecher, *ZA* 63 (1974) 151–85. For an updated discussion, see *ELTS*.

[13] But note that two of the witnesses listed in MVN 10 82 (Lú-GAG+NÁM-sag-tuku and Lugal-geštug) are missing in the other text. On the other hand, MVN 10 83 lists a witness named Gissu-šè, who does not appear in MVN 10 82.

[14] For rig$_9$(DU.TUKU), cf. 1 sag-nita sag-rig$_9$(TUKU.DU) in *RTC* 12 i 2–3 (Fara).

Lagaš (no. 2). The only Pre-Sargonic Lagaš tablet in the Iraq Museum is no. 2, a sale document recorded on a clay cone (gag, Akk. *sikkatu*).

Umma (no. 3). The holdings of the Iraq Museum contain only one Umma tablet of Pre-Sargonic date (no. 3). The Pre-Sargonic economic sources from Umma, numbering approximately one hundred texts, were collected and extensively discussed by M. A. Powell.[15] As proposed by Powell, this lot of tablets (to which no. 3 clearly belongs) seems to derive from the archives of the temple of Innana at Zabalam (modern Ibzaykh),[16] a site located approximately 9 km north of Umma.[17] With the exception of a small group of tablets dating from the 28th to 30th years, which could belong to one of Lugalzagesi's predecessors,[18] these documents date to the reign of Lugalzagesi.

Isin (nos. 4–6). Texts 4–6 and 46 belong to a large group of Sumerian legal documents that appeared on the antiquities market in the 1920s, and are now scattered among various museum collections in the United States and Europe. The institutions that are known to own tablets from this group are the Louvre, Yale University (in the Nies Babylonian Collection), the Free Library of Philadelphia, the Denver Art Museum (one tablet), and the Böhl Collection of the Netherlands Institute for the Near East, Leiden (one tablet: Böhl Coll. 929).[19] To this group also belongs the text published by M. Lambert, whose present whereabouts is unknown.[20]

That all these texts come from the same place is proved beyond doubt by the numerous prosopographic and toponymic links among them, especially the following:

1. BIN 8 80 reappears, practically verbatim, in Lambert Tablet iv 19–v 23.
2. BIN 8 34 parallels closely Lambert Tablet xiii 7–27.
3. The person named É-ki-dùg-ga Da-pi-DU.DU 'E. (son/man of) D.' appears in MAD 4 152 i 8–9 and Böhl Coll. 929:17–18; his father(?) D. is probably identical with Da-pi-DU.DU, father of É-zi, who is mentioned in Lambert Tablet iii 11–12.
4. Ur-gu nigir, listed in Böhl Coll. 929:8, is clearly the same person as Ur-gu nigir-gal, who appears in MVN 3 53 iv 2–3.
5. KA-kug dumu Kur-rí, listed in YBC 8463:12 (unpubl.), is the same person as KA-kug-ga-ni dumu Kur-rí in MAD 4 170:8; he also appears in BIN 8 167:18, 168:5, and 180:7 (in each case written KA-kug Kur-rí).

[15] M. A. Powell, "Texts from the Time of Lugalzagesi: Problems and Perspectives in Their Interpretation," *HUCA* 49 (1978) 1–58.

[16] Ibid., 6–7.

[17] R. M. Adams and H. J. Nissen, *The Uruk Countryside* (Chicago, 1972) 217, 226, site 169.

[18] Powell, "Texts from the Time of Lugalzagesi," 11–13.

[19] The Louvre tablets were published by I. J. Gelb in MAD 4; most of the Yale tablets, by G. G. Hackman in BIN 8; the Philadelphia tablets, by D. I. Owen in MVN 3; the Denver tablet by A. Goetze, *JCS* 20 (1966) 126; and the Leiden tablet, in partial transliteration, in *ELTS* no. 192.

[20] M. Lambert, "Grand document juridique de Nippur du temps de Ur-zag-è, roi d'Uruk," *RA* 73 (1979) 1–22 (henceforth cited as Lambert Tablet).

6. The canal Pa_5-PAD is found in Lambert Tablet xi 2 (misread by Lambert as -GAD+GAR), BIN 8 34:16, MVN 3 13 i 2, ii 3, iii 8, 53 i 2, and NBC 6988 i 2 (unpubl.).
7. The canal Pa_5-dub-sar appears in Lambert Tablet i 3, MAD 4 151:1, and 152:2.
8. The toponym gú-DÍM×SU appears in Lambert Tablet xiii 8 (misread by Lambert as -umbin) and BIN 8 34:1.
9. The toponym $^{giš}kiri_6$ Ti-ti 'orchard of Titi' is found in Lambert Tablet xvi 4 and NBC 6988 i 4–5 (unpubl.).

For other prosopographic links, see commentary to no. 4.

Several of the Yale texts that belong to this group were assigned by F. J. Stephens to Nippur, based on the criteria of paleography and orthography.[21] The Nippur provenience of these documents was subsequently accepted by E. Sollberger, Edzard, and Lambert.[22] The only scholar to dissent from this opinion was Gelb, who expressed doubt as to the correctness of this attribution, and stated that "the evidence linking this group of BIN VIII texts with Nippur needs detailed corroboration."[23]

Gelb's misgivings proved to be fully justified, for there is sufficient evidence to demonstrate that this whole group of documents actually stems from Isin. This evidence, part of which was already communicated by J. N. Postgate,[24] is as follows: (1) the invocation of the goddess Ninisina, the patron deity of Isin, in the oath recorded in BIN 8 158:34 (mu ^{d}Nin-isin$_x$(IN)-na-šè) and Böhl Coll. 929:11–12 (mu ^{d}Nin-isin$_x$(IN)-šè mu lugal-šè); (2) the mention in no. 4 xvii 10′–14′ of the *ḫapūtu* hoes that were dedicated to Ninisina; (3) the oath invoking the temple administrator of Isin in MAD 4 170:1–2 (mu lugal-šè [m]u sanga Isin$_x$(IN)^{ki}-š[è]); (4) the fact that the temple administrator of Isin presides over legal proceedings in three texts belonging to this group: Gissu sanga Isin$_x$(IN)^{ki}-ke$_4$ di-bi si bí-sá (BIN 8 164:7–8, 167:7–8); Ne-sag sanga Isin$_x$(IN)^{ki} (no. 5:7′–8′).

Given that in Old Babylonian legal documents the deity (or deities) invoked in the oath is always the chief god (or gods) of the city in question, the mention of Ninisina in the above examples offers virtually certain proof that these texts come from Isin. In this connection, note that in the Sargonic period the god invoked in the oath at Nippur was Ninurta: ⸢mu ^{d}Nin⸣-urta-šè mu lugal-šè (PBS 9 78:9–10 = Westenholz, *OSP* 2 74). The oath invoking Ninurta and the king also appears occasionally in the Ur III sale documents from Nippur.[25]

In the same way, the fact that the official presiding over the legal cases recorded in these tablets was the temple administrator of Isin establishes that these cases were tried at Isin, since in Pre-Sargonic and Sargonic times the person acting in that capacity was invariably the chief administrator (ensi$_2$ or, less commonly, sanga) of a given city.

[21] F. J. Stephens, in BIN 8, p. 7, group 7.

[22] Sollberger, *BiOr* 16 (1959) 115; Edzard, *SRU*; and Lambert, *RA* 73 (1979) 2–3.

[23] Gelb, MAD 4, p. xviii.

[24] J. N. Postgate, *Sumer* 30 (1974) 209.

[25] P. Steinkeller, *Sale Documents of the Ur III Period* (FAOS 17; Stuttgart, 1989) 73 and n. 209.

Further evidence for the Isin provenience of the texts in question is provided by the fact that, as noted by Postgate,[26] the Louvre and J. B. Nies collections also comprise a major Old Babylonian archive from Isin. The connection between the Old Babylonian Isin texts of the Louvre and its Sargonic material published by Gelb in MAD 4 is confirmed by the fact that the tablets MAD 4 14–15 were included in a lot of Isin texts purchased by the Louvre in 1927.[27]

As regards their date, the Isin texts fall into two distinct groups: the earlier and the later. Earlier texts generally are spheroid and square, while later ones tend to be pillow shaped and oblong. Earlier texts also have more rounded corners, and their lines are shorter and broader than those of the later group. Moreover, in the earlier group the signs ŠU and DA are consistently written with an upward wedge, in contrast to later tablets, where this feature occurs only sporadically. These characteristics are virtually identical to those which distinguish, on the one hand, the late Pre-Sargonic and early Sargonic texts from Nippur (dating to the reigns of Lugal-KISAL-si, Enšakušana, and Sargon) from, on the other hand, the classical Sargonic Nippur texts (Naram-Sin and Šarkališarri).[28]

These are the texts which can be assigned with confidence to the later group: BIN 8 66, 158, 162, 164, 167–68, 171–72, 174–75, 178–80; MAD 4 14–15, 71, 77, 78, 80–81, 150–51, 155, 158, 169–70; MVN 3 25; *JCS* 20 (1966) 126; NBC 10197 (unpubl.), NBC 10198 (= *ELTS* no. 168), NBC 10202 (unpubl.), NBC 10204 (= *ELTS* no. 183), YBC 8463 (unpubl.); and no. 46 in this volume. The dating of these texts to the reigns of Naram-Sin and Šarkališarri is assured by the references to Naram-Sin in BIN 8 162, 164, and MAD 4 14, and to Šarkališarri in MAD 4 15, NBC 10197, and NBC 10202. In addition, this group of documents names the following Isin officials who either presided over legal proceedings or are invoked in the oath: Gissu sanga Isin$_x$(IN)^{ki} (BIN 8 164:7–8, 167:7–8); Li-PI-U(?) (mu lugal-šè mu Li-PI-U(?)-šè; YBC 8463:1–2); Nam-maḫ (MAD 4 158:9′–10′); Lugal-kúš sanga (*JCS* 20 [1966] 126, line 5); and an unnamed sanga of Isin (MAD 4 170:1–2). Of these officials, only Gissu can be assigned to a specific reign (Naram-Sin).

The earlier Isin group comprises the following texts: BIN 8 34, 37, 39, 80; MAD 4 152–53; MVN 3 13, 36, 53, 67; Lambert Tablet; Böhl Coll. 929; NBC 6844 (= *ELTS* no. 165), NBC 6900 (= *ELTS* no. 167), NBC 6988 (unpubl.), NBC 10294 (= *ELTS* no. 194); and nos. 4–6 in this volume. The only clue as to the date of this group is the reference to Ur-zage, king of Uruk (Ur-zag-è [l]ugal [U]nug^{ki}), in Lambert Tablet i 14–15. As suggested by Lambert,[29] this ruler is almost certainly to be identified with Ur-zag-è lugal Kiš^{ki} lugal [Unug(?)^{ki}], who is mentioned in the votive inscription BE 1 93:7–9. Ur-zage's reign belongs to the final phase of the Pre-Sargonic period; insofar as it can be

[26] Postgate, *Sumer* 30 (1974) 209.
[27] D. Charpin, *RA* 74 (1980) 189.
[28] As described by Westenholz, *OSP* 1, pp. 3–4.
[29] Lambert, *RA* 73 (1979) 2 and n. 3.

determined at this time, he should be placed somewhere between Lugal-KISAL-si of Uruk and Lugalzagesi.[30] This permits us to date the earlier group of Isin texts to roughly the end of the Pre-Sargonic period; some of them may even belong to the beginning of the Sargonic period (Sargon, Rimuš?). This conclusion is independently confirmed by the formal similarity of these texts to the late Pre-Sargonic/early Sargonic texts from Nippur, the latter being securely dated to the reigns of Lugal-KISAL-si, Enšakušana, and Sargon.

Unknown Provenience (nos. 7-12). The provenience of six Pre-Sargonic tablets (nos. 7-12) cannot be determined.

Sargonic Texts (nos. 13-74)

Umma (nos. 13-32). The collection of the Iraq Museum contains at least twenty Sargonic tablets of Umma origin (nos. 13-32). In addition, it is possible that a number of the Sumerian texts classified here as of unknown provenience (nos. 52-71) actually come from Umma. Note also that the "Sagub" tablets (nos. 33-45), associated with an Umma official named Mesag, may have formed part of the central Umma archive.

The Umma tablets fall into two distinct groups: earlier (nos. 13-21) and later (nos. 22-32). According to the classification proposed by Foster,[31] nos. 13-21 belong to his group B, while nos. 22-32 belong to his group C. Foster suggested that group B is slightly older than group C, basing this interpretation on the appearance of signs and the shape of tablets.[32] Although conclusive proof that group B is older than group C is as yet lacking, for reasons of convenience we have classified the two groups as "earlier" and "later."

Among the earlier Umma texts, nos. 13-17 correspond to Foster's group B.2, whereas nos. 18-21 belong to groups B.1, B.6, and B.7,[33] these latter three groups forming a single archive that concerns the activities of a certain Ur-Šara, his wife Ama-e, and their associate Ur-Sin.[34] As suggested by Foster, group B.2, which contains exclusively grain records, may belong to the Ur-Šara archive too.[35] It should be noted, however, that the prosopographic evidence adduced by Foster is not completely convincing, and thus this question must be left open for now.

"Sagub" (nos. 33-45). Texts 33-45 belong to a large Sargonic archive, which is associated with Mesag, a high Umma dignitary during the reigns of Naram-Sin and Šarkališarri.[36] All other Mesag tablets presently known are

[30] See, most recently, J. S. Cooper, SANE 2/1, p. 34.
[31] Foster, *USP*, pp. 3-4.
[32] Ibid., 4-6.
[33] Ibid., 55-62 (group B.2); 54-55, 62-72 (groups B.1, B.6, B.7).
[34] Ibid., 77-78.
[35] Ibid., 60-62.
[36] In spite of Foster's objections (*Or.* 48 [1979] 161 n. 56; *Institutional Land*, p. 52), there is a very good chance that this dignitary is identical with Mesag, the governor of Umma. In my opinion, this conclusion is difficult to avoid if one considers the importance of the former Mesag. Note, especially, text BIN 8 291 (plus collations in

housed in the Nies Babylonian Collection of Yale University.[37] The entire Yale group, numbering approximately 140 tablets, has been the subject of an extensive study by S. J. Bridges.[38] The Mesag tablets dealing with fields have also been discussed by Foster.[39]

In her reconstruction of the archive, Bridges utilized 126 texts, comprising 117 previously published (in BIN 8) and 9 unpublished tablets. This estimate is definitely too conservative. For example, it seems certain that the 9 "udu á" tablets, which Bridges excludes from consideration,[40] do in fact belong to the Mesag archive. Thus, together with the 13 Iraq Museum tablets and the 9 "udu á" tablets, the total number of the Mesag texts presently available is at least 148.

The attribution of nos. 33–45 to the Mesag archive is based on their prosopography, which links them with the Yale tablets. It is noteworthy that, with the exception of no. 45, all of the Iraq Museum tablets belonging to this group share the primary accession number 11053, which indicates that they were acquired around the same time and probably from the same source.

The Mesag archive is unique in that it offers exceedingly detailed and varied information on the management of royal estates in southern Babylonia during the classical Sargonic period. Thanks primarily to their rich prosopographic data, these sources permit a comprehensive reconstruction of a local rural economy. The studies of Bridges and Foster make some important contributions toward that objective, but they fall short of utilizing the texts to their full potential.

Given the fact that the field-names appearing in the Mesag tablets are otherwise attested both in sources from Umma and Lagaš, the estate operated by Mesag must have been situated in the general area between Umma and Lagaš/Girsu.[41] As is suggested by text 35, which deals with the distribution of barley seed and animal fodder and places that operation at Sagub (a town belonging to the Lagaš province),[42] there is a great possibility that the administrative headquarters of the estate were situated at Sagub. Two other Mesag tablets, both designating Sagub as a locus of Mesag's activities, support this hypothesis: šu-nigin$_2$ 500 lá 1 udu síg-bi 8 gú 40 ma-na DINGIR-na mu-de$_6$ 270 adda-*su ù* udu è-a *a-na* DINGIR-na sipad *na-zi-iḫ in* dub-*su ù-la ḫu-bu-ut in* Sag-ub^{ki} *ši* Lagaš^{ki} Me-ság *u-na-ki-is*, 'total of 499 sheep, their wool is 8 talents (and) 40 minas, DINGIR-na delivered; 270 of his (sheep) carcasses and expended

Foster, *Institutional Land*, p. 57), according to which he held, in the province of Lagaš, over 400 ha (1176 iku) of purchased land (GANA$_2$ ⸢sa$_{10}$-a⸣) and nearly 900 ha (2424 iku) of prebend land (GANA$_2$ ŠUKU).

37 Most of these tablets were published by G. G. Hackman in BIN 8.

38 S. J. Bridges, *The Mesag Archive: A Study of Sargonic Society and Economy* (Ph.D. diss., Yale University, 1981).

39 Foster, *Institutional Land*, pp. 52–69.

40 Bridges, *Mesag Archive*, pp. 6, 9. This group includes BIN 8 187, which was overlooked by Bridges. Another text belonging to the same group is our no. 34.

41 Cf. ibid., 17; Foster, *Institutional Land*, p. 52.

42 See RGTC 1, p. 141; 2, pp. 162–63.

sheep were deducted for DINGIR-na, the shepherd, from his tablet, which is not a *ḫubuttu* loan; Mesag slaughtered (those sheep) in Sagub, that of (the province of) Lagaš' (BIN 8 141:6–16); 1 kuš udu Sag-ub^{ki}-⌈a⌉ TAG-su ì-šum DINGIR.SUKAL ašgab šu ba-ti *ì-nu a-na* še-ba engar-e Me-ság *ù* Ama-barag dub-sar *i-li-ga-ni*, '1 hide of a sheep (which) TAG-su had slaughtered in Sagub DINGIR.SUKAL, the leatherworker, received; when Mesag and Ama-barag, the scribe, came concerning the barley rations of the farmers' (BIN 8 265:1–8). However, the fact that the Mesag estate appears to have been situated in Sagub does not necessarily mean that the tablets themselves come from the site of Sagub. It is equally possible (and perhaps even more likely) that they formed part of the central Umma archive.

The Sagub tablets are written in a curious mixture of Sumerian and Akkadian (see, especially, the earlier-cited texts BIN 8 141 and 265, and no. 44 in this volume). In contrast to other Sargonic texts written in Akkadian, which generally do not provide Sumerian logograms with the Sumerian grammatical elements, in the Sagub texts Sumerian verbs are fully conjugated and Sumerian nouns are provided with case endings. In some instances the only indication that the text was read in Akkadian is the use of the relative-determinative pronoun *šu* 'that of' (see, e.g., nos. 36–37, 39, and 41) or the prepositions *in* 'in' and *ana* 'for' (see no. 35:28–29). Although it seems likely that all of the Sagub tablets were read in Akkadian, for practical reasons we have transliterated nos. 33–45 in roman, with Akkadian words in italics.

Isin (no. 46). The only Isin tablet in the collection of the Iraq Museum that dates to the Sargonic period is no. 46. For a discussion of the date of the Isin tablets, see pp. 7–8.

Mukdan (nos. 47–49). Texts 47–49 stem from the site of Umm el-Jir in northern Babylonia, which almost certainly is to be identified with ancient Mukdan. Yet another tablet which may come from Mukdan is no. 73. The published Mukdan tablets have been the subject of a recent study by B. R. Foster.[43] For the evidence supporting the Mukdan provenience of nos. 47–49, and possibly no. 73, see the respective commentaries.

Diyala Region (nos. 50–51). Texts 50–51 stem from the Diyala region. Their specific place of origin is probably Ešnunna. I have made a provisional list of the various Sargonic tablets which come from illicit excavations in the Diyala region (to which no. 51 is to be added).[44]

Unknown Provenience (nos. 52–74). The origin of twenty-three Sargonic texts (nos. 52–74) is either unknown or uncertain. Possible attributions are noted in the respective commentaries. Texts 52–71 are Sumerian, and texts 72–74 are written in Akkadian.

[43] B. R. Foster, "An Agricultural Archive from Sargonic Akkad," *ASJ* 4 (1982) 7-51.

[44] P. Steinkeller, "Two Sargonic Sale Documents Concerning Women," *Or.* 51 (1982) 365-66.

Concordance of Texts

Accession Numbers

IM	*Text*	*Plate*	*IM*	*Text*	*Plate*
2886/D	50	24	13369	13	9
5592/4a	22	11	13372	14	9
5592/4b	23	11	13377	21	11
5592/6	31	17	13381	15	9
5592/7	24	12	13383	18	10
5592/8	28	15	13384	19	10
5592/9	26	13	13709	16	10
5592/11	30	16	13710	20	10
5592/16	25	12	13711	17	10
5592/17	29	16	14073	2	2
5592/ . . .	27	14	14182	1	1
10598	7	6	23457/21	54	25
10599	46	23	23459	55	25
10604	52	25	26175	47	23
10613	53	25	30350	56	26
10628	45	22	43381	72	31
10629	3	3	43418	9	7
10630	35	18	43431	57	26
10631	39	–	43451	58	27
11053/21	40	20	43453	61	28
11053/21?	34	–	43483	62	–
11053/23	44	22	43488	73	32
11053/25	36	18	43490	74	32
11053/41	43	21	43612	48	23
11053/44	37	19	43613	49	24
11053/61	8	6	43693	10	8
11053/106	38	19	43702	63	28
11053/118	33	17	43706	64	29
11053/156	4	4–5	43726	66	29
11053/277	51	24	43741	59	27
11053/333	41	20	43749	11	8
11053/337	42	21	43759	60	27

IM	*Text*	*Plate*	*IM*	*Text*	*Plate*
43765	67	30	44025	71	31
44013	12	8	44026	65	29
44018	68	30	55101	32	–
44019	69	30	62813	5	–
44021	70	31	62820	6	–

Previously Published Texts

Publication	*Text*	*Plate*
Gibson-Biggs, *Seals*, p. 51 n. 37	11	8
Sumer 13 (1957) 133 A	61	28
TIM 9 94	2	2
TIM 9 95	62	–
TIM 9 96	6	–
TIM 9 98	10	8
TIM 9 99	61	28
TIM 9 100	5	–
ZA 53 (1959) 6–8	2	2

Concordance with *ELTS*

Text	*ELTS no.*
1	108
2	148
48	234
50	245
57	216
58	219
59	220
61	215

Texts 1–74

Transliteration and Translation

No. 1. (IM 14182) Pl. 1

Tablet on display; could not be collated.

Obverse

i	1)	13 urudu ma-na	13 minas of copper
	2)	sám é	(is) the price of the house;
	3)	41 urudu ma-na	41 minas of copper
	4)	níg-dirig	(is) the additional payment
	5)	é-dù	for the house;
	6)	2 síg ma-na túg	2 minas of wool (as the equivalent of) a garment,
ii	1)	15 ⸢ninda⸣	15 ⸢breads⸣,
	2)	15 gúg	15 cakes,
	3)	4 PAB ḪI×DIŠ	4 PAB-measures of soup,
	4)	4 PAB LAGAB×ḪA+A	4 PAB-measures of the . . . fish,
	5)	1 ì sila$_3$	(and) 1 liter of oil
	6)	RI-ti(!)	(for) RI-ti(!);
	7)	1 túg-ME-gál	1 . . . garment
	8)	Nin-GAG(?)-NI	(for) Nin-GAG(?)-NI;
	9)	lú sám kú	(they are) the recipients of the price.
	10)	20 lá 2 ninda	18 breads,
iii	1)	20 lá 2 gú[g]	18 cak[es],
	2)	4 PAB ḪI×DIŠ	4 PAB-measures of soup,
	3)	4 PAB LAGAB×ḪA+A	(and) 4 PAB-measures of the . . . fish
	4)	⸢KA⸣-TAR-zi	(for) ⸢KA⸣-TAR-zi,
	5)	Nin-⸢MU/ŠEŠ⸣-mu-SILA$_4$	Nin-⸢MU/ŠEŠ⸣-mu-SILA,
	6)	Ur-ur	Ur-ur,
	7)	Mim-ma	(and) Mima.
	8)	5 ninda	5 breads,
	9)	5 gúg	5 cakes,
	10)	1 PAB ḪI×DIŠ	1 PAB-measure of soup,
	11)	1 PAB LAGAB×ḪA+A	(and) 1 PAB-measure of the . . . fish
iv	1)	^{I}Ga-⸢ga(?)⸣	(for) Ga-⸢ga(?)⸣
	2)	⸢Sum$_4$-mú⸣	(and) Summu.
	3)	^{I}Ur-túl(LAGAB×U(!))-sag	Ur-tulsag,

	4)	ka-guru$_7$	the granary superintendent;
	5)	^{I}Šeš-kur-ra	Šeš-kura,
	6)	na-gada	the shepherd;
	7)	^{I}Lú-na-NAM	Lu-na-NAM,
	8)	dub-sar	the scribe;
	9)	^{I}Ur-⸢MIR(?)⸣	Ur-⸢MIR(?)⸣;
v	1)	⸢^{I}Ur(?)-BU(?)-DU(?)⸣	⸢Ur(?)-BU(?)-DU(?)⸣;
	2)	^{I}⸢DUN(?)-SAG(?)-x⸣	⸢DUN(?)-SAG(?)-x⸣,
	3)	ad-NE	the . . . ;
	4)	^{I}Zag-^{d}⸢Sùd⸣-ta	Zag-⸢Sud⸣-ta,
	5)	MAŠ.GAG	the . . . ;
	6)	^{I}Lugal-KISAL-si	Lugal-KISAL-si,
	7)	gala	the lamentation priest;
	8)	^{I}Sag-⸢an(!)-tuku(!)⸣	Sag-⸢antuku⸣;

Reverse

vi	1)	^{I}Inim(!)-^{d}Sùd-⸢da⸣-zi	Inim-Sud-⸢da⸣-zi;
	2)	^{I}É-⸢ki-ba⸣	E-⸢kiba⸣,
	3)	sipad	the shepherd;
	4)	^{Id}Gú-lá-an-dùl	Gula-andul,
	5)	ašgab	the leather-worker;
	6)	^{I}Ur-é(!)-^{d}Saman$_3$(NUN.ÉŠ.ŠE.BU)	Ur-e-Saman;
	7)	^{I}É-úr-bi(!)-[dùg]	E-urbi[dug];
vii	1)	^{I}Lugal-lirum(ŠU.KAL)	Lugal-lirum;
	2)	^{I}Dingir-a-mu	Dingir-amu;
	3)	^{Id}Sùd-da-lú	Sudda-lu;
	4)	^{I}Šu-i	Šui;
	5)	^{Id}Nin-me-šu-du$_7$	Nin-mešudu;
	6)	^{Id}Sùd-á-maḫ	Sud-amaḫ,
	7)	unud$_x$(ÁB.KU)	the cowherd;
	8)	^{I}PAB.NU.LAL	PAB.NU.LAL;
	9)	^{I}Amar-⸢má⸣	Amar-⸢ma⸣,
viii	1)	dub-sar	the scribe;
	2)	lú-ki-inim	(these are) the witnesses.
	3)	1 urudu ma-na	1 mina of copper
	4)	gal-nigir	(for) the chief herald.
	5)	½ urudu ma-na	½ mina of copper,
	6)	5 ninda	5 breads,
	7)	5 gúg	5 cakes,
	8)	1 PAB ḪI×DIŠ	1 PAB-measure of soup,
	9)	1 PAB LAGAB×ḪA+A	(and) 1 PAB-measure of the . . . fish
	10)	Nam-maḫ	(for) Nammaḫ,
ix	1)	um-mi-a	the master
	2)	lú-é-éš-gar	house-surveyor.
		(space)	

x	(space)	
	1) Zag-^{d}Sùd-ta	Zag-Sudta,
	2) unud$_{x}$(ÁB.KU)	the cowherd,
	3) lú é sa$_{10}$	(is) the one who bought the house.
	4) Ki-uzug$_{2}$(KA×Ú)	(The city-quarter of) Kiuzug.
	5) bala	The tenure of
	6) Abzu(ZU.AB)-ki-dùg	Abzu-kidug.

---

ii 3–4. For the capacity-measure PAB, possibly to be read kúr, see most recently Krecher, *ZA* 63 (1974) 179–80. The commodities ḪI×DIŠ and LAGAB×ḪA+A, which are characteristic of Fara sale documents, have not until now been satisfactorily explained. The former commodity, written  and measured in liters (sila$_{3}$), appears already in UET 2 18 iii′ 3, an archaic tablet from Ur. In Fara texts, the word is written either 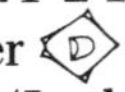or ; since the latter sign is ḪI×DIŠ,  must be analyzed as ḪI×DIŠ too. (In the alleged ḪI×U in PBS 9 3 ii 6, v 2, 9, and pl. lxviii [so reads Edzard, *SRU*, pp. 19, 64–65], U is probably a slanted DIŠ.) The reading of ḪI×DIŠ in this context depends on the broader question of the relationship of ḪI×DIŠ to the signs ḪI×AŠ and KAM(ḪI×TIL), which seem to have been used interchangeably with ḪI×DIŠ in early texts. Table 1 shows the distribution of the values of these three signs, according to the date and origin of the sources; it also includes the attestations of KAM$_{4}$, due to the importance of this sign for the origin of the value /kam/ of ḪI×DIŠ and KAM.

Even though the data in table 1 hardly offer a complete picture of the usage of ḪI×DIŠ, ḪI×AŠ, KAM, and KAM$_{4}$ in third-millennium texts, they do allow us to make a number of observations. The most obvious point here is that, with the exception of the Ebla material, which shows both ḪI×DIŠ and KAM (but note that ḪI×DIŠ occurs only twice at Ebla, both attestations coming from lexical texts), ED texts use either ḪI×DIŠ or KAM. On the other hand, the sign ḪI×AŠ occurs together with ḪI×DIŠ, but is mutually exclusive with KAM (the exception here are the Ur texts, which use both ḪI×AŠ and KAM). These facts suggest that there were two different scribal traditions in ED times: one, at home at Fara, Abu Salabikh, Adab, Nippur, and Isin, which used ḪI×DIŠ and ḪI×AŠ as two distinct signs to express different values; and the other, documented at Ebla and Lagaš, which knew only one sign, KAM, combining the values of ḪI×DIŠ and ḪI×AŠ. (Is it possible, therefore, that KAM is actually a combination of ḪI×DIŠ and ḪI×AŠ?) It appears that in Sargonic times ḪI×DIŠ went out of use, having been everywhere replaced by KAM. As suggested by Biggs (*JCS* 24 [1971] 2) ḪI×DIŠ actually coalesced with the sign ŠIR; this is evident from the fact that the ED spelling ^{d}Aš$_{x}$(ḪI×DIŠ)-gi$_{4}$ was replaced in Sargonic times by $^{d\ aš}$Aš$_{7}$(ŠIR)-gi$_{4}$. In contrast, ḪI×AŠ (= sùr) seems to have survived the Sargonic scribal reform. Although we lack unequivocal attestations of ḪI×AŠ in Sargonic and Ur III texts (but see UET 2 suppl. 44 i 2, iii 8 [cited in table 1 under no. 23], which may belong to Sargonic times), its continued usage is indicated

[*text continues on p. 19*]

TABLE 1. Distribution of the Values of ḪI × DIŠ, ḪI × AŠ, KAM, and KAM$_4$

		ḪI × DIŠ 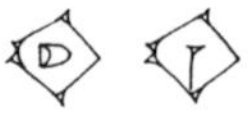	ḪI × AŠ 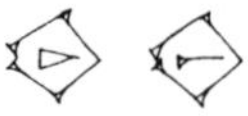	KAM(ḪI × TIL) 	KAM$_4$ 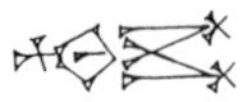
Archaic Ur		1. tu$_7$(?)			
Fara		2. aš$_x$ 3. tu$_7$(?)	4. sùr		5. -kam$_4$
Abu Salabikh		6. -kam 7. aš$_x$	8. sùr(?)		9. -kam$_4$
Ebla		10. aš$_x$		11. sùr	12. -kam$_4$ 13. gàm
Pre-Sargonic	Lagaš			14. sùr (utul$_2$) 15. -kam 16. gám 17. tu$_7$	
Pre-Sargonic	Adab Nippur Isin	18. -kam 19. aš$_x$ 20. utul$_2$			21. -kam$_4$
Pre-Sargonic	Umma	22. umma(?)			
Pre-Sargonic	Ur		23. sùr	24. -kam	
Classical Sargonic			25. sùr(?)	26. -kam 27. tu$_7$ 28. utul$_2$	
Ur III				29. -kam 30. tu$_7$ 31. utul$_2$	

Key

1. 7 sila$_3$ tu$_7$(?) () '7 liters of soup(?)' (UET 2 18 iii′ 3); PN KI:AN:  :EN (UET 2 67 ii 1). The value tu$_7$ may be related to utul$_2$ 'bowl' (see no. 20 below). I owe this suggestion to M. Civil, who contributes the following comments: "The difference between tu$_7$ and udul$_2$ I find obscure. Note that Proto-Ea 371:1f. seems to have only one value, then there is Hh. X 47f. with ^{dug}du$_7$, ^{dug}KAM; as a matter of fact there seems to be no evidence for tu$_7$ = *ummaru* except for the reconstruction in Ea V. Note that udul$_2$ has a variant utul$_2$ in Ea V, more authoritative than the udul$_2$ of Nabnitu. I would not be surprised if there is a connection with utu$_2$, old awuzu (<a+utu?); see *OA* 21, 15, where I did not mention this possibility, though it had crossed my mind."

Key to Table 1 (CONT'D.)

2. DN ^{d}Aš$_{x}$-gi$_{4}$ (*SF* 39 vii 17, 58 ii 6, 63 i 8–9). For the reading aš$_{x}$ of ḪI×DIŠ, see Biggs, *JCS* 24 (1971) 1–2; cf. also Steinkeller, in Gibson-Biggs, *Seals*, p. 51 n. 44.
3. x PAB tu$_{7}$(?) 'x PAB measures of soup(?)' (present text and passim in Fara sale documents).
4. a sùr () sùr e-sig$_{10}$-gim 'like ditchwater, filling the ditch' (Krebernik, *Beschwörungen*, pp. 382–83 viii 1–2 = *SF* 54). For sùr (Akk. *sūru*, *ḫarru*) 'depression, ditch', see CAD S, p. 415; Ḫ, p. 114.
5. 1 uzu šáḫ-kam$_{4}$ (Jestin, *Šuruppak*, 515 v 6); (property) PN-kam$_{4}$ (*RTC* 12 i 4–5). See also the occurrences of -kam$_{4}$ in *SF* 37 xii–xiii and 38 ii′ 6, which are replaced by -kam in OIP 99 248 rev. and 114 iii 11′ respectively. Cf. Krebernik, *Beschwörungen*, p. 332.
6. See the examples of -kam cited above under no. 5.
7. PN Amar-^{d}Aš$_{x}$-gi$_{(4)}$ (Names and Professions List lines 45 and 220 = Archi, *SEb* 4 [1981] 182 + *RA* 78 [1984] 173).
8. Possibly attested in Sùr(ḪI×[x])-gal^{ki} in the AbS version of the Geographical List line 111 (OIP 99 94 v 5′), corresponding to Sùr(KAM)-gal^{ki} in the Ebla manuscript (MEE 3, p. 233 line 111). My transliteration of these two entries in *Vicino Oriente* 6 (1986) 34 is to be corrected accordingly.
9. ka ù-sar-kam$_{4}$ (OIP 99 256 ii 3); éš-kiri$_{3}$ GABA.LUM-kam$_{4}$ (OIP 99 256 v 2). Cf. Alster, *Instructions*, pp. 11–12.
10. PN Amar-^{d}Aš$_{x}$-gi (4) (Names and Professions List lines 45 and 220 = Archi, *SEb* 4 [1981] 182 + *RA* 78 [184] 173). The sign ḪI×DIŠ also occurs in the lexical text MEE 3 53 vii 9 (note that the same text lists KAM in vi 21).
11. GN Ga-sùr^{ki} (e.g., ARET 2 4 vi 8, xii 6); PN A-sùr-Ma-lik (e.g., ARET 4 6 rev. xi 18); ⌜me⌝-[n]e sùr-ru$_{12}$ (MEE 3 63 i 5; cf. Civil, *OA* 21 [1982] 3); gud an gír sùr-mi-nu-kam$_{4}$ (ARET 5 20 i 1–2, 21 i 1–2); etc. The reading sùr of KAM is confirmed by SE 66 (MEE 3, p. 193): KAM = su-ru$_{12}$-um. Against Pettinato (MEE 3, p. 204), the sign is not ḪI×MAŠ but simply ḪI×TIL. See, for example, ARET 2 pls. IV and V no. 4 vi 8, xii 6; ARET 4 pl. XII no. 6 rev. xi 18.
12. gud-ninda$_{2}$ urum$_{x}$(Ú.ÚR)-ma-kam$_{4}$ (ARET 5 20 ii 1, 21 ii 2; and passim in cols. i–ii there).
13. Logographically: 10 gàm za-gìn (MEE 3 45–46 i 16), corresponding to gi-mu 10 in MEE 3 61 ii 6. Civil (in Cagni, *Ebla 1975–1985*, 147) translates gàm as 'ring' and connects it with *kamkammatu*. Another possible identification would be gàm (Akk. *šikru*) 'handle'; see no. 16 below. Syllabically: GIŠ.KI.SI.GA = *kas-gàm-mu* (VE 484 = MEE 4, p. 254); *zi-gàm* (Sollberger, *SEb* 3/9–10 [1980] fig. 27b rev. vi 2); *i-da-gàm* (Sollberger, *SEb* 3/9–10 [1980] fig. 27b rev. x 13). The reading of KAM$_{4}$ is given in SE 18 (MEE 3, p. 191): KAM$_{4}$ = ga-mu-um.
14. (Field) sùr-ri ús-sa 'adjoining a depression' (*RTC* 74 i 2); (field) sùr-ri lá-a 'overhanging a depression' (*RTC* 74 ii 2, 4; cf. Ba-gara$_{2}$ é íd-dè lá-a in Gudea Cylinder A ii 7); (field) sùr-ra lá-a (*RTC* 74 iv 1, v 1); (field) šag$_{4}$ sùr-ra '(located) in a depression' (*RTC* 74 iii 2); 26 giš ú sùr-ra (*DP* 449 iii 3). Note also the obscure 10 giš-sag KI.SAG.Ú (= ki-uzug$_{2}$?) sùr-ra in *DP* 433 iii 6. Yet another occurrence of sùr is probably found in the Lagaš toponym KAM-gal^{ki} (*DP* 159 iii 4; VAS 14 93 viii 11), for which see the northern Babylonian Surgal (Steinkeller, *Vicino Oriente* 6 [1986] 34). The reading Utul$_{2}$-gal^{ki} (given in RGTC 1, p. 188) is theoretically also possible. Finally, note PN KAM-ba-e (*DP* 339 i 3), whose reading remains uncertain.

Key to Table 1 (CONT'D.)

15. kurušda-kam (*DP* 201 iii 3); and passim in economic texts and royal inscriptions. Note the form in Sollberger, *Corpus* Ean. 2 viii 7, which preserves the archaic form of TIL (see Steinkeller, *ZA* 71 [1981] 23).
16. 7 á gud PN simug gám gír-šè ba-de$_6$ 'PN, the smith, took away 7 ox-horns for dagger handles' (VAS 14 15 i 1–ii 1). See ga/ka-am GÀM = *šikru* (S^b 373); ga-am GÀM = *šikru ša* GÍR (Aa VIII/1:92; cf. Ea VIII 37).
17. x (sila$_3$) tu$_7$ 'x (liters of) soup' (no. 2 ii′ 3′, 7′, iii′ 2′, 4′, 6′ in this volume and passim in sale documents and economic texts).
18. ud 1-kam (OIP 14 58 i 2, 5–6, ii 1); see also OIP 14 72:3, 76 ii 8, iii 2 (all Adab); ì-du$_8$ èš-kam (Westenholz, *OSP* 1 85:2); see also Westenholz, *OSP* 1 101 i 5, ii 3, 106 i 2, ii 3, etc. (all Nippur); mu nu-gál-la-kam (BIN 8 170:21); see also BIN 8 164:12, 168:10, 16, 17, 19, etc. (all Isin).
19. PN Ur-^{d}Aš$_x$-gi$_4$ (OIP 14 51 iii 7, vii 1, 74 iii 8; all Adab; BIN 8 7 i 3; Isin?); Ur-$^{d\ aš}$Aš$_x$-gi$_4$ (TuM 5 38 i 5 = *ECTJ*, pl. II; Nippur).
20. é ^{d}Nin-utul$_2$-la (PBS 9 8:18 = Westenholz, *OSP* 2 57). As far as I know, the DN Nin-utul$_2$(-la) 'Lady-of-the-Bowl' is not otherwise attested. Further, note 10 ^{giš}utul$_2$ '10 wooden bowls' (BIN 8 272:7; courtesy of M. Civil; cf. also BIN 8 271:12). For utul$_2$ (Akk. *diqāru*) 'bowl', see CAD D, pp. 157–58.
21. níg-sám GANA$_2$ PN-kam$_4$ (Foxvog, in Alster, *Death*, p. 68 i 5–6; Adab).
22. ḪI×DIŠ$^{(ki)}$ = Umma(?)$^{(ki)}$, passim in the royal inscriptions from Umma. For the occurrences, see Behrens and Steible, FAOS 6, p. 419.
23. PN Sùr-maḫ (UET 2 suppl. 44 i 2, iii 8). Alberti and Pomponio, *Pre-Sargonic and Sargonic Texts from Ur* (Studia Pohl, Series Maior 13; Rome, 1986) p. 97, interpret it as an object. Cf. x-kam-ma-ka in i 5, ii 1, 4, 7, iii 4 of the same text.
24. See no. 23. Also PN-kam (UET 2 suppl. 13 iv 5, 15:2, 43:5, etc.).
25. Possibly found in PN La-ba-sùr(?)( )-šum (Gadd, *Early Dynasties*, pl. 3 BM 114703 iii 2). But see Gelb's suggestion (MAD 2^2, p. 99 no. 233) that the sign in question may be a defective AḪ.
26. *i-li-kam* ( ) (BIN 8 146:16); a-rá x-ka-ma-kam (no. 26 i 12 and passim there; ud 25-kam ( ) (ITT 1 1338:2; etc.).
27. 1440 lá 5 sila$_3$ tu$_7$ ( ), followed by 1183 (pieces of) ku$_6$-dar-ra and 3 gur 170 liters of ku$_6$-ḫád (PBS 9 23:2′–4′, photo pl. lxxii; Nippur); 90 tu$_7$ ( ) ga-ríg '90 ga-ríg-bowls of soup' (ITT 1 1243:5); 120 tu$_7$ ga-ríg (ITT 1 1285:9, transliteration only; both Lagaš). For ga-ríg, see commentary to no. 26 i 3. Alternatively, in the Lagaš examples KAM could be read utul$_2$ and interpreted as a qualification of ga-ríg. Since, however, both texts are lists of foodstuffs (bread, cakes, beer, pig and sheep meat, and ÙR), the first reading is preferable. Note also x sila$_3$ še tu$_7$, possibly 'porridge', in Pinches, *Amherst* 14:3; ITT 1 1308, 1311 (all Lagaš, late Sargonic or early Ur III).
28. 1 utul$_2$ ( ) ì-nun (Pinches, *Amherst* 9:7; Lagaš); 2 utul$_2$ ì (Pinches, *Amherst* 9:9).
29. 2 kam-kam-ma-tum kug-babbar '2 silver rings' (UET 3 392:1; etc.); a-rá 9-kam-aš (BIN 3 7:8; etc.).
30. 16 sila$_3$ tu$_7$ úš 'blood soup', 10 sila$_3$ tu$_7$ gú 'pea soup', 30 sila$_3$ tu$_7$ ku$_6$ 'fish soup' (Pinches, *Amherst* 17 i 4′–6′); x sila$_3$ tu$_7$ (Pinches, *Amherst* 17 i 12′, 16′, and passim there).
31. 1 utul$_2$ ì-nun ku$_6$ (BE 3 106:1, 3); 105 dug-utul$_2$ gal, 201 dug-utul$_2$ murub$_6$ (ITT 2 892 rev. ii 15′–16′), 4 dug-utul$_2$ 5 sila$_3$ (ITT 2 892 rev. iii 12′).

by the fact that Proto-Ea still rigorously distinguishes between ḪI×AŠ and KAM (see MSL 14, p. 46 lines 369–72).

To return now to the question of the commodity ḪI×DIŠ, the only Fara value of ḪI×DIŠ that is documented beyond doubt is aš$_x$. Other values that can be posited for ḪI×DIŠ at Fara (by analogy with the usage of ḪI×DIŠ, KAM, and ḪI×AŠ in later texts) are tu$_7$ and utul$_2$. (That ḪI×DIŠ could be read as kam at Fara seems to be precluded by the fact that the Fara texts consistently use KAM$_4$ to express the genitive + copula chain; the value kam of ḪI×DIŠ and KAM thus appears to be a slightly later development, which occurred in Abu Salabikh or another scribal center.) Of these two values, tu$_7$ is the most likely candidate for the reading of this commodity, for tu$_7$ 'soup' is frequently included among the commodities distributed as gifts in the Pre-Sargonic sale documents from Lagaš (see commentary to no. 2 ii′ 3′). It is noteworthy that in the latter texts tu$_7$ is often given together with ku$_6$-dar-ra 'dried fish' (tu$_7$ and ku$_6$-dar-ra are mentioned side by side also in PBS 9 23, cited in table 1 under no. 27), thus paralleling the association of ḪI×DIŠ with the fish product LAGAB×ḪA+A (see below) in Fara sale documents.

As concerns the commodity LAGAB×ḪA+A (occasionally written also LAGAB×ḪA, see, for example, MVN 10 83 ii 4, iii 6), it is probably to be equated with the fish product GÁ×ḪA+A, mentioned in the ED Word List D line 56 (MEE 3, p. 172). In the syllabic version of this list (ARET 5 23 ii 4), GÁ×ḪA+A appears as ⸢a⸣-da-⸢gú-wa⸣ (see Civil, ZA 74 [1984] 161). See also VE 078 (MEE 4, p. 354): GÁ×ḪA+A = *ti*-LUM ḫu-a, where ḫu-a is possibly a gloss of GÁ×ḪA+A. As is shown by the spelling in ARET 5 23 ii 4, GÁ×ḪA+A is the same as the later adakuʾa/edakuʾa: LAGAB×A+DA+ḪA or GÁ×A+DA+ḪA, which is translated as *siḫil nūni* 'fish bone' (CAD S, p. 237b; MSL 14, p. 115 line 41; see already Civil, *OA* 21 [1982] 2 and n. 3). Assuming that adakuʾa/edakuʾa is to be analyzed as /adda-kuʾa/ 'fish meat/carcass', it is possible that GÁ/LAGAB×ḪA+A originally described dried or similarly processed fish. In this connection, note the association of ku$_6$-dar-ra 'dried (lit., split) fish' with tu$_7$ 'soup' in the Pre-Sargonic sale documents from Lagaš and in the Sargonic text PBS 9 23.

ii 6. The form of TI is unusual, as it has two extra wedges ("LIŠ") at its end. However, since the PN RI-ti is well attested in Fara and Pre-Sargonic texts (see Edzard, *SRU*, p. 209; Pomponio, *Prosopografia*, p. 209), the sign is undoubtedly TI.

iii 5. Perhaps to be read Nin-⸢mu⸣-sila$_4$-mu.

iii 7. This PN is also found in MVN 10 85 v 2.

iv 2. For Sum$_4$-mú 'Bearded', which is characteristically a feminine name, see now VE 199–200: SUM$_4$.DÙ (gloss su-mu(-du-ù)) = *ša-ga-núm*, *ša-gu-*⸢*nu*⸣*-um* /*ḏaqānum*/; SUM$_4$.MÚ (gloss šum-mú) = *du-uš-da-gi-núm/nu-um* /*ḏqn*/, *da-ra-ru*$_{12}$*-um* /*ṭarārum*/. Cf. Krebernik, ZA 73 (1983) 8; idem, *BiOr* 41 (1984) 646. Further, note sum$_4$-lá = *ziq-na-n*[*u*] (MSL 12, p. 105 line 34), mèš$^{\text{mi-iš-su-lá}}$sum$_4$-lá = *ba-du-lu* EME.SAL (MSL 12, p. 126 line 83). To the occurrences of this name collected by Krecher, ZA 63 (1974) 204, add Westenholz, *OSP* 1 23 xii 5′(?), 24 v 3, and no. 12 iii 2 in this volume. The usual form of SUM$_4$ in

ED texts (as is the case here and in no. 12 iii 2) is KA×KID(*-tenû*), corresponding to LAK-328 and LAK-332. Exceptions are the Pre-Sargonic texts from Lagaš, which generally use KA×GANA$_2$-*tenû* (= LAK-324; see Rosengarten, *Répertoire*, p. 38 no. 206). Note, however, that the standard ED form of SUM$_4$ is found in Sollberger, *Corpus* Urn. 49 ii 5 ("Plaque de diorite").

iv 3. Ur-túl(LAGAB×U)-sag: in late Pre-Sargonic and Sargonic texts this PN is consistently written with LAGAB×TIL (e.g., BIN 8 37 iii 1, 82 iii 10; VAS 14 71 ii 1); cf. Steinkeller, *ZA* 71 (1981) 26. In Fara texts, however, the spelling with LAGAB×U (or LAGAB×DIŠ) is predominant (e.g., Jestin, *NTSŠ* 496 x 5′; *WO* 8 [1976] 180 v 3; cf. also *JCS* 29 [1977] 213 x′ 9′—Ur-Nanše of Lagaš). But note the clear Ur-LAGAB×TIL-sag in Jestin, *NTSŠ* 65+159 rev. v 4′.

v 3. ad-NE: For other attestations of this occupation/title in Fara texts, see M. Lambert, *Sumer* 10 (1951) 161, and note also ad-NE in *SF* 47 vii 6. Outside of the Fara material, ad-NE is found in CT 50 30 v′ 2 (Pre-Sargonic, Lagaš) and in ED Lu List C line 53 (MSL 12, p. 15). Evidently the same word, written lú-^{giš}ad-NE, appears in no. 3 ii 4 below, a Pre-Sargonic tablet from Umma. As suggested by the last example, the element ad (or the whole ad-NE) was a wooden object of some sort. This object is possibly the same as GIŠ.AD = *a-tum/du* in VE 390 (MEE 4, p. 243); cf. also ^{giš}ad-maḫ in MEE 3 45–46 rev. iii 14. The VE entry should probably be compared with ^{giš}ad-má = *ud-di e-lep-pi* 'the . . . of a ship' in Hh. IV 363 (MSL 5, p. 181). Alternatively, the Semitic *a-tum/du* could be connected with *addu/atû* (a type of javelin), written GIŠ.RU in Sumerian (see CAD A/1, p. 111; A/2, p. 518a). The translation 'javelin(-thrower)' would provide good sense for (lú-^{giš})ad-NE; I cannot, however, explain the presence of -NE in the term.

v 5. The interpretation of MAŠ.GAG is not without difficulties. While the present occurrence is unique, as far as I know, in Fara texts, MAŠ.GAG is well documented in the Pre-Sargonic texts from Lagaš, where it appears as a PN (for examples, see HSS 3, p. 25; Bauer, *Lagasch*, p. 554; the occurrences in Nikolski 1 313 ii 4 and "Figure aux Plumes," which Edzard [*SRU*, p. 217] interprets as a title/profession, probably also involve a PN). Based on the entries ma-áš-da MAŠ.GAG, MAŠ.EN.GAG = *muš-ke-nu* in A I/6:130–31 (MSL 14, p. 228), Edzard (*SRU*, p. 131) reads the Lagaš PN as maš-dà and sees in it a Sumerian term for *muškēnu*. One suspects, however, that the reading /mašda/ of MAŠ.EN.GAG = *muškēnu* resulted from the misinterpretation of MAŠ.GAG, an abbreviated spelling of MAŠ.EN.GAG, as mašda = *ṣabītu* 'gazelle'. Therefore, if the Fara and Pre-Sargonic MAŠ.GAG is in fact connected with *muškēnu*, its reading would more likely be maš-ga$_x$(GAG), an abbreviation of maš-ga$_x$-en. For the latter term, see now MAŠ.EN.GAG = *mu-sa-ga-i-núm*, *mu-zu*(perhaps *sug*$_6$ = SU)*-i-nu-um* in VE 1306′ (MEE 4, p. 334). Alternatively, MAŠ.GAG could be read mašda and connected with *ṣabītu*. Note, however, that in the present example MAŠ.GAG appears to be an occupation or title, which favors, at least in this particular instance, the first solution.

v 8. For this PN, to be analyzed as /sag-i-n-tuku/ (for other occurrences, see Edzard, *SRU*, p. 209; Westenholz, *OSP* 1, p. 97; Pomponio, *Prosopografia*,

p. 47), compare Sag-ab-tuku-a /sag-i-b-tuku-a/ in PBS 9 8:17 = Westenholz, *OSP* 2 57.

vi 2–3. The same person appears as a witness in the sale of a field in Jestin, *Šuruppak* no. x iv 5–6 (= Edzard, *SRU* no. 1).

vi 6. This PN is also attested in Jestin, *Šurruppak* 66 iv 2 (= Edzard, *SRU* no. 24, with collations); TuM 5 78 vi 6 (= Edzard, *SRU* no. 28).

vii 3. This PN could alternatively be read Lú-^{d}Sùd-da.

vii 7. For unud$_{x}$(ÁB.KU) 'cowherd', see now the exhaustive discussion by Waetzoldt, in *Kraus AV*, pp. 386–97.

viii 10–ix 2. The same official acts as the house-measurer in *RTC* 13 vii 4–6 (= Edzard, *SRU* no. 26).

x 4. The same location is also given in the Fara sale documents in TuM 5 71 vii 5 (= *ECTJ* no. 71) and *RA* 32 (1935) 126 vii 5, which are also concerned with houses. Ki-uzug$_2$ thus appears to have been a city quarter (cf. Edzard, *SRU*, p. 62), probably in Šuruppak. For this toponym, cf. the Lagaš field-names GANA$_2$-ki-uzug$_2$(KA×Ú)-ga-ka (locative) (Nikolski 1 194 viii 3; Pre-Sargonic) and GANA$_2$-^{d}Ab-ú-ki-uzug$_2$(KA×Ú) (*STTI* 168 iii 4′; Sargonic). For the reading uzug$_2$ of KA×Ú, see Diri IV 44–45: [ú]-zu-ug Ú.[K]A, [ú-zu-u]g Ú.[SAG] = *ú-su-uk* (cited in CAD M/2, p. 239 lexical section of *musukku*). The sign KA×Ú is also found in lú-uzug$_2$-ga in Gudea Statue B iii 15; elsewhere in Gudea's inscriptions the same word is written either ^{ú}uzug$_{x}$(KA×UD) (Cylinder B xviii 1) or ú-sig (Statue B vii 34). Further, see uzug$_2$(Ú.KA) é-kur-ra in *JNES* 32 (1973) 30 xi 3′, a literary text from Pre-Sargonic Lagaš. Later texts usually show the spelling ^{ú}uzug$_{x}$(KA×LI) (see Gordon, *Proverbs*, p. 424). It appears that uzug$_2$ is to be analyzed as uzug$_{x}$(KA)^{ú}; note that KA has a value zuḫ, which is probably a derivative of (or at least is related to) uzug$_2$.

No. 2. IM 14073 Pl. 2

Previously published by Sollberger, ZA 53 (1959) 6–8 (transliteration); Edzard, *SRU*, pp. 74–76 no. 32a (transliteration); van Dijk, TIM 9 94 (copy). Recopied.

i′		(beginning destroyed)	(too broken for translation)
	1′)	[. . .] SAL	
	2′)	[. . .] TÚG	
	3′)	[. . .] ⸢DU⸣	
	4′)	[. . .] ⸢x x⸣	
	5′)	[. . .] ⸢GAR⸣	
		(rest destroyed)	
ii′		(beginning destroyed)	
	1′)	⸢dumu⸣ [X(-x)]-šag$_5$-[(x)]-me	⸢sons⸣ of [X(-x)]-šag-[(x)]
	2′)	šu ba-ti	received;
	3′)	3 ninda 1 tu$_7$	3 breads (and) 1 (measure of) soup
	4′)	Ur-^{d}Nin-gír-su	(for) Ur-Ningirsu,

	5′)	ì-du$_8$	the doorkeeper of
	6′)	Ti-ra-áš(ÁŠ.RA)	Tiraš;
	7′)	3 ninda 1 tu$_7$	3 breads (and) 1 (measure of) soup
	8′)	GÌR(?)	(for) GIR(?),
	9′)	⸢engar⸣	the ⸢farmer⸣;
		(rest destroyed)	
iii′		(beginning destroyed)	
	1′)	dumu AB.É-ke$_4$	son of AB.E;
	2′)	3 ninda 1 tu$_7$	3 breads (and) 1 (measure of) soup
	3′)	Ur-me	(for) Ur-me;
	4′)	3 ninda 1 tu$_7$	3 breads (and) 1 (measure of) soup
	5′)	En-DU	(for) En-DU;
	6′)	3 ninda 1 ⸢tu$_7$⸣	3 breads (and) 1 (measure of) ⸢soup⸣
	7′)	Ur-b[i(?)]-⸢x⸣-[(x)]	(for) Ur-b[i(?)]-⸢x⸣-[(x)],
	8′)	du[mu . . .]	so[n of . . .];
	9′)	⸢x⸣ [. . .]	⸢x⸣ [. . .]
		(rest destroyed)	
iv′		(beginning destroyed)	
	1′)	⸢x⸣ [. . .]	⸢x⸣ [. . .]
	2′)	3 [ninda]	3 [breads]
	3′)	U[r- . . .]	(for) U[r- . . .];
	4′)	⸢3⸣ [ni]nda	⸢3⸣ [bre]ads
	5′)	U[r(?)]-ú	(for) U[r(?)]-u,
	6′)	ugula	the foreman;
	7′)	3 ninda	3 breads
	8′)	Lugal-an-ni	(for) Lugal-ane;
	9′)	3 ninda	3 breads
	10′)	Ḫa-ma-ti	(for) Ḫamati;
	11′)	3 ninda	3 breads
	12′)	^{d}Ba-ú-ig-gal	(for) Bau-iggal;
	13′)	ìr Sig$_4$-zi-me	these are the servants of Sig-zi;
	14′)	[x] še	[x] barley,
	15′)	[1(?) kas] dug	[1(?)] jug of [beer],
		(rest destroyed)	
v′		(beginning destroyed)	
	1′)	[gag-bi é-gar$_8$-ra bi-dù]	[This peg was driven into the wall].
	2′)	[ì-bi zag-g]i	[The oil on the si]de
	3′)	bi-ak	was spread.
	4′)	[u]d-ba	On that day
	5′)	[Ur]u-KA-gi-na	[Ur]u-KA-gina
	6′)	lugal	(was) the ruler of
	7′)	Lagaš^{ki}	Lagaš
	8′)	La-la	(and) Lala
	9′)	nigir Gír-su^{ki}	(was) the herald of Girsu.
	10′)	lú am$_6$-⸢ma⸣-dù-da	(If) someone else holds it (i.e., the sold property) in possession,

11′)	gag-bi ka-ka e-gaz	this peg (i.e., the peg on which the cone is mounted) will be driven through (the seller's) mouth.
	(space)	
12′)	[it]i-ezen-[. . .]	[Mon]th Ezen-[. . .].

The present text is recorded on a hollow clay cone, which can be identified with the "peg" (gag, Akk. *sikkatu*) that is referred to in the clauses appearing in v′ 1′ and v′ 10′–11′. Identical documents are *DP* 31–32; Nikolski 1 317–18; BiMes 3 11. For a discussion of the functions of these documents, see Steinkeller, *Sale Documents*, pp. 238–41 commentary to no. 62.

The preserved portions of the cone record the foodstuffs which were presented by the buyer to the secondary sellers (or the witnesses; columns ii′–iv′), final clauses, and the date (column v′). Although the object of sale is not preserved, it assuredly was either a field or a house, since other Lagaš sale documents recorded on such cones deal exclusively with real property.

ii′ 3′. For the reading of ḪI×TIL as tu$_7$ and the interpretation 'soup' (Akk. *ummaru*), see commentary to no. 1 ii 3–4. Since in *DP* 32 and Nikolski 1 317 tu$_7$ is measured in sila$_3$ 'liters', the unexpressed measure used in the present text was probably sila$_3$, too.

iv′ 14′–15′. These lines probably record the gift of the "herald" (nigir), who performed the ceremonial acts described in v′ 1′–3′; cf. *DP* 31 vi 9–15, 32 vii 4–9.

v′ 1′–3′. For this clause, see most recently *ELTS* § 8.12.5.2.

v′ 10′–11′. For this clause, see most recently Steinkeller, *Sale Documents* § 2.7.1.5.

No. 3. IM 10629 Pl. 3

Obverse

i 1) 3½(iku) gana$_2$ 15(gur) še
2) Ur-sag-dingir Lugal-ezen
3) ¾(iku) gana$_2$ 4(gur) lá 1(pi) še
4) Šeš-kur-ra Ga-du$_6$
5) 1¼(iku) gana$_2$ 5(gur) še
6) É-ni-šè Ur-^{d}Nin-ildum$_3$ ì-du$_8$
7) 3½(iku) gana$_2$ 13(gur) 2(pi) še
8) É-ni-šè
9) ¾(iku) gana$_2$ 2(gur) še Kiš-a-bí-LUL

ii 1) ¼(iku) gana$_2$ 1(gur) 1(pi) še GANA$_2$-rig$_9$(DU.ḪÚB)-GAN^{ki}
2) 1 lá ⅛(iku) gana$_2$ 3(gur) še
3) En-kalam-e
4) 1(iku) gana$_2$ 5(gur) še lú-^{giš}AD.NE

5) 2(iku) $gana_2$ 5(gur) še Gala sur-gu
6) 1(iku) $gana_2$ 5(gur) Gala É-⌜maḫ-da⌝
7) ½(iku) $gana_2$ 3(gur) še Giš-$šag_4$ Lugal-íb-ta-ni-è

Reverse

iii 1) ⅜(iku) $gana_2$ 1(gur) 2(pi) še Amar-^{d}$Ezinu_2$
2) 1¼(iku) $gana_2$ 4(gur) 2(pi) še Lugal-ḫur-sag
3) (blank) 6(gur) še Kum-tuš-šè
4) (blank) 3(gur) zíz NE.SAL-an-da

iv 1) še è-a
2) ud 6

A record of land areas and the corresponding grain volumes. For the text type, see Powell, *HUCA* 49 (1978) 16 (group C. Small-Format Land-Grain Texts), and 22–24.

This group of the Pre-Sargonic Umma texts is characterized by the pattern (1) land area, (2) volume of grain, and (3) personal name (in some instances, more than one name is listed; see, e.g., i 2 and i 4 in the present text). Also typical for these texts is the subscript še è-a 'expended grain' (as in this text) or še ág(-gá) 'measured out grain'.

Powell, *HUCA* 49 (1978) 22–24, believes that these texts are records of grain owed to the temple by renters or holders of land allotments of some type. As he himself acknowledges, however, this interpretation is complicated by the fact that in some instances the ratio between land and grain is as high as five gur per iku. Given what is known about grain yields in third-millennium Mesopotamia, the figure of five gur per iku must represent the total crop, and not a third or half of the harvest that was customarily paid by the renter. On the other hand, the designation še è-a seems to connect these texts with the records of rental payments from Pre-Sargonic Lagaš, which use the same expression (see Diakonoff, *Šumer*, p. 40; Steinkeller, *JESHO* 24 [1981] 138; Foster, *USP*, p. 92). I can offer no ready solution for this problem.

The present text can be dated securely to the reign of Lugalzagesi. This is shown by the fact that at least seven of the persons listed in it also appear in BIN 8 82 and 86, both of which specifically name Lugalzagesi:

É-ni-šè	i 6, 8	BIN 8 82:2, 86:19
Ur-^{d}Nin-$ildum_3$ ì-du_8	i 6	BIN 8 86:53, 91
Kiš-a-bí-LUL	i 9	BIN 8 82:26
En-kalam-e	ii 3	BIN 8 86:83
É-maḫ-da	ii 6	BIN 8 86:86
Giš-$šag_4$	ii 7	BIN 8 82:10
Lugal-íb-ta-ni-è	ii 7	BIN 8 82:25, 87

i 9. This name, attested also in BIN 8 82:26 and *HUCA* 49 (1978) 40 no. 4 ii 9 (Kiš-a-bí⟨-LUL⟩), is a graphic variant of Kiš-a-bí-tuš 'He/she-Dwells-in-Kiš', well documented in Pre-Sargonic texts from Lagaš (see, e.g., HSS 3 20 ii 7, 21 iv 3, 22 iv 5, 23 v 9). In this context, LUL must therefore be interpreted as tuš$_x$ (the reading luk$_x$(LUL) is excluded by the fact that the root luk$_x$ is restricted to the singular subject of the class of animals; see Steinkeller, *SEL* 1 [1984] 5-10). Cf. Uru-kug-a-bí-tuš$_x$(LUL) in Nikolski 1 19 iii 13.

ii 1. It is not clear whether GANA$_2$-rig$_9$-GAN^{ki} is a personal name or a toponym. The same word is spelled GANA$_2$-rig$_9$ in BIN 8 120:8.

ii 4. For this occupation or title, see commentary to no. 1 v 3.

No. 4. IM 11053/156 Pls. 4-5

Obverse

i–iii		(completely destroyed)	
iv		(beginning destroyed)	(cols. iv–vii too broken for translation)
	1′)	10+⌜2(?)⌝ kug gín	
	2′)	[(X-)]^{d}Nin-sún	
	3′)	[x] ⌜x⌝ [(. . .)]	
		(rest destroyed)	
v		(beginning destroyed)	
	1′)	⌜X⌝-[. . .]	
	2′)	dumu [. . .]	
	3′)	É [. . .]	
	4′)	NI ⌜x⌝ [. . .]	
	5′)	⌜x⌝ [. . .]	
		(rest destroyed)	
vi		(completely destroyed)	
vii		(beginning destroyed)	
	1′)	[. . .] ⌜x⌝ SAG	
	2′)	[. . .] MA	
		(rest destroyed; only traces)	
viii		(beginning destroyed)	
	1′)	[x] ⌜x⌝ [x]	⌜. . .⌝
	2′)	MI-AB.[SI$_4$]	(of ?) MI-AB.[SI];
	3′)	[níg]-sám-bi	its price,
	4′)	[⅓ kug ša]-na gín	⌜20⌝ shekels of [silver],
	5′)	10(gur) še gur	10 gur of barley,
	6′)	6 urudu [ma-na]	6 [minas] of copper,
	7′)	4 kug [gín-kam]	(valued at) 4 [shekels] of silver,
		(rest destroyed)	
ix		(only traces)	(too broken for translation)
x		(completely destroyed)	

Reverse

xi–xii		(completely destroyed)	
xiii		(beginning destroyed)	
	1′)	⌜níg⌝-s[ám-bi/pi]	[its] ⌜price⌝,
	2′)	10 k[ug gín]	10 [shekels] of silver

xiv		(beginning destroyed)	
	1′)	⌜šu(?)⌝ [. . .]	⌜. . .⌝
	2′)	1(iku) [. . .]	1 iku of [land?],
	3′)	gú [. . .]	(located) on the bank of [. . .];
	4′)	níg-s[ám-bi/pi]	[its] price,
	5′)	1 ⌜x⌝-[. . .]-NI[N(?) (. . .)]	1 ⌜. . .⌝,
	6′)	11+[x . . .]	11+[x . . .],
	7′)	Ur-[. . .]	Ur-[. . .],
	8′)	dumu [. . .]	son of [. . .],
	9′)	šu ba-[ti]	received.
	10′)	1(eše) 1+[x(iku)] gana$_2$	7+[x] iku of land,
	11′)	GANA$_2$-En-n[a]-D[U]	(located) in the field GANA-Enn[a]-D[U],
	12′)	GANA$_2$ Ka$_5$[a]	the field of Ka,
	13′)	šeš sanga	brother of the temple administrator,
xv		(beginning destroyed)	
	1′)	1(eše) 1+[x(iku)] gana$_2$	7+[x] iku of land,
	2′)	GANA$_2$-En-na-D[U]	(located) in the field GANA-Enna-D[U],
	3′)	ki-ba Šag$_4$-an-zu	in its midst (is the property of) Šag-anzu;
	4′)	níg-sám-pi	its price,
	5′)	8(gur) še gur-sag	8 gur of barley (measured by) gsg(?),
	6′)	2(gur) 2(pi) A še gur	2 gur 120 liters of . . . barley,
	7′)	⌜Ur-TAR⌝	⌜Ur-TAR⌝
	8′)	šu ba-ti	received;
	9′)	8(gur) še gur-sag	8 gur of barley (measured by) gsg(?),
	10′)	2(gur) 2(pi) A še gur	2 gur 120 liters of . . . barley,
	11′)	dam DINGIR-LU-maḫ-ke$_4$	the wife of DINGIR-LU-maḫ
	12′)	šu ba-ti	received;
	13′)	8(gur) še gur-sag	8 gur of barley (measured by) gsg(?),
	14′)	2(gur) 2(pi) A še gur	2 gur 120 liters of . . . barley,
	15′)	dam Ur-ki	the wife of Ur-ki
	16′)	šu ba-ti	received.
	17′)	iš-gana$_2$-pi	Its additional payment
	18′)	šag$_4$-ba an-šid	he (i.e., the buyer) included (lit.: counted) in it (i.e., the price).
	19′)	sám GANA$_2$-En-na-DU-kam	The price of the field GANA-Enna-DU
	20′)	dumu Šag$_4$-an-zu-ke$_4$-ne	the children of Šag-anzu [received.]
xvi		(beginning destroyed)	
	1′)	⅓ kug ša-na gín	20 shekels of silver
	2′)	Si$_4$-si$_4$	Sisi
	3′)	šu ba-ti	received;
	4′)	12 ì-šáḫ UMBIN	12 UMBIN-jars of pig fat,
	5′)	2 kug gín-kam	(valued at) 2 shekels of silver,
	6′)	8(gur) še gur	8 gur of barley,

	7′)	⸢Si$_4$-si$_4$⸣	⸢Sisi⸣,
	8′)	⸢dumu⸣ Amar-^{d}Ezinu$_2$(ŠE.TIR(!))	⸢son⸣ of Amar-Ezinu,
	9′)	Nin-ur$_x$(EN)-ra	(and) Nin-ura,
	10′)	ama-ni	his mother,
	11′)	šu ba-ti	received.
	12′)	1(bùr) lá 2(iku) gana$_2$	16 iku of land,
	13′)	Pa$_5$-Ḫa-ti	(located) on the canal Pa-Ḫati;
	14′)	níg-sám-pi	its price,
	15′)	½(!) kug ma-na	½ mina of silver,
	16′)	Ga-la-su-ni	Kalašuni
	17′)	Ur-Ab-zu	(and) Ur-Abzu,
	18′)	dumu Me-gud-e-me	sons of Me-gude,
	19′)	šu ba-ti	received.
xvii		(beginning destroyed)	
	1′)	[x(iku) ^{giš}]kiri$_6$	[x iku] of an orchard,
	2′)	[^{giš}kiri$_6$(?)] ⸢Ur⸣-gu	bordering on the [orchard(?)] of ⸢Ur⸣-gu;
	3′)	[a]b-ús	
	4′)	[x á]b(?)-šè	in lieu of [x co]ws(?)
	5′)	ab-ši-gar	was pledged(?);
	6′)	1(eše) ^{giš}kiri$_6$	6 iku of an orchard,
	7′)	^{giš}kiri$_6$ Lú(!)-dingir-ke$_4$	bordering on the orchard of Lu-dingir;
	8′)	ab-ús	
	9′)	níg-sám-bi	its price,
	10′)	30 lá 1 urudu ma-na	29 minas of copper—
	11′)	ḫa-bù-da^{urudu}	(of this copper) the *ḫapūtu* hoes
	12′)	íb-ta-dé-dé	were cast
	13′)	mu ^{d}Nin-isin$_x$(IN)-na	(and with) the name of Ninisina
	14′)	bí-sar	were inscribed—
	15′)	10 kug gín	10 shekels of silver,
	16′)	[. . .] LAL	⸢. . .⸣
	17′)	[. . .] ⸢LAL⸣	⸢. . .⸣
	18′)	[. . .]	[. . .]
xviii		(beginning destroyed)	
	1′)	[x] ⸢x⸣ SAR	⸢. . .⸣
	2′)	Ur-^{d}Nin-isin$_x$(IN)	Ur-Ninisin
	3′)	ab-šuš	branded(?).
	4′)	1(eše) ^{giš}kiri$_6$	6 iku of land,
	5′)	^{giš}kiri$_6$	bordering on the orchard of Mezuanda;
	6′)	Me-zu-an-da-ke$_4$	
	7′)	[a]b-ús	
	8′)	[níg]-sám-bi	its price,
	9′)	[x kug] ⸢x⸣ še gín	[x] shekels (and) ⸢x⸣ grains(?) [of silver],
	10′)	[x x] GAR IGI KE$_4$ [. . .] gín	⸢. . .⸣ shekel(s),

11′) [. . .] NE [. . .] ⌜x⌝ ⌜. . .⌝
(rest destroyed)
xix–xx (completely destroyed)

A very large tablet, resembling in shape a plano-convex brick. It is estimated that the tablet originally had twenty columns of writing, ten on the obverse (flat), and ten on the reverse (convex). Most of the obverse is at present illegible. As far as its content is concerned, no. 4 is a *Sammelurkunde*. Its extant sections record at least nine separate transactions, all of which seem to involve sales.

This tablet is closely related to Lambert Tablet (see above pp. 5–6), which also stems from Isin and is a *Sammelurkunde*. The latter text is also very large; it bears eighteen columns, eleven on the obverse and seven on the reverse. In contrast to no. 4, however, Lambert Tablet is flat on both sides. It records thirty-two transactions (A through FF, according to Lambert's designations), dealing exclusively with field and orchard sales, plus a colophon (GG), listing four persons, identified as 'bailiffs' (maškim). As far as we can tell, the transactions name only sellers and no buyers. This suggests that all of the parcels listed in Lambert Tablet were purchased by the same unnamed buyer, and that this document is a composite record of his individual transactions. That the Lambert Tablet was in fact compiled from such individual records is demonstrated by the existence of tablets that match some of its transactions (see p. 5 above).

Since the extant transactions of no. 4 likewise do not name sellers, we may speculate that this document, like Lambert Tablet, is a composite record of the purchases made by a single buyer. It cannot even be excluded that both texts involve the same buyer. This possibility is suggested by the demonstrable prosopographic links that exist between these two documents (see below).

viii 2′. Presumably the same MI-AB.SI$_4$ is mentioned in Lambert Tablet v 20 (= BIN 8 80:30), xiii 15. See also the comment to xv 1′–20′. In Fara sources and in Pre-Sargonic texts from Lagaš, this PN is spelled MI-SI$_4$.AD (Pomponio, *Prosopografia*, p. 177; *DP* 141 ii 1; VAS 14 95 ii 1), where AB is replaced by AD. I cannot explain this alternation. For the name pattern, cf. Ur-AB.SI$_4$ in no. 5 rev. 3′.

xv 1′–20′. The 'children of Šag-anzu' (line 20′) were Ur-TAR and his two sisters, who are identified in the text by the names of their husbands. Ur-TAR also appears in Lambert Tablet x 25–26 (^{I}Ur-TAR Šag$_4$-an-zu 'U. (son of) Š.'), where he acts as a witness. Ur-ki, husband of one of Šag-anzu's daughters, is probably the same person as Ur-ki, son of MI-AB.SI$_4$, who is attested in Lambert Tablet v 19–20 (= BIN 8 80:29–30), xiii 14–15. Note also the mention of Barag-mezida, daughter of Ur-ki, in Lambert Tablet vi 29–30.

xv 3′. For this line, cf., in an identical context, ki-ba Ur-gu dumu Nigin$_3$-kam in Lambert Tablet xiv 2–3.

xv 6′, 10′, 14′. The meaning of A še gur, standing in apposition to še gur-sag (lines 5′, 9′, 13′), is unclear. The same expression appears in Lambert Tablet ix 20 (likewise contrasted with še gur-sag), xiii 25. Tentatively, I interpret gur-sag as an abbreviation for gur-sag-gál, but, in view of its consistent association with A še gur, it is possible that a completely different term is involved here.

xvi 4′. UMBIN (reading unknown) was a type of jar used for storing pig and sheep fat. For its occurrences, which are limited to Pre-Sargonic texts, see *ELTS* no. 14 passim (ì-udu); Lambert Tablet vii 13, viii 2, 12, 17 (ì-udu); Fish, *Catalogue* 22 i 3 (ì-šáḫ); M. Lambert, *RA* 70 (1976) 191 i 1 (bur-UMBIN—donated ex-voto). Based on the occurrences from *ELTS* no. 14, it can be established that the UMBIN had a capacity of two sila$_3$. See *ELTS* note to no. 14 i 7.

xvii 9′–14′. The copper was apparently paid in the form of inscribed hoes. This type of information is completely unique in third-millennium sale documents. For the use of copper/bronze objects as currency in the later periods, see the Nuzi text HSS 9 106:12, where part of the payment was made *ina libbi* ZABAR *ḫaṣṣinnū* ‘in bronze axes’. For the votive inscriptions on weapons/tools, see the copper axe(?) dedicated for the life of Šu-Sin to Šara (Limet, *Textes sumériens* 2 = Hallo, *HUCA* 33 [1962] 38 Šu-Sin 16) and the tin *ḫaṣṣinnu* axe dedicated to Nergal (TuM 4 45).

xviii 6′. Attested also in Lambert Tablet xi 3.

No. 5. IM 62813 no copy

Published by van Dijk, TIM 9 100 (copy). Collated by J. A. Black. Collations are indicated by asterisks.

Obverse

(destroyed; only some traces preserved on the right edge of reverse)

Reverse

(beginning destroyed)

1′)	⸢X-x-x⸣ [. . .]	⸢PN⸣,
2′)	dumu Ur-ur	son of Ur-ur;
3′)	¹Lú-dingir-ra dumu Ur-⸢AB*.SI$_4$*⸣	Lu-dingira, son of Ur-⸢AB.SI⸣;
4′)	lú-ki-inim-ma-bi-me	these were the witnesses.
5′)	¹Lugal-KISAL-e dumu Úr*-ra-ni	Lugal-KISAL, son of Urani,
6′)	maškim-bi	was the bailiff.
7′)	Ne-sag sanga Isin$_x$(IN)^{ki}	Nesag, the temple administrator of Isin,
8′)	di-bi si bí-sá	tried this case.

9′)	Lugal-níg-zu Ur-LI-ke$_4$* [(. . .)]	(After?) Lugal-nigzu, (son) of Ur-LI,
10′)	en-na-sa$_{10}$ in-til-la [(. . .)]	had bought (the slave?) and completed (the transaction/price),
11′)	Lugal-ma*-DU-e (empty (space*)	Lugal-ma-DU (declared?):
12′)	sag-nu in-šub-ba [(. . .)] (rest destroyed)	"He is not a slave, he was . . ."

Lugal-nigzu (line 9′) is almost certainly the same person as his namesake, son of Ur-LI, who appears in no. 6. The two texts probably come from Lugal-nigzu's archive, as is suggested by the prominent role he plays in both of them.

7′. For the title and role of the sanga of Isin, see p. 6 above.

9′–12′. Due to the fragmentary condition of the text, our rendering of these lines is only tentative.

10′. The spelling with en-, instead of the expected in- or ì-, is highly unusual.

12′. For the suffix -nu 'is not', serving as a negative enclitic copula, see Thomsen, *Sumerian*, pp. 191–92. The meaning of šub in this context is unclear.

No. 6. IM 62820 — no copy

Published by van Dijk, TIM 9 96 (copy). Collated by J. A. Black. Collations are indicated by asterisks.

Obverse

i		(beginning destroyed)	
			[(x shekels of silver)]
	1′)	[x(iku) gana$_2$ ^{giš}]kiri$_6$-šè	for [x iku/sar] of an orchard
	2′)	[Lu]gal-níg-zu	[Lu]gal-nigzu,
	3′)	dumu Ur-LI	son of Ur-LI,
	4′)	nigir-ke$_4$	the town crier,
	5′)	⌜A-pú(?)*-lú⌝	(to) ⌜A-pu(?)-lu⌝,
	6′)	dumu ⌜UM/MES-x⌝-[x]-⌜ra*⌝	son of ⌜UM/MES-x⌝-[x],
	7′)	⌜mu⌝-na-sum	gave.
	8′)	⌜ud(?)*⌝-bi-t[a]	⌜After(?)⌝
	9′)	⌜X*⌝-LU ba-⌜úš*⌝-a	⌜PN died⌝
	10′)	⌜GIŠ⌝ MI NA NI ⌜ḪI(?)*⌝	⌜. . .⌝
		(rest destroyed)	
ii		(beginning destroyed)	
			[PN]
	1′)	dumu [. . .]	son of [. . .],
	2′)	Lugal-[níg-zu(?)-ra]	[to] Lugal-[nigzu(?)]

3′)	ba-gi$_4$	replied:
4′)	[l]ul*-lam	"This is a [l]ie!
5′)	[še]š*-mu	To my brother
6′)	kug nu-na-sum	you did not give (that) silver"—
7′)	in-na-dug$_4$	he told him.
8′)	Lugal-níg-zu	Lugal-nigzu
9′)	é ^{d}En-ki-ka	in the temple of Enki
		[took an oath?].
	(rest destroyed)	(rest too broken for translation)

Reverse

iii (beginning destroyed)

1′) [(x)] ⸢x⸣ íd-d[a(?)* . . .]

(space)

(rest destroyed; only traces)

iv (beginning destroyed)

1′) ⸢x x⸣ zu

(rest destroyed)

Left Edge

[. . .]-na ba-dé ⸢x (x)⸣

As far as one can ascertain, this document deals with a legal claim which was raised against Lugal-nigzu (see no. 5) concerning the silver he had paid for an orchard. It appears that the action was initiated by the seller's brother, and that Lugal-nigzu was subsequently required to take a declaratory oath in the temple of Enki. The mention of íd in iii 1′ may indicate that he was also subjected to a river ordeal.

i 4′. The lacuna in front of nigir is not large enough to permit the reconstruction [gal]- (information courtesy of Black).

i 6′. Against van Dijk's copy, -⸢ra⸣ belongs to this line (information courtesy of Black).

i 9′. One would expect to find here the name of the seller, that is, ⸢A-pú(?)-lú⸣ (i 5′). However, the last sign is clearly LU and not LÚ. The possibility that -LU is a syllabic writing seems unlikely.

i 10′. Perhaps to be analyzed as a PN: Gissu-na-ì-dúg.

ii 1′. The destroyed patronymic is evidently that of the seller, that is, ⸢UM/MES-x⸣-[x] (i 6′).

ii 2′. If this line mentions not Lugal-nigzu but some other person whose name also began with Lugal (e.g., a judge), the verb in ii 6′ should perhaps be translated 'he did not give (that silver to my brother)'.

No. 7. IM 10598 Pl. 6

Obverse

i	1)	2 urudu ma-na	2 minas of copper,
	2)	3 ^{urudu}šen	3 caldrons,
	3)	2 ^{urudu}URI	2 URI-containers,
	4)	5 zabar	5 "bronzes,"
	5)	11 kug gín	11 shekels of silver,
	6)	2(gur) še gur	2 gur of barley,
	7)	35(gur) še gur	35 gur of barley,
	8)	15 túg	15 garments,
	9)	4 ì-ir dug	4 pots of scented oil,
ii	1)	4 gír	4 daggers,
	2)	1 ^{urudu}gu	1 . . . ,
	3)	5 sag-nita	5 slaves,
	4)	1 sag-SAL	1 slave woman,
	5)	1 ^{giš}dúr-gar erin	1 chair of cedar,
	6)	1 ^{giš}dúr-gar mes	1 chair of mes-wood,
	7)	1 ur_5	1 grinding slab,
	8)	1 ^{giš}ná	1 bed,
	9)	4 ì-ir $sila_3$	4 bowls of scented oil;
	10)	níg-è-a(written MIN) Šu-ni-ba-sum	the expenditure of Šuni-basum.

Reverse

(uninscribed)

The composition of this listing suggests a personal inventory; cf. *DP* 507 (Pre-Sargonic), TuM 5 147 (Sargonic), Nies, *UDT* 1 (Ur III), and no. 21 in this volume. However, the key phrase in inventories usually is níg-gur_{11} PN 'property of PN', and not, as in the present text, níg-è-a PN. It is possible that níg-è-a 'expenditure' or the like, here denotes movables received as part of the division of an estate.

i 3. URI is a type of metal container. As shown by the following examples, it could be of considerable size: 2 ^{urudu}URI ki-lá-bi 20 lá 2½ ma-na '2 URI, their weight (is) 17½ minas (i.e., 8¾ minas per one URI)' (*STTI* 8 rev. 6′–7′); 1 URI^{urudu} zabar ki-lá-pi 4 ma-na '1 bronze URI, its weight (is) 4 minas' (Westenholz, *OSP* 1 95:4–5). The reading of URI in this context and its Akkadian equivalent are unknown. For the problems involved in the interpretation of URI/KINDA, see Kraus, *Sumerer und Akkader*, pp. 61–82.

i 4. zabar can also denote 'mirror'. See my comments in *ASJ* 9 (1987) 347–49, and cf. no. 21:5.

ii 2. The sign GU is possibly an error for NAGAR, that is, ^{urudu}$bulug_4$ (Akk. *pulukku*) 'chisel' (suggestion of Powell).

ii 7. ḪAR could alternatively be interpreted as ḫar (Akk. *šewiru*) 'ring, coil (of metal)', for which see Powell, in *Matouš Festschrift* 2, pp. 211–43.

No. 8. IM 11053/61 Pl. 6

Obverse

i 1) [. . .] še [g]ur-⸢sag-gál⸣
2) Su$_{4}$-pi-lí
3) 3+[x(?) (gur)] 2(pi) [. . .]
4) [. . .]

ii 1) [. . .]-NE-⸢x⸣
2) ⸢5(gur)⸣ 2(pi) Zag-mu
3) 7+[x(?)(gur) x(pi)(?)] ⸢X⸣-[. . .]-⸢x⸣
4) 2(gur) 1(?)(pi) [. . .]

iii 1) 1+[x(gur) x(pi)(?)] Lugal-ur-mu
2) 5(gur) 2(pi) Lum-[m]a-mu
3) 2(pi) ⸢SAG/KA-lú⸣-[. . .]
4) [. . .]

Reverse

iv 1) [. . .] ⸢x x⸣
2) 1(gur) Áš-⸢DUB(?)-SI(?)⸣
3) 1(gur) I-bí-il
4) 1(gur) ⸢X⸣-[. . .]
5) 2(gur) [. . .]

v 1) 1(gur) KAS$_{4}$.⸢GUR⸣-[. . .]
(space)

vi 1) ⸢šu⸣-nigin$_{2}$(!)(KU) ⸢še⸣ gur-sag-gál 40+⸢2(?)(gur)⸣ 2(pi)
(rest destroyed; probably nothing missing)

A record of barley distributed(?) among several individuals. The tablet is very poorly preserved. Note the name Su$_{4}$-pi-lí /*Šu-bēlī*/ in i 2, for which see MAD 3, p. 247.

No. 9. IM 43418 Pl. 7

Obverse

i	1) 1 SAL-u$_{8}$ sila$_{4}$ nim	1 ewe (with) a spring lamb
	2) Lú-⸢x⸣-ke$_{4}$	Lu-⸢x⸣,
	3) 1 u$_{8}$ si[la$_{4}$ (x)]	(on account of) 1 ewe (with) a [(x)] lamb,
	4) DINGIR-na	(to) DINGIR-na

	5)	mu-na-ši-sum	gave;
	6)	1 SAL-u$_8$ è-li	1 . . . ewe
	7)	DINGIR-na	(with) DINGIR-na
	8)	an-da-luk$_x$(LUL)	remains;
	9)	udu Ur-UD.BU-kam	the sheep of Ur-UD.BU.
	10)	1 u$_8$ ama	1 mature(?) ewe
ii	1)	DINGIR-na	DINGIR-na
	2)	in-šum	slaughtered;
	3)	lú(!)-éš-GANA$_2$-gíd-kam	(the sheep) of the field surveyor.
	4)	⸢1⸣ SAL-u$_8$ è-li	⸢1⸣ . . . ewe
	5)	Ur-UD.[B]U	(of) Ur-UD.[B]U
	6)	DINGIR-[n]a	(with) DINGIR-[n]a
	7)	an-da-⸢luk$_x$(LUL)⸣	⸢remains⸣.
	8)	2 sil[a$_4$] ama	2 mature(?) lambs,
	9)	1 kuš udu	1 sheep hide,
	10)	Ur-UD.BU	(of) Ur-UD.BU
	11)	Du-du	(with) Dudu
	12)	an-da-luk$_x$(LUL)	remain.
iii	1)	1 sila$_4$ è-li	1 . . . lamb
	2)	Sag-an-tuku	(to) Sag-antuku (he gave);
	3)	(erasure)	
	4)	1 udu-nita	1 ram
	5)	Igi-ni-šè	(to) Iginiše,
	6)	Ad-da	Adda,
	7)	Pù-gul	(and) Pu-gul
	8)	in-na-sum	he gave;
	9)	lú-éš-GANA$_2$-gíd⟨-kam⟩	(the sheep of) the field surveyor.
	10)	1 SAL-u$_8$ sila$_4$	1 ewe (with) a lamb

Reverse

iv	1)	É-gá	Ega
	2)	Ur-AŠ.DUN	(to) Ur-AŠ.DUN,
	3)	dumu Ur-Ap-ra	son of Ur-Apra,
	4)	in-⸢na⸣-sum	gave.
	5)	1 u$_8$ 2 sila$_4$	1 ewe (with) 2 lambs
	6)	Ur-UD.BU	(of) Ur-UD.BU
	7)	DINGIR-na⟪-n[a]⟫	(with) DINGIR-na
	8)	an-da-luk$_x$(LUL)	remains.
	9)	1 SAL-u$_8$ sila$_4$	1 ewe (with) a lamb
	10)	ba-úš	died;
	11)	Ur-An-tu[m]	(the sheep of) Ur-Antu[m].
v	1)	1 u$_8$ sila$_4$ ⸢dù-a⸣	1 ewe which has (already) lambed
	2)	Ur-UD.BU-kam	of Ur-UD.BU
	3)	Ur-AŠ.DUN	(with) Ur-AŠ.DUN
	4)	an-da-⸢luk$_x$(LUL)⸣	remains.

	5) 1 SAL-u_8 ⌜è⌝-li	1 . . . ewe
	6) É-zi	(of ?) Ezi,
	7) bar ⌜RU(?)⌝ [. . .]	on account of ⌜. . .⌝
	8) B[U(?) . . .]	⌜. . .⌝
	(rest destroyed)	
vi	(uninscribed)	

The text is a composite record of several transactions concerning sheep that belonged to at least four different persons: Ur-UD.BU (i 1–9, ii 4–7, ii 8–12, iv 5–8, v 1–4), lú-éš-GANA$_2$-gíd (i 10–ii 3, iii 1–9), Ega (iii 10–iv 4), and Ur-Antum (iv 9–11). The sheep were entrusted to several shepherds, among whom the most conspicuous are DINGIR-na (i 1–5, i 6–9, i 10–ii 3, ii 4–7, iv 5–8) and Ur-AŠ.DUN (iii 10–iv 4, v 1–4). For the text type, cf. no. 47.

i 1. For sila$_4$ nim (Akk. *ḫurāpu*) 'spring lamb', see CAD Ḫ, p. 245.

i 5. For other examples of the use of the infix -ši- with sum, see Edzard, *WO* 8 (1976) 165–66, who translates -ši- in such forms by "dafür."

i 6. The meaning of è-li, describing ewes and lambs (iii 1), is unknown. Cf. *ŠL* 381.254. Note that in MVN 3 66 i 2 (Pre-Sargonic) è-li appears by itself (following u_8 and preceding udu-nita).

i 8. For luk$_x$ (or lug$_x$), a suppletive stem of the verb ti 'to live', reserved for the singular subject of the class of animals, see Steinkeller, *SEL* 1 (1984) 5–10. To the examples cited there (pp. 6–7) add 1 sila$_4$ ga sub-ba PN kurušda-da mu-da-luk$_x$(LUL)-ka-am$_6$ (*DP* 338 i 1–4, courtesy of H. Behrens). Note that in ii 8–12 luk$_x$ is used anomalously in reference to a plural subject. Another example of the same anomaly is found in MCS 4 (1954) 12 i 1–ii 3, a Pre-Sargonic tablet from Lagaš: 91 ama ùz 1 [SAL]-áš-gàr šag$_4$-dùg 1 maš-nita šag$_4$-dùg PN PN$_2$-da e-da-luk$_x$.

The conjugational prefix a-, attested here, is characteristic of Fara, Pre-Sargonic, and, though to a lesser extent, Sargonic texts. Available data show that a- appears predominantly in sentences where the agent is implied but not spelled out. See, for example, animals sipad-ra an-na-sum 'were given to PN (by PN$_2$)' (MVN 3 66 i 1–ii 2; Pre-Sargonic). For other examples, see *ECTJ*, p. 8, and no. 62:6 in this volume. It needs to be emphasized that this type of sentence is distinctly different from the standard absolutive construction of the type uru-Ø ba-ḫul 'the town perished/was destroyed' (as contrasted with the ergative construction lugal-e uru-Ø mu-ḫul 'the town was destroyed by the king)'.

Since the usual conjugational prefix used in the sentence 'X lives/remains with Y' is ì- (see *Or.* 48 [1979] 55 n. 5; *SEL* 1, pp. 5, 14 n. 2), it is possible that the examples with a- (as in the present text and in BiMes 3 18 iii 4: an-da-se$_{12}$-àm; and ITT 1 1100:4, 11: an-da-ti), are to be understood as containing an implied agent: 'X (was made by Z) to live with Y.'

i 9. Ur-UD.BU is possibly to be interpreted as Ur-ud-sud(!).

i 10. The qualification ama (cf. ùz ama in MAD 4 40:4, 44:5, etc., as well as áb ama, discussed by Bauer, *Lagasch*, p. 292) probably means '(sexually) mature, adult'; cf. Foster, *USP*, p. 63, who translates it "adult (having had young)." Alternatively, this term could be interpreted as 'pregnant'. The combination sil[a$_{4}$] ama, appearing in ii 8, is troublesome.

iv 3. For the divine element Ap-ra, see Gelb, MAD 3, p. 57 under *aprum*, who cites the names Ap-ra-il and Ur-Ap-ra. Cf. also J. J. M. Roberts, *The Earliest Semitic Pantheon* (Baltimore, 1972), pp. 12–13. Yet another example of Ur-Ap-ra is found in OIP 99 478 colophon.

iv 7. Against the copy, there is no sign following the second NA.

iv 11. Cf. the Sargonic name Šu-An-tum (MAD 3, p. 251). Note that Antum is mentioned already in the Abu Salabikh god list OIP 99 82 iii 6.

v 1. For u$_{8}$ sila$_{4}$ dù-a 'ewe which has (already) lambed', see Landsberger, MSL 8/1, p. 27 n. to lines 190ff.

No. 10. IM 43693 Pl. 8

Previously published in copy by van Dijk, TIM 9 98. Transliterated and translated by C. Wilcke in *Geschlechtsreife und Legitimation zur Zeugung* (ed. E. W. Müller; Munich, 1985), p. 240. Recopied.

Obverse

1)	[^{I}G]eme$_{2}$-^{d}Ma-[mi]	[G]eme-Mami
2)	⌜é⌝-gi$_{4}$-a	is the daughter-in-law of
3)	⌜Ur⌝-Kèš(DINGIR.U.RÉC-215(!))^{ki}-⌜kam(?)⌝	⌜Ur⌝-Keš;
4)	^{I}Nin-giš-da-na-ni	Nin-gišdanani
5)	ù Šeš-⌜gu⌝-la	and Šeš-gula
6)	^{ú}mussa$_{x}$(SAL.UŠ)-me	were the (competing?) suitors.
7)	⌜KA(?) x (x) TUM(?)⌝	⌜. . .⌝
	(rest destroyed)	

Reverse

	(beginning destroyed)	
1′)	[n]íg-mussa$_{x}$(SAL.UŠ)-bi	The bridal gift
2′)	in-ak	he gave (lit.: made).
3′)	Dug$_{4}$-ga-ni	Dugani,
4′)	⌜arad$_{2}$(?) X-pum(?)⌝	⌜slave(?) of X-pum(?)⌝,
5′)	^{I}Lugal-iti-da	Lugal-itida,
6′)	dumu Ur-⌜^{d}⌝TUR	son of Ur-TUR,
7′)	Lugal-[. . .]	Lugal-[. . .],
8′)	⌜x⌝ [. . .]	⌜. . .⌝
9′)	[. . .]	[these were the witnesses?]

The context suggests a litigation over the non-fulfillment of a marriage agreement. If lines 4–6 do in fact involve two "bridegrooms" (see commentary to line 6), this text possibly concerns a breach of contract by the father of the bride against the intended bridegroom, in favor of another suitor. This particular theme is dealt with by Ur-Nammu Code §12 and Lipit-Ištar Code §29. See in detail Finkelstein, *JCS* 22 (1969) 74–76.

3. For other occurrences of the name Ur-Keš, see RGTC 1, p. 85. In the present example KÈŠ, usually written U.DINGIR.RÉC-215, has a reversed order of the composite signs. Cf. also the spelling Ur-DINGIR.RÉC-215[ki] in OIP 14 192:6. We may note here parenthetically that KÈŠ has a syllabic value kèš in Old Akkadian, which is attested in the toponym Ur-kèš[ki] (i.e., Urkiš) (AOAT 3/1 69:4, misread as Ur-na?-ŠÁR×GAD(RÉC-215)[ki] in RGTC 1, p. 180).

6. The Sumerian term for 'son-in-law', usually written $mussa_x$(SAL.UŠ)[sá], has recently been discussed by Bauer, "Altorientalische Notizen (21–30)" (photocopy; Hochberg, 1985), pp. 22–24. This term contains the logogram SAL.UŠ (more correctly: GAL_4.GÌŠ 'vagina + penis'), which is used in third-millennium (primarily ED) sources to write various words connected with the idea of heterosexual intercourse. Bauer also recognizes here, in addition to $mussa_x$(SAL.UŠ)[sá], $giš_x$(SAL.UŠ) . . . dug_4/e 'to copulate', $geme_2$-$karkid_x$(SAL.UŠ)[kar-kìd] 'prostitute', nitadam(SAL.UŠ)[dam] 'husband', and [mi]$nigirsi_x$(SAL.UŠ)[si] 'groom's companion'. To be added to this list is (*a*) SAL.UŠ (reading unknown) 'sheath (of a dagger)', attested in Ur III texts from Ur (for the examples, see UET 3 indexes, p. 150); and (*b*) SAL.UŠ.KID[mušen] (Fara) or SAL.UŠ.DI.KID[mušen] (Pre-Sargonic and later), to be read gambi or gam(m)u (note also the syllabic spelling ga-i[mušen] in MEE 3, p. 110 line 2), Akkadian ***kumû***, ***atān nāri***, a type of equatic bird. While the sexual symbolism of sheath is obvious (cf. the dual sense of Latin *vagina*, German *Scheide*, Polish *pochwa*, etc.), the choice of this logogram for the ***kumû*** bird is unclear. In this connection, we may also mention the logogram UŠ.TUŠ (more correctly: GÌŠ.DÚR 'penis + anus'), standing for gala, which is clearly the "homosexual" equivalent of SAL.UŠ.

In support of Bauer's suggestion that SAL.UŠ.DI is a logogram, with DI representing a phonetic indicator, the following evidence may be adduced: (*a*) the fact that the oldest spelling of this term, attested in Fara texts, is simply SAL.UŠ (e.g., *SF* 7 vii 27; *WF* 22 i, 25 iv, 121 iii; Jestin, *Šuruppak* 1 viii 10; note also níg-SAL.UŠ in Jestin, *Šuruppak* 515 iv 5); (*b*) the occurrences in which the order of signs is reversed: SAL.DI.UŠ (OIP 14 49 vi 4); UŠ.SAL.DI (Çiğ-Kizilyay, *NRVN* 1 5:5; *NATN* 131:23, 893:2); (*c*) the occasional addition of the phonetic indicator ú, as in [ú]SAL.UŠ[sá] and SAL.[ú]UŠ in ED Lu List E line 156 (MSL 12, p. 19) and [ú]SAL.UŠ-me in the present text; (*d*) the fact that the expected complement of the verb ús is -sa and not -sá (see Falkenstein, *Or.* 19 [1950] 110), which excludes the interpretation SAL-ús-a 'he who follows the woman' (CAD E, p. 156a).

The fact that the basic form of the term is SAL.UŠ also precludes the interpretation munus[ús]-sá 'he who buys a woman', where -sá would be a syllabic spelling of sa_{10} 'to buy' (Landsberger, in *David AV*, p. 95). Lexical texts are consistent in assigning to SAL.UŠ.DI the pronunciation mussa; for the evidence, see CAD E, p. 154 lexical section of *emu*, and, further, note the "syllabic" logogram NÍG.MU.SÁ which stands for níg-$mussa_x$ in Ebla texts (for examples, see ARET 3, p. 379; 4, p. 317; etc.), and the spelling níg-[mu]SAL.UŠ[sá]-a in BIN 7 173:8 (early OB). The presence of double /ss/ in the term shows that it cannot be etymologized as /mí-ús-a/. It seems equally unlikely that mussa could contain the word munus. In all probability, therefore, mussa is a primary kinship term which has no relation to the words 'woman' and 'to follow.' It is of interest, however, that in later periods this term was analyzed by scribes as containing the verb ús. This is shown by Emesal Voc. III 51, where níg-SAL.UŠ.DI is written with SA instead of DI; the corresponding Emesal pronunciation is èm-mu-lu-ús-sa (in reflection of the etymology níg lú ús-a?!).

4′. The reading [x] ÚS.X.SI, proposed for this line by Wilcke, in *Geschlechtsreife und Legitimation zur Zeugung*, p. 240, is not confirmed by the collation.

No. 11. IM 43749 Pl. 8

Previously published by Steinkeller, in Gibson-Biggs, *Seals*, p. 51 n. 37 (transliteration and translation); drawing of the seal on p. 42 (made by M. Matoušóva).

Obverse

1) 90 u_8	90 ewes,
2) 90 udu-nita	90 rams;
3) Mu-NI-NI	(the property? of) Mu-NI-NI;
4) É-GAM.GAM^{ki}	(in) E-GAM.GAM

Reverse

(top destroyed; could contain one line; remainder uninscribed)

Seal

^{d}Nin-urta	Ninurta,
$ensi_2$ Nibru^{ki}	the governor of Nippur.

A memo concerning 180 sheep, belonging(?) to Mu-NI-NI. Alternatively, Mu-NI-NI could be the shepherd to whom the sheep were entrusted for herding. As indicated by the fact that Ninurta is afforded the title of the "governor of Nippur" in the seal inscription, the provenience of the text is probably Nippur (or its vicinity). Further, note that the toponym É–GAM.GAM, mentioned in line 4, seems to have been situated near Nippur (see commentary to line 4).

3. In Gibson-Biggs, *Seals*, p. 51 n. 37, I interpreted this name as the Akkadian MU-ì-lí. However, since there are no certain examples of the use of the logogram MU (for *šumu*) in Old Akkadian personal names, it is safer to analyze it as a non-Akkadian name. The same name appears in the Nippur text Westenholz, *OSP* 1 29 ii′ 5 (Pre-Sargonic).

4. É-GAM.GAM is mentioned in the Nippur tablets TuM 5 24 i 6, 45 i 4′ (both Pre-Sargonic; cf. Westenholz, *OSP* 1, p. 117 under X_2; RGTC 1, p. 41

under é-GAM$^{?ki}$), and thus appears to have been a satellite of Nippur. The reading of GAM.GAM in this toponym probably is simply gam-gam; see R. D. Biggs, *RA* 69 (1975) 185–86. Note, however, that GAM (= LAK-180) is given the reading a-zu-tum in SE 71 (MEE 3, p. 198).

seal. For Ninurta's epithet "governor of Nippur," cf. his title "great governor of Enlil," discussed by me in Gibson-Biggs, *Seals*, p. 51 n. 37. Apart from the examples cited there, the latter title also occurs in an Ur III brick inscription from Nippur: ^{d}Nin-urta, ensi$_2$-gal, ^{d}En-líl-lá (Goetze, *Iraq* 22 [1960] 151 n. 3). For another example of an ED seal belonging to a diety, see E. Heinrich, *Fara* (Berlin, 1931) pl. 42c, invoking ^{d}Anzud$_x$(IM.MI.MUŠEN) and ^{d}Sùd.

No. 12. IM 44013 Pl. 8

Obverse

i	1)	1 dug-maḫ	1 large pot,
	2)	2 dug-KU.ZI kaš(!)-sur	2 goblets(?) of . . . beer,
	3)	1 sag šáḫ	1 pig head,
	4)	3 uzu(LAK-350)	3 (pig?) flitches,
ii	1)	6 ninda	6 breads,
	2)	1(bán) zíd 80 AB.TU	10 liters of flour, 80 . . . ;
	3)	gurum$_2$ nu-tuku	(these goods) were not inspected.

Reverse

iii	1)	níg-X-a	The gift(?) of
	2)	Sum$_4$-mú-kam	Summu.
	3)	níg-gur$_{11}$ Kur-ra	The property of Kura.
	4)	La-la	Lala
iv	1)	ì-de$_6$	brought (it).

A list of foodstuffs, which were presented(?) by Kura to Summu. Lala acted as the conveyor.

i 2. In all probability, dug-KU.ZI is a variant spelling of dug-gú-zi / dug-ka-a-su (Akk. *kāsu*) 'goblet, bowl' (CAD K, pp. 253–56). The latter word is attested already in the Ebla lexical text MEE 3 45–46 v 8 (gú-zi). Note also dug-KA.ZI in no. 26 i 7 and passim and in no. 32:1, 5, 7 (both Sargonic), which evidently denotes the same vessel.

M. A. Powell (personal communication) questions the traditional interpretation of kaš sur as 'pressed' or 'poor quality beer' (see, e.g., Bauer, *Lagasch*, p. 217), and wants to see in this beer a Pre-Sargonic equivalent of kaš 3-ta-àm, that is, a beer whose given volume required three times as much barley to make.

i 4. For the identification of LAK-350 as the ancestor of uzu, see Civil, *ZA* 74 (1984) 161–62. It is characteristic that the early attestations of uzu = LAK-350 invariably involve pig meat: 1 uzu šáḫ-kam$_4$ (Jestin, *Šuruppak* 515 v 6; Fara); 2 uzu šáḫ (ITT 1 1243:2; Sargonic); [x]+1 uzu šáḫ 15 sagdu(SAG×DU) šáḫ mu-šeg$_6$ 10(?) uzu šáḫ (L. 30304:1–4, courtesy of I. J. Gelb; Sargonic); and probably in the present text, given the mention of a pig head in i 3. This evidence suggests that uzu originally denoted the cured side of a hog, that is, "flitch."

As noted by Pettinato (MEE 3, p. 134) and Archi (*SEb* 4 [1981] 189, 203) the interchange a-bù-ká (Ebla) = a-LAK-350-ká (Abu Salabikh) in lines 286–87 of the ED Names and Professions List points to LAK-350 having a syllabic reading bu$_x$. This reading is possibly also found in the Abu Salabikh personal name A-LAK-350-BÀD (OIP 99 495 v 7: A-LAK-350-B[ÀD] engar; 511 iv 2: A-LAK-350-PA:BÀD = A-LAK-350-BÀD ugula), which can be analyzed as A-bu$_x$-dūrī. Cf. A-bù-BÀD in ARET 7, p. 179.

ii 2. The reading and meaning of AB.TU are unknown to me.

iii 1. The sign read as X is probably a ligature of ŠU and TAG$_4$ (suggestion of M. Civil). If so, the word could be connected with níg-šu-taka$_4$-a 'gift', for which see most recently Whiting, AS 22, pp. 26, 113–17. The alternative reading níg-zag-a does not yield any satisfactory meaning.

iii 2. For this PN, see commentary to no. 1 iv 2.

No. 13. IM 13369 Pl. 9

Obverse

1)	[. . .] ⸢še gur⸣-[sag-gál DÙL]	[x gsg of] barley, [(measured by the gsg DÙL)],
2)	[. . .]	[. . .],
3)	[x]+13(gur) 3(pi) zíz ⸢gur⸣	[x]+13 gsg 180 liters of emmer,
4)	10(gur) gig gur	10 gsg of wheat:
5)	Ur-^{d}Ab-ú	Ur-Abu;
6)	270(gur) 2(pi) še gur	270 gsg 120 liters of barley,
7)	30 lá 1(gur) zíz gur	29 gsg of emmer:
8)	Inim-ma-ni	Inimani;
9)	545(gur) 2(pi) še gur	545 gsg 120 liters of barley,
10)	22(gur) zíz gur	22 gsg of emmer:
11)	Lugal-še	Lugal-še;
12)	511(gur) 2(pi) še gur	511 gsg 120 liters of barley,
13)	1(gur) zíz gur	1 gsg of emmer:
14)	É-e	E-e;
15)	203(gur) 2(pi) še gur	203 gsg 120 liters of barley,
16)	[x(gur)] zíz gur	[x] gsg of emmer
17)	[Á]-kal-li	[A]kali;

Reverse

18)	205(gur) [x(pi)(?) še gu]r	205 gsg [x(?) liters of barley],
19)	10+[x(?)(gur) x(pi)(?) zíz g]ur	10+[x(?) gsg x(?) liters of emmer],
20)	1(gur) [2(pi) gig] gur	1 gsg [120 liters of wheat]:
21)	U[r- ^{giš}]gigir$_2$	U[r]-gigir;
22)	280(gur) 2(pi) še gur	280 gsg 120 liters of barley:
23)	Ur-$^{⸢d⸣}$TUR	Ur-TUR;
	(space)	
24)	šu-nigin$_2$ 2464(gur) 1(pi) še gur-⸢sag⸣-gál DÙL	the total of 2464 gsg 60 liters of barley (measured by) the gsg DÙL;
25)	šu-nigin$_2$ 177(gur) 2(pi) zíz gur	the total of 177 gsg 120 liters of emmer;
26)	šu-nigin$_2$ 11(gur) 2(pi) gig gur	the total of 11 gsg 120 liters of wheat;
27)	[še] giš ra-a	the threshed [grain]
28)	[Agar$_2$(SIG$_7$)]-a-šag$_4$-^{d}En-líl-lá	[of the field Agar]-ašag-Enlila.
29)	[še] ḫal-bi íb-ta-zi	Its . . . [barley] was deducted,
30)	[zíz ús]-⸢bi(!)⸣ šag$_4$-ba ì-gál	⸢its⸣ [. . . emmer] is (still) included in it.
31)	[ugula Ur]-$^{⸢d⸣}$Ab-ú	[Under the supervision of Ur]-Abu.
32)	[4] iti	[4th] month.

This and the following four texts belong to Foster's group B.2 (*USP*, pp. 55–62), which comprises records of grain. The majority of the group B.2 tablets (including the present text and nos. 14 and 16) deal with the collection and disposition of the harvest. In spite of a certain variation in form, all of the harvest texts show basically the same structure: (1) volumes of barley, emmer, and wheat, followed by personal names; (2) the phrase še giš ra-a 'threshed barley'; (3) field-name; (4) additional information concerning the disposition of the grain (optional).

Foster (*USP*, p. 57) thinks that these texts are "records of individuals' payment of rent or other dues on land which did not belong to them." According to him, they show "how much grain a lessee . . . delivered from a certain field . . . , whether the grain was threshed . . . , what was done with it . . . , and when" (p. 57).

The possibility that the documents in question are records of rental payments is precluded by the fact that the volumes of grain involved are far too large to represent the rent (or even the total yield from a rented field). See, for example, the total of 1643 gur and 120 liters of barley, emmer, and wheat, associated with Ur-Abu in MAD 4 48:1–4 (the same person appears in no. 13:5, 31), which, at an average yield of 30 gur per bùr of land, must have entailed ca. 55 bùr (= 990 iku of land). Needless to say, a field of that size never would have been leased out to a single individual!

It is also noticeable that the people mentioned in the harvest texts form a very narrow circle; the same few individuals appear in one text after another, often in association with different fields. For example, five of the men listed in no. 13, Lugal-še, E-e, Akali, Ur-gigir, and Ur-TUR, where they are associated with the field Agar-ašag-Enlila, are also found in MAD 4 66, in conjunction with the field Agar-ašag-gibil.

These facts make it quite certain that we are dealing here with the records of harvest (specifically: threshing) conducted on some type of demesne land. The men listed therein can, accordingly, be identified as the officials responsible for the harvest. Rather revealingly, in MAD 4 167 several of those individuals appear in charge of work teams: E-e, in charge of 24 men (lines 1–3), Lugal-še, in charge of 16 men (lines 4–5), Ur-Abu, in charge of 25 men (lines 9–10), and Ur-gigir, in charge of 22+[x] men (lines 15–16). It is not unreasonable to see in these work teams the labor force employed on the harvest.

Text 13 closely parallels MAD 4 39, with which it shares the same structure and formulary. Like no. 13, MAD 4 39 concerns the harvest on the field Agar-ašag-Enlila, though it mentions different harvest officials. The great formal similarity between these two texts, on the one hand, and the fact that each lists different officials, on the other hand, suggest that they are complementary records, dealing with the same harvest operation.

1. The meaning of the term DÙL, which occasionally qualifies the capacity measure gur-sag-gál in the Sargonic texts from Umma (see Gelb, MAD 4, p. xxi, for a complete listing of occurrences), is unknown. Since the same documents sometimes qualify the gur-sag-gál as si-sá 'standard' (e.g., no. 14:1), DÙL possibly denotes a nonstandard variety of the gur-sag-gál. Unfortunately, however, the available attestations of the gur-sag-gál DÙL do not permit us to draw any conclusions regarding its size.

5. Ur-Abu supervises a harvest/threshing on the field Agar-ašag-Enlila also in MAD 4 144:7. His other attestations are MAD 4 48:4 and 167:10.

11. Attested also in MAD 4 66:9, 14 (ugula), and 167:5.

14. Attested also in MAD 4 26:8, 66:2, 7 (ugula), 144:2, and 167:3.

17. Attested also in no. 17:3, MAD 4 26:6, and 66:4.

21. Attested also in MAD 4 66:13 and 167:16.

23. Attested also in MAD 4 66:6.

28–32. Reconstructed after MAD 4 39:15–19.

29–30. The meaning of še ḫal-bi and zíz ús-bi is unclear. Foster (*USP*, p. 59) suggests that ḫal and ús may denote some parts of the threshing process. M. A. Powell (personal communication) concurs with this opinion, at least as far as ḫal is concerned, pointing out that ḫal is lexically equated with ***bêšu*** and ***petû***, both of which denote part of the threshing operation. For ***bêšu*** and ***petû***, see now M. Civil, *The Farmer's Instructions* (forthcoming), commentary to lines 95–96. Alternatively, ḫal and ús could describe the quality of grain. For še ḫal, see še ḫal-la, appearing in the Umma texts MAD 4 85:1 and 91:1, and further, note x $sila_3$ še gig-ta ḫal-la 'x liters of barley mixed(?) with(?) wheat', and x $sila_3$ še zíz-ta ḫal-la 'x liters of barley mixed(?) with(?) emmer'

(BE 3 101 iii 6, 18; Ur III). The meaning of ús in zíz ús-bi could be 'second quality, inferior'.

No. 14. IM 13372 Pl. 9

Obverse

1)	144(gur) še gur-sag-gál si-sá	144 gsg of barley, (measured by) the standard gsg,
2)	Lugal-KA	(the property? of) Lugal-KA,
3)	Nam-tar-ri-e	Namtare
4)	šu ba-ti	received.
5)	dub ús	The additional(?) tablet.

Reverse

(uninscribed)

A receipt of barley. Other occurrences of Lugal-KA in Umma grain texts are MAD 4 62:7, 67:13, 103:5, 108:5, 120:5, and 125:5. Cf. Foster, *USP*, pp. 58–61. The meaning of ús in line 5 is unclear.

No. 15. IM 13381 Pl. 9

Obverse

1)	338(gur) 2(pi) še gur-sag-gál DÙL	338 gsg 120 liters, (measured by) the gsg DÙL:
2)	Sag-du$_5$	Sagdu;
3)	486(gur) 2(pi) 3(bán) še gur	486 gsg 150 liters of barley,
4)	30(gur) 1(pi) 3(bán) zíz gur	30 gsg 90 liters of emmer:
5)	[X]-⌈x⌉-[x]-⌈x⌉	[X]-⌈x⌉-[x]-⌈x⌉;

Reverse

6)	(erasure)	
7)	4(gur) 2(pi) zíz gur	4 gsg 120 liters of emmer:
8)	Lugal-kur	Lugal-kur;
	(space)	
9)	šu-nigin$_2$ 1913(gur) 2(pi) 3(bán) še gur-sag-gál DÙL	the total of 1913 gsg 150 liters of barley;

10) šu-nigin$_2$ 50(gur) 3(pi) 3(bán) zíz gur-⌜sag(?)⌝	the total of 50 gsg 210 liters of emmer;
11) še giš ra-a	the threshed grain of
12) Agar$_2$-bar-DU	the field Agar-bar-DU.

A record of threshed grain. For the text type, see no. 13.

2. Sagdu is associated with the field Agar-bar-DU also in MAD 4 48:7. In MAD 4 39:18 and 115:5 he is in charge (ugula) of threshed barley from the field Agar-ašag-Enlila (cf. no. 13:28).

5. Possibly to be reconstructed [Ur]-⌜d⌝[A]b-⌜ú⌝. Cf. no. 13:31.

9–10. Both totals exceed the amounts listed in the text.

No. 16. IM 13709 Pl. 10

Obverse

1) 222(gur) 1(pi) še gur-sag-gál	222 gsg 60 liters of barley;
2) še giš ra-a	the threshed grain of
3) Áš-bí(?)-um	(the field?) Ašbiʾum(?);
4) ^{d}Šara$_2$-an-dùl	Šara-andul (was the responsible official).

Reverse

(uninscribed)

A record of threshed grain. For the text type, see no. 13. Other sources mentioning Šara-andul are MAD 4 136:5 and BIN 8 292:6. In the first text, he is in charge of threshed grain from the field Ašag-Lagaš; in the second, he authorizes(?) an expenditure of barley to a certain Ama-e.

Since Áš-bí(?)-um is not attested elsewhere as a toponym, one should perhaps analyze it as a personal name. Note, however, that in the še giš ra-a texts this section of the document invariably identifies the field from which the barley came.

No. 17. IM 13711 Pl. 10

Obverse

1) 73(gur) lá 3(bán) še gur-sag-gál	72 gsg 210 liters of barley,

2) 5(gur) zíz gur	5 gsg of emmer,
(space)	
3) Á-kal-li	Akali
4) ì-ág	measured out.

Reverse

5) šag$_4$-bi-ta	Out of it
6) 2(gur) lá 4(bán) še gur-sag-gál	1 gsg 200 liters of barley
7) ba-ta-zi	were expended.

An account of barley and emmer. For Akali, see no. 13:17.

No. 18. IM 13383 Pl. 10

Obverse

1) 2 udu-nita	2 rams
2) ^{d}Utu-mu-e	Utu-mu⟨gi⟩
3) ba-laḫ$_4$	took away.
4) Ur-^{d}Šara$_2$-ka-kam	(The sheep) of Ur-Šara.

Reverse

5) 4 mu 10 lá 1 iti	4th year, 9th month.

A record of the withdrawal of two sheep, belonging to Ur-Šara, by the shepherd Utu-mu⟨gi⟩. For Ur-Šara, see above p. 8. For other occurrences of ^{d}Utu-mu-gi$_4$, see no. 20:5 and Gelb, MAD 4, p. 119. His name is usually abbreviated as ^{d}Utu-mu (as in the present text and in no. 20:5).

No. 19. IM 13384 Pl. 10

Obverse

1) 2 kuš u$_8$	2 ewe hides
2) Lugal-ég-gi	Lugal-eg
3) nag-kud Inim-ma-ni-zi-da-ka	at the nag-kud irrigation-device of Inimanizi
4) Ur-^{d}EN.ZU-ra	for Ur-Sin

Reverse

5) ì-na-gíd	flayed(?).
6) Ur- ^{d}Šara$_2$	(The property of) Ur-Šara.
7) 23 mu 2 iti	23d year, 2d month.

An account of hides. For Ur-Šara and Ur-Sin, see above p. 8.

2. Lugal-ég "flays" hides also in MAD 4 93:2, 99:3, and 111:6. Cf. also MAD 4 73:15, 119:5, 138:11, and 168:6. For the interpretation of the name as 'King-of-the-Dike,' see the divine name ^{d}Lugal-ég-ga (Steible, FAOS 5/2, p. 345: Anonym 10:1; Pre-Sargonic), and, further, note the Sargonic personal name Ur-ég-ga (ITT 1 1195:2; Westenholz, *OSP* 2 84 iii 6, 96–97 v 12).

3. For nag-kud, probably a type of canal-regulator, see most recently Steinkeller, *BSA* 4 (1988) 74–79.

5. When said of hides, gíd apparently means 'to flay' (lit., 'to pull') (against Foster, *USP*, p. 71, who, following Jacobsen's suggestion, translates gíd in such contexts as "to haul upstream"). See already Oppenheim, *Eames Collection*, p. 5 and n. 10, and, more recently, *SVS* 1/3, p. 120. This sense of gíd seems fairly certain in the Ur-Šara texts (for examples, see Foster, *USP*, p. 71), in UET 2 suppl. 30:9, as well as in the following Ur III examples: dead sheep kuš-bi é-gal-šè gíd-da 'their hides were flayed for the palace' (Legrain, *TRU* 14:2); adda kuš (nu-)gíd-da 'carcass whose hide was (not) flayed' (Chiera, *STA* 9 i 11′, ii 15′; Reisner, *Telloh* 28 iv 25, 82 rev. 20); (cows) kuš gíd-da (Reisner, *Telloh* 39 rev. 2); (sheep) ri-ri-ga adda(!) kuš-bi gíd-dam (MVN 11 98:24, also line 19). Admittedly, however, in all these examples gíd could mean simply 'to pass along, to transfer'. The latter sense of gíd is well attested in economic texts; see, for example, UET 2 suppl. 19 (said of beer), 35 (said of birds), 44 (said of sheep), etc.

No. 20. IM 13710 Pl. 10

Obverse

1) 26 ma-na síg ùz-da	26 minas of goat hair,
2) Ur-^{d}Šara$_2$-ka-kam	(the property) of Ur-Šara;
3) 14(ma-na) síg ùz-da	14 (minas) of goat hair,

Reverse

4) Ur-^{d}EN.ZU-ka-kam	(the property) of Ur-Sin;
5) ^{d}Utu-mu sipad	(due from) Utu-mu⟨gi⟩, the shepherd.
6) 6 mu 4 iti	6th year, 4th month.

A record of goat hair due to Ur-Šara and Ur-Sin from the shepherd Utu-mu⟨gi⟩. For Ur-Šara and Ur-Sin, see p. 8. For Utu-mu⟨gi⟩, see no. 18.

1. The spellings of ùz with the complements -da and -dè led Landsberger (MSL 8/1, p. 28 n. to line 192a) to introduce the reading ud$_x$, and to suggest that "ùz is a spirantization of ud$_x$." In contrast, Alster (*Or.* 41 [1972] 352) retained the reading ùz, assuming that "z in Sumerian may represent sd, as is the case in classical Greek." The entry ùz = a-sa-tum in SE 67 (MEE 3, p. 198) allows us now to reconstruct the reading of ùz as /uzud/ (the alternative reconstruction /uzd/ is precluded, in my opinion, by the fact that Sumerian does not tolerate consonantal clusters in the final position). For this interpretation, see already Sollberger in TCS 1, p. 188b. When followed by a vowel, /uzud/ loses the second vowel due to contraction and becomes /uzd/, in the same way as /kalag-a/ contracts to /kalga/. For the latter transformation, note the gloss šag$_4$-gal-ga of šag$_4$-kalag in VE 592 (MEE 4, p. 266).

No. 21. IM 13377 — Pl. 11

Obverse

1)	20 lá 2 túg	18 garments,
2)	1 gada bar-dul$_5$	1 linen bar-dul$_5$ garment,
3)	1 gada šag$_4$-gi-da$_5$	1 linen šag$_4$-gi-da$_5$ garment,
4)	1 ^{urudu}šu-lá	1 šu-lá container,
5)	4 ^{urudu}zabar	4 copper mirrors,
6)	20 bar-si síg gíd-da	20 long woolen bands,
7)	30 bar-si gada	30 linen bands,
8)	1 gír	1 dagger,
9)	1 kug-bi gín	its silver (value) is 1 shekel,

Reverse

10)	1 ^{urudu}SAG×GAG PÚ(LAGAB×U) 6-lá	1 copper cup(?), (decorated with?) . . . ,
11)	ki-lá-bi 1 ma-na	its weight (is) 1 mina,
12)	1 ⌜níg(?)⌝-gul	1 pick,
13)	½(!) kug-bi gín	its silver (value) is ½ shekel,
14)	1 pisan gíd-da	1 long basket;
15)	Ur-^{d}EN.ZU ba-úš-a	when Ur-Sin died,
16)	ba-de$_6$	(these objects) were taken away.

This text is an inventory of the belongings of Ur-Sin, one of the associates of Ur-Šara (see p. 8 above). Another text from the Ur-Šara archive which refers to Ur-Sin's death is MAD 4 87. The latter document lists three goats, the property of Ur-Šara, which were 'disbursed when Ur-Sin died' (Ur-^{d}EN.ZU ba-úš-a ba-zi, lines 3–4). Cf. Foster, *USP*, pp. 66, 75.

2. For bar-dul$_5$, a type of elaborate garment, see *PSD* B, pp. 119–21 bar-dul$_5$ A.

3. The garment šag$_4$-gi-da$_5$ is common in Sargonic sources (e.g., OIP 14 145:5; *STTI* 49:3, 82:11; *JCS* 26 [1974] 78 no. 4:1′). It is not to be confused with šag$_4$-ga-dù (Akk. *šakattû*) 'loin-band', for which see most recently Steinkeller, *Or.* 51 (1982) 362. šag$_4$-gi-da$_5$ appears to be a loanword from *šaqītu* 'high'; if so, it probably denotes a "long, full-length garment." The same word possibly occurs in the Ebla literary texts ARET 5 1 and 3, as suggested by the comparison of the following passages: *a-gu-du*, TÚG-*gi-tum* (1 vi 6–7) = *la-mu-gu-du*, *ša-gi-tum* (3 iii 5–6).

4. šu-lá is a type of metal container. Note, especially, *JAOS* 88 (1968) 58, 6N-T662 i 8–10, which lists šu-lá with capacities of 1, ½, and ¼ liter: ⸢1⸣ šu-lá^{urudu} 1 sila$_3$, 3(?) šu-lá^{urudu} ½ sila$_3$, ⸢1(?)⸣ šu-lá^{urudu} igi-4. Other attestations of this container include Westenholz, *OSP* 1 95:7; OIP 14 103:4; TuM 5 147:3; BIN 8 145:5; and ITT 5 6747:4′, 9262:4′. The translation "hand-cuff," proposed by Westenholz, *OSP* 1, p. 52, is obviously incorrect.

5. For the meaning 'mirror' for zabar, see Steinkeller, *ASJ* 9 (1987) 347–49. To the examples cited there, add [1] zabar nim urudu ki-lá-bi 2 ma-na (Westenholz, *OSP* 2 49 i 10–11), probably denoting a mirror decorated with 'flies' (nim).

6. For bar-si 'band, sash', see *PSD* B, pp. 126–27 bar-si A.

10. SAG×GAG is probably to be read here as múḫ or muḫ(ḫ)um; see CAD M/2, pp. 172–73 lexical section of *muḫḫu*. Since the Akkadian equivalent of múḫ/muḫ(ḫ)um is *muḫḫu* 'cranium, top of the head' (note SAG×GAG(!) = *mu-ḫu* SAG in VE 264 [MEE 4, p. 228]), the object in question appears to have been a cup or bowl. For the sign SAG×GAG (= LAK-312), quite rare in third-millennium texts, note the occupation/title SAG×GAG.DU$_8$ 'cupbearer(?)' (perhaps related to SILA$_3$.ŠU.DU$_8$ = sagi), which is found in the Pre-Sargonic text *DP* 135 iv 17. The phrase PÚ 6-lá, which qualifies SAG×GAG in the present text, is obscure.

12. For níg-gul (Akk. *akkullu*) 'pick' or 'mattock', see CAD A/1, pp. 276–77; Limet, *JESHO* 15 (1972) 11; Foster, *USP*, p. 35.

No. 22. IM 5592/4a Pl. 11

Obverse

1) 1(bùr) 1(eše) 4 lá ¼(iku) gana$_2$
2) Šag$_4$-é-TUR gala
3) 2(eše) 3½(iku) gana$_2$
4) Ur-DUN
5) 1(eše) 4½(iku) gana$_2$
(rest destroyed)

Reverse

(uninscribed)

Probably a fragment of the listing of land allotments.

No. 23. IM 5592/4b Pl. 11

Obverse

1)	900 ninda-30-du$_8$ 1(bán)(?!)	900 breads, baked (at the rate of) 30 (breads) per 10(?) liters (of barley),
2)	30 kaš ⸢3(bán)(?)⸣ dug	30 jugs of beer, (at the rate of) ⸢30(?)⸣ liters (of barley per one 30-liter jug of beer),
3)	erin$_2$ Ì-lí-TAB.BA-ke$_4$	the soldiers of Ilī-tappê
4)	šu ba-ab-ti	received;
5)	1(bán) zíd 1(bán) kaš 5(bán) ⟨dug⟩	10 liters of flour, 10 liters of beer, (at the rate of) 50 liters (of barley per one 30-liter jug of beer),
6)	lú-tukul Ì-lí-TAB.BA	the man-at-arms of Ilī-tappê (received);

Reverse

	(space)	
7)	šu-nigin$_2$ 5(gur) 3(pi) 2(bán) 6 sila$_3$ še ⸢x (x) ninda⸣ gur-sag-[g]ál	the total of 5 gur 206 liters of barley, . . . , (and) bread (measured by) gsg.
8)	2 mu 2 iti 16 ud(!)	2d year, 2d month, 16th day.

A record of barley used to produce bread, beer, and flour rations. This text falls under the Umma beer-and-bread texts (see discussion of no. 24), though it differs from the latter documents in two respects. First, in contrast to the standard beer-and-bread texts, which tend to be quite long, it records only two expenditures. Second, it has a verb following the names of ration recipients (line 4), a feature not found in other beer-and-bread texts. As argued recently by Kraus, (*Verfügungen* pp. 253–55), what is meant by "beer" in these texts is actually beer mix (Akk. *billatu*).

The amounts recorded in the body of the text do not agree with the total. Note, however, that in line 1 the interpretation of the last sign is open to question.

1. The sign which I tentatively interpret as 1(bán) looks like 2(pi).

The formula ninda-30-du$_8$ describes the grain/flour content of bread: from every 10 liters of grain/flour 30 loaves of bread were baked. See Blome, *Or.* 34–35 (1928) 129ff.; Foster, *USP*, p. 15.

2, 5. In the Sargonic texts from Umma, beer is measured in jugs (dug) of 30 liters each. See Powell, *RA* 70 (1976) 98–100.

7. The reading of ⸢x (x)⸣ as kaš zíd, suggested by the context, is not confirmed by the collation.

No. 24. IM 5592/7 Pl. 12

Obverse

1) 120 ni[nda 2(dug) 1(bán) kaš 1(pi) 1(bán) (dug) . . .]
2) 90+[x(?) ninda x] kaš [5(bán) (dug) . . .]

3) 2(bán) kaš 5(bán) ⸢x(-x)⸣-lá
4) 60 ninda 1(dug) 4(bán) kaš 5(bán) dug
5) lú Ga-súr^{ki}
6) 60 ninda 2(bán) kaš 5(bán) dub-sa[r]
7) ⸢60⸣ [nin]da 2(bán) kaš 5(bán) lú-e[me(?)]
8) [10(?)]+20 ninda 1(bán) kaš 5(bán) má[š-šu-gíd-gíd]
9) 40 ninda 1(bán) kaš 5(bán) a-z[u(?)]
10) 30 ninda 1(bán) kaš 5(bán) šeš šagina
11) 30 ninda 1(bán) kaš 5(bán) sukal šagina
12) 30 ninda 1(bán) kaš 5(bán) sipad-anše
13) 15 ninda 5 sila$_3$ kaš 5(bán) geme$_2$ Gù-dé-a
14) 15 ninda 5 sila$_3$ kaš ⸢5(bán)⸣ geme$_2$ Šu-Eš$_4$-dar
15) 40 ninda 2(bán) kaš 5(bán)
16) lú Lagaš^{ki} 2-bi
17) 120 ninda 1(dug) kaš 1(pi) 1(bán) dug 1(dug) kaš 5(bán) dug
18) [n]u-banda$_3$ Lagaš[^{ki}(-me)]

Reverse

19) [20]+20 ninda 5(dug) kaš 5(bán) dug
20) [. . .] AŠ-inversum(?)-bi
21) ⸢2(?)(bán)⸣ kaš 5(bán) Gala nagar-gal
22) 2 ninda-banšur lú Ga-súr^{ki}
23) 1(ninda-banšur) Amar-si$_4$ 1(ninda-banšur) ^{d}En-líl-lá 1(ninda-banšur) Ab-ba
24) 1(ninda-banšur) Lú-^{d}Šara$_2$ 1(ninda-banšur) Zag-mu
25) 1(ninda-banšur) Gu-ti-um 1(ninda-banšur) šabra-bi
26) 12 ninda dumu-dumu 2-bi
27) 270 ninda-30-du$_8$ 2(dug) kaš 1(pi) 1(bán) dug
28) 2(dug) 1(pi) kaš 5(bán) dug šagina
29) 3+[1] ninda IŠ(?!) 2(ninda) Ur-^{d}⸢X⸣-[. . .]
30) 31 ninda-20-du$_8$ dug ⸢x⸣
31) 4(bán) zíd lú Ga-sú[r^{ki}]
32) šu-nigin$_2$ 1160+[x ninda-50-du$_8$]
33) 276 ⸢ninda⸣-[30-du$_8$]
34) 31 ninda-⸢20⸣-[du$_8$]
35) 5(dug) 1(bán) k[aš 1(pi) 1(bán) dug]
36) 14+[x(dug) kaš 5(bán) dug]
37) 1+[x . . .]
(rest destroyed)

Left Edge

⸢4(?)⸣ mu 4 iti 5 ud

A record of beer and bread rations. For the text type, see Foster, *USP*, pp. 110–11, group C.3.3.II. Another text belonging to the same group is no. 25; cf. also no. 23.

The Umma beer-and-bread texts are the Sargonic equivalent of Ur III "messenger tablets." Like the latter documents, they record expenditures of travel provisions to various state officials and their dependents. In the present text, of special interest is the mention of the 'man of Gasur' and his retinue (lines 4–5, 22–26, 31). Note also the presence of a group of people from Lagaš (lines 15–18), as well as that of a 'general' (šagina) (lines 10–11, 28).

1. The amount and the type of beer are reconstructed on the basis of the total in line 35, as compared with lines 17 and 27.

33. The total corresponds to lines 27 and 29.

No. 25. IM 5592/16 Pl. 12

Obverse

(beginning destroyed)
1′) [x] kaš 3(bán) dug Ur-^{d}Nin-a-zu
2′) 60 ninda 6 sag-ninda 15(sila$_3$) kaš 1(pi) dug
3′) ⸢15(sila$_3$)⸣ kaš 3(bán) dug Ì-lí-en-nu
4′) 60 ninda 6 sag-ninda 15(sila$_3$) kaš 1(pi) dug
5′) ⸢15(sila$_3$)⸣ kaš 3(bán) dug ⸢Pù⸣-ì-lí
6′) 30 ninda 3 sag-ninda
7′) ⸢15(sila$_3$)⸣ kaš 1(pi) dug Šu-na-KU(?)-K[A(?)]
8′) 30 ninda 3 sag-ninda
9′) 15(sila$_3$) ⸢kaš⸣ 1(pi) dug Ama-bar[ag(-gi)]
10′) ⸢30⸣ ninda 3 sag-[ninda]
11′) [15(sila$_3$) k]aš 1(pi) ⸢^{d}EN.ZU⸣-[. . .]
12′) 30 ninda ⸢3⸣ sag-ninda
13′) ⸢15(sila$_3$)⸣ kaš 1(pi) [dug . . .]-⸢šag$_5$(?)⸣
14′) 10+[20(?) ninda] 2+[1(?) sa]g-ninda

Lower Edge

15′) 1(bán) ka[š] 1 še ⸢x⸣ [. . .]-ì-lí

Reverse

16′) 15(sila$_3$) kaš 1(pi) dug Gissu
17′) 2+[x . . .] Ì-ma-rí(?)-su-ni
18′) ⸢20⸣+[x] ⸢sag⸣-ninda
19′) ⸢2(bán) kaš(?)⸣ [l]ú-tukul TU(?)-⸢x⸣
20′) ⸢1⸣ ninda-banšur Lú-^{d}[N]anna
21′) 1(ninda-banšur) Sar-⸢um⸣-ì-lí 1(ninda-banšur) L[ú- . . .]
22′) 1(ninda-banšur) Ì-lí-en-nu 1(ninda-banšur) [. . .]
23′) [1(ninda-banšur)] ⸢lú-uru⸣ 1(ninda-banšur) lú ⸢x⸣-[. . .]
24′) [1(?)(ninda-banšur L]ú-⸢barag(?)⸣-ab-du 5(ninda-banšur) ⸢x⸣-[. . .]
25′) [x(ninda-banšur)] nar 5(ninda-banšur) ⸢sukal⸣ lú Túl-t[a(?)]
26′) 1(ninda-banšur) lú Ku-li

27′) šu-nigin$_2$ 570 ⸢ninda⸣-50-du$_8$
28′) [10(?)]+30 ninda-30-du$_8$ 4 ninda-šu(?)
29′) [. . . k]aš 1(pi) dug 2(dug) kaš 3(bán) dug
30′) [. . .] ⸢x⸣
(rest destroyed)

A record of beer and bread rations. The tablet is very poorly preserved. For the text type, see no. 24.

No. 26. IM 5592/9 Pl. 13

Obverse

i 1) [x]+20 ⸢dug-ŠID⸣
2) [20(?)]+40 dug-gur$_8$-gur$_8$
3) [x]+⸢60(?)⸣ ga-ríg
4) [x]+⸢60(?)⸣ sila$_3$
5) [x]+⸢60(?)⸣ U.LAL
6) [a-r]á 1-kam
7) [x du]g-KA.ZI
8) [x]+12 dug-gur$_8$-gur$_8$
9) [x]+⸢60(?)⸣ ga-ríg
10) [x] sila$_3$
11) [x]+⸢120(?)⸣ U.LAL
12) [a-r]á 2-ka-ma-kam
13) [x]+36 dug-ŠID
14) [x]+⸢10(?)⸣+6 dug-gur$_8$-⸢gur$_8$⸣

ii 1) 240 ga-[ríg]
2) 300 [sila$_3$]
3) 120 U.LAL
4) a-rá 3-ka-ma-kam
5) 70 dug-KA.ZI
6) 20 dug-gur$_8$-gur$_8$
7) 360 ga-ríg
8) 600 sila$_3$
9) 100 U.LAL
10) a-rá 4-ka-ma-kam
11) 26 dug-gur$_8$-gur$_8$
12) 80 ga-ríg
13) 300 sila$_3$
14) 70 U.LAL
15) a-rá 5-ka-ma-kam
16) 20 dug-gur$_8$-gur$_8$
17) 80 ⸢ga-ríg⸣

Reverse

iii 1) 60+[x sila$_3$/U.LAL]
2) a-rá ⸢6⸣-[ka-ma-kam]
3) 20 du[g- . . .]
4) [x]+20 [dug(?)- . . .]
5) [. . .]
6) 120+[x . . .]
7) ⸢a-rá⸣ [7]-⸢ka⸣-[ma-kam]
8) [x d]ug-⸢gur$_8$⸣-[gur$_8$]
9) [x g]a-r[íg]
10) [x]+240 ⸢sila$_3$⸣
11) [x]+240 [U].LAL
12) ⸢a⸣-r[á 8]-ka-ma-kam
13) 30 dug-KA.⸢ZI⸣
14) 24 [du]g-gur$_8$-[gur$_8$]
15) 140 ga-[ríg]
16) [x]+180 [sila$_3$]
17) [x]+240 U.LAL
18) [a]-rá 10 lá 1-k[a-ma-kam]

iv 1) [blank(?)]
2) [(šu-nigin$_2$) x]+40 dug-KA.ZI
3) [x]+136 d[ug-ŠID]
4) [x]+290 lá 2 d[ug]-⸢gur$_8$-gur$_8$⸣
5) 2120+[x] ⸢ga⸣-[ríg]
6) ⸢4080(?)⸣ si[la$_3$]
7) [x]+30 lá 2 ⸢U.LAL⸣
8) [X]-DÙL-kug-ke$_4$
9) [ì(?)]-kú [(x)]
10) [z]i-ga ⸢X⸣-[. . .]
(rest destroyed)

This unusual text concerns nine separate issues of various pots. The large numbers of pots involved suggest that we find here a record of the potter's output. The partly preserved colophon (iv 8–10) should perhaps be translated: '[X]-DUL-kug received (the pots); the expenditure of ⸢PN(?)⸣.' A related text is no. 32, which also concerns pots. For similar documents in later periods, see MVN 1 231–32 (Ur III), edited and discussed by Waetzoldt, *WO* 6 (1971) 7–41; Edzard, *Tell ed-Dēr* no. 198 (OB).

i 1, 13. dug-ŠID: A type of pot. Note 3 ì-šáḫ ŠID '3 ŠID pots of lard' in CT 50 52 iii 4 (Sargonic).

i 2. dug-gur$_8$-gur$_8$: A large earthen container, used for storing beer (Akk. ***kurkurru***). In Pre-Sargonic texts this word is spelled dug-gur$_4$-gur$_4$ (e.g., Nikolski 1 318 ii′ 2) or gur$_4$-gur$_4$ (e.g., VAS 14 21 i 1, 48 i 1). See also DUG.GUR$_4$ = *gú-gú-ru$_{12}$-tum/du-um*, DUG.GUR$_4$.GUR$_4$ = *gu-ra-ru$_{12}$/lu* ŠE+DIN in VE 938–39 (MEE 4, p. 304). Sargonic sources use the form gur$_8$-gur$_8$, usually without dug (e.g., Nikolski 2 25:1, 26:1; CT 50 52 ii 6; MCS 9 232:30; *RTC* 221 i 2, 222 i 3, 223 i 4). In later periods one finds the spellings dug-gur$_4$-gur$_4$ and dug-níg-ta-gur$_4$ (see CAD K, pp. 563–64 under *kurkurru* A). The Ur III kur-ku-dù/ku-kur-dù = /kud͡rkud͡ru/ (for examples, see CAD K, p. 564a) and the OB and NA *gugguru/gukkuru* (= dug-níg-ta-gur$_4$, see CAD G, pp. 122–23) evidently denote the same pot. It is generally believed that, in Pre-Sargonic Lagaš, *kurkurru* had a standard size of 10 liters (see Bauer, *Lagasch*, p. 214; read as nigin), but this view has recently been questioned by Powell, *RLA* 7 (forthcoming) *sub* "Masse und Gewichte" § IV.B.2.e, who suggests that *kurkurru* "may have contained the equivalent of 9 sila$_3$ in the dry capacity system, but the size remains elusive." *kurkurru* is used as a standard beer-measure also in the Sargonic beer-and-bread texts from Umma (Nikolski 2 25–32; Foster, *USP* nos. 3–4), its size there being unknown (see Foster, *USP*, p. 14). The Ur III kur-ku-dù/ku-kur-dù ranged in capacity between 30 and 600 liters, though 100 liters seems to have been its usual size (see Waetzoldt, *WO* 6 [1971] 16–17).

i 3. ga-ríg: Probably a type of bowl (any connection with ga-ríg 'comb'?). Note that in the Lagaš Sargonic texts ITT 1 1243:5 and 1285:9 ga-ríg are used to store soup (tu$_7$) (see p. 18 under no. 27). The same container may also occur in the following examples: 6 ga-ríg (among various pots and containers—ITT 2/2, pp. 31–31 4570, transliteration only); ga-ríg kug-babbar (A 30744, unpubl.; courtesy of M. Civil); 1 ga-ríg zabar (listed following a bronze šu-ša-lá, for which see below under i 5) (TCS 1 364:5).

i 4. sila$_3$: A type of bowl (Akk. *qû*); see CAD Q, pp. 288–90.

i 5. U.LAL: Probably to be read šuš-lá and connected with šu-sal-la, a type of bowl (suggested by M. Civil). See šu-sal za, šu-sal bur (MEE 3 45–46 iii 10′, iv 6 = Civil, in Cagni, *Ebla 1975-1985*, pp. 143–44); na$_4$-bur-šu-sal-la = ŠU-*u* (Hh. XVI 277 = MSL 10, p. 12). The same word, spelled syllabically, appears in TCS 1 364:4: 1 šu-ša-lá zabar (following a bronze ga-ríg).

i 7. dug-KA.ZI: Attested also in no. 32:1, 5, 7. Probably the same object as dug-gú-zi/dug-ka-a-su (Akk. *kāsu*) 'goblet, bowl' (CAD K, pp. 253–56). For the latter word, note the spelling dug-KU.ZI in no. 12 i 2. The early occurrences of (dug-)KA.ZI include: 12 urudu zabar KA.ZI (Nikolski 1 304 i 1; Pre-Sargonic); 1 zabar KA.ZI ki-lá-bi 1⅓ ŠA ma-na (ITT 1 1370:1–2; Sargonic); and 2 ì-šáḫ dug-KA.ZI (BIN 8 312:1; Sargonic).

No. 27. IM 5592/ . . . Pl. 14

Collated by J. A. Black.

Obverse

i 1) [1] udu-niga
2) ⸢1⸣ šeg$_9$-bar
3) 8 mašda(MAŠ.GAG)
4) 2 ba-ba-az uz
5) ⸢10⸣ uz

6) [1(?)]+4 mušen
7) [1]+1 dug ga
8) [x] ⸢1(pi)⸣ 1(bán) 5 sila$_3$ še ar-[za-n]a gur A-ga-dè^{ki}
9) [x] ⸢1(pi)⸣ imgaga$_3$(ZÍZ.AN)
10) [x] ^{giš}ḫašḫur
11) [. . .] ŠIM×ÙḪ
12) [. . .]-⸢x⸣-[. . .]

ii 1) 20(gur) 3(pi) 1(bán) 4 [sila$_3$ . . .]
2) 1(gur) še g[ur] ⸢x x⸣ [. . .]
3) 1(pi) še zíd-⸢sig$_{15}$(?)⸣
4) 2(pi) 3(bán) še zé-i[r- . . .]
5) 10(gur) še gur ba-ba-[munu$_4$]
6) 3(gur) imgaga$_3$ g[ur]
7) 3 sila$_3$ ì-nun
8) 1 sila$_3$ làl
9) ⸢2⸣ ma-na erin
10) 1 ma-na šim-GÍR-*gunû*
11) ⅓ ma-na ŠIM×ÙḪ
12) Puzur$_4$-Ma-ma
13) 5(gur) imgaga$_3$ gur
14) 3(gur) še gur
15) [. . .] ⸢še-li⸣

Reverse

iii 1) [PN]
2) [x(gur)] ⸢še⸣ g[ur]
3) 2(bán) ì-nun
4) 1(bán) làl
5) 1(pi) 3(bán) zú-lum
6) 2 dug ga
7) 3(bán) ba-ba-munu$_4$
8) 5(?)(bán) gú-gú-gal-gal
9) 5(bán) gú-gú-TUR-TUR
10) 2(bán) gú-gú-KU-mašda
11) 4(bán) še-giš-ì
12) 2(bán) lá 3 sila$_3$ lam-gal-gal
13) 5 sila$_3$ lam-TUR-TU[R]
14) 5 sila$_3$ [. . .]
15) 2⅓ sila$_3$ g[i$_4$- . . .]
16) ⸢2 x⸣ [. . .]

iv (one line missing, if anything)
1) [. . .] ⸢x⸣
2) [x ^{giš}ḫaš]ḫur(?) šè-ir-gu
3) [x ^{giš}pè]š(?) šè-ir-gu
4) [x m]a-na erin
5) [x m]a-na šurmin$_x$(ERIN)$^{\text{šu-me}}$

6) [x m]a-na šim-GÍR-*gunû*
7) [x m]a-na ŠIM×ÙḪ
8) [nar(?)]-me
9) [x]+3 dug ga
10) [. . .]
11) [(ki)] ⸢balag-bi⸣-šè
12) [Sa]r-ga-lí-LUGAL-rí
13) [Ki]-en-gi-šè
14) [b]a-gin-na-a
15) [uz-ga-n]e
16) [. . .]-⸢x⸣
17) [1 mu x iti]

A list of foodstuffs and spices expended to several persons in connection with Šarkališarri's journey to Sumer. The issuing party appear to have been the uz-ga personnel (iv 15–16). If our reconstruction is correct, the recipients were three(?) individuals (i 12, ii 12, iii 1) and a group of singers(?) (iv 8). The latter also received additional provisions 'for their balag-instrument' ([(ki)] ⸢balag-bi⸣-šè, iv 11). Note that the first group of provisions (i 1–12) includes a number of animals: barley-fed sheep (udu-niga), deer (šeg$_9$-bar), gazelles (mašda), *paspasu* birds (ba-ba-az uz), *ūsu* birds (uz), and some other birds (mušen) without specific identification.

This text is closely related to the Umma tablets MCS 9 247 and CT 50 52, which record similar expenditures and concern the same occasion: lugal Ki-en-gi-šè ì-im-gin-na-a uz-ga-ne [. . .] (MCS 9 247:28′–30′); lugal Ki-en-gi-šè ì-gin-na-a Zabalam^{ki}-a ì-gíd-da-am (CT 50 52:46–49). The first of them, dated 1 mu 6 iti, lists various foodstuffs and spices expended to four persons; the latter, dated four months earlier, is a record of provisions (nidba) disbursed on behalf of the king, the queen, and possibly a prince. Other tablets belonging to the same group are MCS 9 232 (not dated), a list of expended foodstuffs and spices, and BRM 3 26, dated to the 7th month of year 1, a pisan-dub-ba label, which concerns 'records of the disbursements which were made (when) the king went to Nippur' (im-sar-ra zi-ga lugal Nibru^{ki} im-gin-a). For other documents relating to Šarkališarri's journey to Sumer, stemming from Lagaš and possibly also from Isin, see Foster, *JANES* 12 (1980) 37–40.

The fact that, as shown by MCS 9 247, CT 50 52, and BRM 3 26, Šarkališarri traveled to Sumer during the "first year," has, I believe, interesting implications for the meaning of the mu-iti dating system. Early studies on the mu-iti texts (e.g., Ungnad, *RLA* 2, p. 132) generally assumed that this particular dating system is based on regnal years. This view was recently contested by Foster (*USP*, p. 7), who asserted that "since the Pre-Sargonic mu-iti system referred to the rule of the énsi of Umma, the numeration of the mu-iti texts studied here must also refer to the era of the ensi of Umma." But Foster failed to offer any hard evidence in support of this supposition. In fact, the testimony of MCS 9 247, CT 50 52, and BRM 3 26 is a compelling argument in favor of interpreting the mu-iti dates as regnal years, since there is independent evidence that Šarkališarri's journey actually took place during the first year of his reign (see Foster, *JANES* 12 [1980] 39–40, with a conclusion that "the occasion for this journey was his [i.e., Šarkališarri's] coronation as king of Sumer and Akkad"). It is theoretically possible, of course, that *both* the ensi$_2$ of Umma and the king of Akkade assumed their respective offices in the same year; but, until this has been fully demonstrated, a simpler and more logical explanation must be that the "first year" recorded in the tablets in question is that of Šarkališarri.

i 4. I assume that ba-ba-az uz corresponds to UZ.TUR (Akk. *paspasu*) 'duck', with ba-ba-az representing a loanword from *paspasu*. The ba-ba-az birds occur also in the Sargonic text *USP* no. 26:20 (an issue of barley for ba-ba-az) and in the Ur III text ITT 5 6794:1–4 (an issue of barley for 120 ^{mušen}ba-ba-za(!), brought from Adamdun). The Sumerian /babaz(a)/ should probably be recognized in the gloss bi-bad, which is assigned to UZ.TUR in Diri V 220 (see MSL 8/2, p. 131 note to line 200). If so, the reading of UZ.TUR could be reconstructed as /bazbaz/, allowing in turn one to interpret the present occurrence as $^{\text{ba-ba-az}}$bazbaz$_x$(UZ). Since the following line mentions uz (Akk. *ūsu*), which is also translated as 'duck' (*AHw*, pp. 1438–39), *paspasu* and *ūsu* must have denoted two different (though probably related) bird species.

i 8. For (še) ar-za-na 'barley groats', a loanword from Akkadian *arsānu*, see CAD A/2, pp. 306–7; Postgate, *BSA* 1 (1984) 108.

i 9. For imgaga$_3$ (or udra) (Akk. *kunāšu*) 'emmer', see CAD K, pp. 536–38. imgaga$_3$ is also equated with the emmer products *buṭuttu* and *dišiptuḫḫu* (see CAD B, p. 359; D, p. 160). As suggested by Powell (*BSA* 1 [1984] 51), in third-millennium texts imgaga$_3$ does not seem to be used for "emmer" but only for partially processed emmer.

i 10. Despite the objections raised by Gelb (in *Kraus AV*, pp. 67–82, 484), ḫašḫur almost certainly denotes a type of apple (crab apple?), and not apricot. Gelb's main argument against this interpretation was the alleged absence of archeological and ethnographic data for apples being threaded on strings, which disagrees with the usage of strings (*šerku*) to preserve the ḫašḫur fruits, as documented in third-millennium texts. See, however, Ellison et al., *Journal of Archaeological Science* 5 (1978) 167–77 (cited in addenda to Gelb's article, *Kraus AV*, p. 484), who write that small crab apples, cut in half and threaded on a string, were discovered in ED graves at Ur. See now also Postgate, *BSA* 3 (1987) 117–19; Civil, in *Reiner AV*, p. 45 n. 13.

i 11. The reading of ŠIM×ÙḪ (= LAK-658), a type of aromatic, is uncertain. For other attestations, stemming from Pre-Sargonic and Sargonic texts, see *ŠL* 223. As demonstrated by the spellings da ŠIM×ÙḪ-ga-šè and da ŠIM×ÙḪ-ga-ta in ITT 1 1175:2, 4 (Sargonic), where ŠIM×ÙḪ is a toponym, and the writing ŠIM×ÙḪ-ga in *Šulgi* X 18, the word ends in /g/. With Klein, (*Hymns*, p. 148), I assume that ŠIM×ÙḪ is an early graph of šimbulug (Akk. *ballukku*), which appears as ŠIM×BULUG, ŠIM×MUG, ŠIM×ŠI, or ŠIM.BALA in later texts (see CAD B, p. 64). In turn, šimbulug may be identical with šim-buluḫ(ḪAL) (Akk. *baluḫḫu*; see CAD B, pp. 74–75; see also ḪAL = *bu-lu/ru-uḫ* in Proto-Ea 143), though note that *baluḫḫu* and *ballukku* occur together in MAD 1 286:3, 5. At any rate, in ŠIM×ÙḪ the sign ÙḪ appears to be a phonetic complement, that is, ùḫ or ug_x. Compare the spelling $šimbi_x$(ŠIM×PI), occurring in Gudea Cylinder A xviii 21, xix 6, and in the Ur III PN Ama-ŠIM×PI (Limet, *Anthroponymie*, p. 376), which replaces the usual šimbi(ŠIM×SIG_7).

ii 3. For zíd-sig_{15}(KAL) (Akk. *ḫišiltu*), a type of flour, see CAD Ḫ, p. 205; Bauer, *Lagasch*, p. 423.

ii 4. Reconstruction uncertain. Cf. perhaps *ṣirpētu* (a dish made with barley and milk or fat) (CAD Ṣ, p. 208). Any connection with *sirdu* 'olive' would be most unlikely.

ii 5. For ba-ba(-za)-$munu_4$ (Akk. *pappāsu*) 'milled malt' or the like, see Hrozný, *Getreide*, pp. 101–7; *AHw*, p. 824.

ii 10. For (šim-)GÍR-*gunû* (Akk. *asu*) 'myrtle', see CAD A/2, pp. 342–44. For the evidence suggesting that in this context GÍR-*gunû* has a reading $kišik_2$/g, see Biggs, OIP 99, pp. 69–70.

ii 15. For še-li (Akk. *kikkirânu*), an aromatic, see CAD K, pp. 351–52.

iii 1. Since iii 2 lists another issue of barley, and since barley is mentioned just two lines earlier, I assume that this line records a personal name.

iii 8. gú-gú-gal-gal (also in no. 41:11) (Akk. *ḫallūru*), lit., 'big pulse', is usually identified as 'chick-pea'. Stol (*BSA* 2 [1985] 127–30) now considers 'broad bean' (*Vicia faba*) as a possible identification. Note, however, the evidence which he cites in addendum (ibid., p. 133), which may favor the choice of 'chick-pea'.

iii 9. gú-gú-TUR-TUR (also in no. 41:12) (Akk. *kakku*), lit., 'small pulse', is 'lentil', or, as suggested recently by Stol (*BSA* 2 [1985] 129–30), 'common pea' (*Pisum sativum*). Note that no. 42 i 8 lists simply gú-gú, which probably combines the "big" and "small" pulses.

iii 10. gú-gú-KU-mašda is evidently a type of pulse, but I am not aware of any other attestations of this vegetable. Civil suggests the reading $še_{10}$-mašda, 'droppings of the gazelle' and cites as parallels a-gar-gar mašda (Akk. *piq(q)an ṣabīti*; CAD Ṣ, p. 44a) and AḪ.AḪ.AḪ.ḪI (probably to be read $agargar_x$) mašda (TuM n.s. 1/2 358 i 8). The interpretation tukul-mašda, '"weapon" of the gazelle' appears less likely.

iii 11. For the meaning 'sesame' for še-giš-ì, see now the contributions of Waetzoldt, Stol, Postgate, and Bedigian in *BSA* 2 (1985).

iii 12–13. Although it is clear that lam-gal-gal and lam-TUR-TUR are varieties of nuts, their identification is uncertain. The Sumerian and Akkadian terms for nuts were discussed recently by Postgate (*BSA* 3 [1987] 133–35), who, following Stol (*On Trees*, pp. 1–16), identifies lam-gal-gal with (GIŠ.)LAM.GAL (Akk. *buṭuttu*) 'terebinth'—previously translated as 'pistachio'. However, the third-millennium nut terminology is much more complicated than the picture drawn by Postgate, and so a review of this whole problem is in order. Beginning with the Akkadian terminology, the following words for nuts occur in third-millennium texts:

1. *šiqdu* 'almond' (the identification is based on good Semitic etymology; for examples, see Waetzoldt, *BSA* 2 [1985] 90 n. 8).
2. *buṭuttu* 'terebinth'; see GIŠ.$EŠ_{22}$(LAM×KUR) = bu_x(NI)-*du-du* VE 462, followed by GIŠ.LAM (without a translation) (MEE 4, p. 251).

3. *lupānu* (a type of nut); see MCS 9 232:11, collated by Westenholz, *OSP* 2, p. 30 (*lu-ba-nu*), listed following lam.

The Sumerian terms for nuts are:

1. lam-gal-gal (the present occurrence and ITT 2/2 4658, transliteration only—in both instances, lam-TUR-TUR is also mentioned).
2. eš$_{22}$ (or ešu, see S^{b} I 217), which is identified with *buṭuttu* in VE 462, and listed together with giš-lam in Westenholz, *OSP* 2 1:3–4, rev. 2′–3′.
3. (giš-)lam; see (*a*) GIŠ.LAM in VE 463, which is listed separately from GIŠ.EŠ$_{22}$ = *buṭuttu* in VE 462; (*b*) lam, listed with *lupānu* in MCS 9 232; and (*c*) giš-lam, listed together with giš-eš$_{22}$ in Westenholz, *OSP* 2 1.
4. lam-tur-tur (the present occurrence and ITT 2/2 4568—both also mention lam-gal-gal—and *STTI* 44:4).

The relevant lexical evidence is as follows (for the references, see CAD and *AHw sub voce*):

1. eš$_{22}$ = *lupānu*, *šiqdu*, and *lammu*.
2. lam = *šiqdu*, *lammu*, and *lukʾu*.
3. lam-gal = *buṭuttu* and *lupānu*.
4. lam-ḫal = *lupānu*.
5. giš-lam-TUR = *tu/arʾazu* (Hh. III 137 = MSL 5, p. 103, where it is listed separately from giš-lam-ḫal = *lupānu* and giš-lam-gal = *buṭuttu*; cf. also *šerʾaz*(*z*)*u*, listed in *AHw*, p. 1216a).
6. Finally, note the sequence lam, ⸢lam⸣-TUR, ⸢lam⸣-gal, and ⸢šag$_{4}$⸣ lam-gal, which appears in an OB forerunner to Hh. XXIV (MSL 11, p. 161 v′ 28–31).

These data allow us to make the following observations:

1. lam-gal-gal is different from lam-TUR-TUR.
2. eš$_{22}$ is different from lam (the evidence of VE and Westenholz, *OSP* 2 1).
3. eš$_{22}$ may be *buṭuttu* (if VE is correct).
4. lam is different from *lupānu* (MCS 9 232).
5. *lammu* is a loanword from lam.
6. *lukʾu* is a loanword from lug$_{x}$(LAM) (see lu-ug ⸢GIŠ.LAM⸣ = *lukʾu*, *lammu*, *šiqdu* in Diri II App. Bogh. 222a–23b, cited in CAD L, p. 67b).
7. lam-ḫal is probably a phonetic variant of lam-gal (note especially Hh. III 135, where giš-lam-gal interchanges with giš-lam-ḫal).

For an evaluation of these data, of basic importance, naturally, is the equation eš$_{22}$ = *buṭuttu* in VE 462. Assuming that this identification is correct and that *lammu* and *lukʾu* are synonymous with *šiqdu*, we would arrive at the following distribution of the third-millennium terminology:

1. eš$_{22}$ = *buṭuttu* 'terebinth'.
2. lam = *šiqdu*, *lammu* '(a type of) almond'.
3. lug$_{x}$(LAM) = *šiqdu*, *lukʾu* '(a type of) almond'.

4. lam-gal-gal = *lupānu* (a type of nut).
5. lam-TUR-TUR = *tu/arʾazu* (a type of nut).

It goes without saying that the above interpretation must be considered highly tentative, because it is evident from the lexical evidence that there was a general confusion of the various words.

iv 2–3. Since the signs are preserved incompletely, it is impossible to tell which line records ḫašḫur and which, pèš. For *šerku* 'string', see Gelb, in *Kraus AV*, pp. 67–78. The spelling šè-ir-gu is new. In this connection, note that the writing ÉŠ.ŠER$_7$.GU (MCS 9 232:20, 21, 247:13′, 14′), which Gelb (in *Kraus AV*, p. 75), analyzed as éš 'rope' + *šerku*, is simply to be explained as ^{šè}šer$_7$-gu.

iv 5. For šurmin$_x$(ERIN)$^{šu\text{-}me}$ (Akk. *šurmēnu*) 'cypress', see now VE 379 (MEE 4, p. 242): GIŠ.ŠU.ME = *šè-rí-mi-nu, ša-mi-nu*. For other writings of this word in third-millennium texts, see Civil, *OA* 22 (1983) 3.

iv 15. Reconstructed on the basis of MCS 9 247:30′. The term uz-ga is notoriously difficult; see most recently Foster, *USP*, p. 105; Cooper, *Agade*, p. 256; Michalowski, *Lamentation*, pp. 104–5. The earliest attestations of uz-ga come from Sargonic texts (e.g., *USP* nos. 26:2, 3, 5, 10, 14; BIN 8 336:3 [lú-uz-ga]; OIP 14 113:2 [uz-ga-me], 118:8 [uz-ga-ne]), where it denotes a profession or title. The Ur III texts from Drehem mention a building or establishment é-uz-ga, probably located at Nippur, which was a recipient of small numbers of livestock and birds (see Jones-Snyder, pp. 227–32). Contrary to common belief, there is absolutely no evidence that the Drehem é-uz-ga was involved in fattening animals, and thus the reconstruction *bīt* [*marî*] in the translation of [udu] é-uz-ga in Hh. XIII 92a, proposed by Landsberger (MSL 8/1, p. 15), is obviously wrong (this is also M. Civil's opinion—private communication). Since the occurrences of uz-ga in literary texts suggest a cultic locus of some sort, van Dijk's suggestion (*Götterlieder*, p. 125) that uz-ga was "ein heiliger Bezirk im Bereich des Tempels" is probably correct. Accordingly, the uz-ga people of Sargonic texts very likely represent personnel of that shrine. Here one notes the term uš-ga, equated in lexical texts with *uškû*, *girseqû*, and *šerru* (Lu IV 89–90; Diri IV 156; Antagal C 236 [written UŠ$^{bu\text{-}ug\text{-}ga}$GÁ]; *AHw*, p. 1441), all denoting a type of servant, which may be a variant spelling of uz-ga.

No. 28. IM 5592/8 Pl. 15

Obverse

i 1) [x ma-n]a síg
2) [. . .]-barag
3) [dumu U]r-^{d}Nu-muš-da
4) 14 ma-na síg
5) G[Á(?)-x]-⌜x⌝-TUR
6) [dumu . . . -A]B
7) [x ma-na sí]g

8) [. . .]
9) [x ma-n]a síg
10) [Ur]-^{giš}gigir$_2$-e
11) [dumu . . . -A]B
12) [x ma-na s]íg
13) [. . .]-⸢x⸣
14) [. . . D]A(?)-KAB
15) [. . . G]IŠ(?) ⸢x⸣
16) [. . .]-⸢x-ke$_4$(?)⸣
17) [. . .]-lá-a

ii 1) 34½ ma-na s[íg]
2) Ur-^{d}Ba-ú
3) 8 ma-na síg
4) Me-zu
5) 1 gú 4 ma-na síg
6) Ab-ba
7) dumu Ur-UM+ME-ga
8) 3⅓ ma-na síg
9) Sig$_4$-zi
10) 4 ma-n[a síg]
11) DINGIR-ni
12) dumu Šeš-šag$_5$
13) 3½ ma-na ⸢síg⸣
14) Ur-^{d}Alla(NAGAR)
15) dumu Ur-mes
16) 16½ ma-na ⸢síg⸣
17) KA-⸢kug⸣
18) dumu Lugal-èš
19) 1 gú 25⅓ ma-na ⸢síg⸣

Reverse

iii 1) En-zi
2) 30 ma-na síg
3) A-ba-mu-na
4) dumu Gissu
5) 30 lá ⅔ ma-na síg
6) Al-lú
7) dumu Ur-^{d}Saman$_3$(NUN.ŠE.ÉŠ.BU)
8) 6 ma-na síg
9) Lugal-nisag-e
10) 2⅔ ma-na síg
11) É-[. . .]
12) 20 ma-[na síg]
13) Íd-⸢pa(?)⸣-[è(?)]
14) 10 ma-n[a síg]
15) Ur-ni[gin$_3$]

16) dumu Ur-^{d}Iškur
17) 20 lá 1 ma-na [síg]
18) É-ú-šim-[(e)]
19) 30 lá 2 ma-n[a síg]
20) Ur-^{d}A[b-ú]
iv 1) [dumu Lu]gal-èš
2) [x m]a-na síg
3) [. . .]-GAN
4) [dumu X-^{d}Ni]n-pirig
5) [x ma]-na síg
6) [Šeš(?)]-šag$_5$
7) [dumu . . .]-gú
(space)
8) [šu-nigin$_2$ x]+12½ [(x)] ma-na síg
9) [l]á-u$_x$(NI)
10) ⸢sipad⸣ ensi$_2$-ka
11) è-è-dam
(space)
12) [x m]u 8 iti

A record of wool due from the shepherds of the governor (of Umma). The text is composed of twenty-three identical entries, each recording an amount of wool followed by a personal name. In one case (i 12–17), the entry contains some additional information, now largely lost. The colophon (iv 8–12) is to be translated: '[total of x]+12½ [(x)] minas of wool; the arrears of the ⸢shepherds⸣ of the governor; to be delivered; [x] ⸢year⸣, 8th month.' The text was briefly discussed by Foster, *USP*, pp. 81, 131.

ii 7. As I suggested in *ASJ* 3 (1981) 90, the word UM+ME-ga 'wet nurse' is to be read eme-ga and distinguished from emeda(UM+ME.DA) 'nursemaid'. Further evidence in support of the reading eme-ga is provided by the Sargonic name Ur-me-ga (e.g., BIN 8 152:12, 165:13, 190:8, 194:4), which almost certainly is a syllabic spelling of Ur-UM+ME-ga.

ii 9. Though it would be tempting to connect this name with the Sargonic PN Sig$_4$-gi (*STTI* 20:7; BIN 8 158:25), the second sign is clearly ZI and not GI. Further, note that Sig$_4$-zi is documented in the Pre-Sargonic sources from Lagaš (Nikolski 1 108 i 2 and no. 2 iv′ 13′ in this volume).

ii 14. For the reading of NAGAR as alla, see W. G. Lambert, *BSOAS* 32 (1969) 595. This divine element, spelled ^{d}Al-la, occurs in the Ur III names ^{d}Al-la-gu-la and Ur-^{d}Al-la (Limet, *Anthroponymie*, p. 154), and Alla-šar(rum) (MAD 3, p. 288).

iv 9. For the reading lá-u$_x$ of lá-NI 'balance (positive or negative), arrears', see my remarks in *Aula Orientalis* 2 (1984) 137–39.

No. 29. IM 5592/17 Pl. 13

Obverse

1) ⸢1⸣ gín kug-si[g$_{17}$]	⸢1⸣ shekel of gol[d],
2) kug-babbar-bi 3 gín	its silver (equivalent is) 3 shekels;
3) ⅓ ŠA ma-na lá 1 gín igi-3-gál ur[udu z]abar([U]D.KA.BAR)	18⅔ shekels of cop[per (and) br]onze,
4) kug(-babbar)-bi [x] gín	their silver (equivalent is) [x] shekels;
5) še 1(pi) ⸢gur⸣-s[a]g-gál	(at that time, for 1 shekel of silver) 60 liters of barley
6) ág-gá-a	were measured out;
7) 4(gur) še gur-sag-gál	(total(?) of) 4 gsg of barley.

Reverse

(space)	
8) ⸢6⸣ mu 6 iti	⸢6th⸣ year, 6th month.

An account of gold, copper, and bronze. The rate of 1 shekel of silver per 60 liters of barley (lines 5–6) is high, but even higher rates are attested in Sargonic times. See, for example, ud-ba še 1 g[ín-ta] 1(bán)-àm ì-ág 'at that time, for 1 shekel (of silver) one measured out 10 liters (of barley)' (Serota Coll. A 15, unpubl.); ud-ba še 1 gín kug-babbar 3(bán) ì-ág 'at that time, for 1 shekel of silver one measured out 30 liters (of barley)' (MVN 3 100:13–14).

However, if we were to assume that the grain amount in line 7 represents the total equivalent of gold, copper, and bronze listed in lines 1–4, the numeral in line 5 would have to be interpreted not as 1(pi) but as 1 (gín); otherwise, the value of the copper and bronze would be an impossible 13 shekels of silver. The resulting rate (1 shekel of silver = 1 gsg of barley) would then permit us to reconstruct the missing numeral in line 4 as [1] (shekel of silver).

The rate of 3 shekels of silver per 1 shekel of gold (lines 1–2) is the lowest of the gold tariffs extant from ancient Mesopotamia. See the data compiled by Leemans, *RLA* 3, pp. 512–13 (Sargonic through Persian), and Young, in *Studies Jones*, pp. 214–15 (Ur III), which show that the prices of gold ranged from a low of 3:1 to a high of 20:1.

No. 30. IM 5592/11 Pl. 16

Obverse

i 1) ᴵLugal-banšur-e ugula
2) ᴵLum-ma
3) dumu Ama-IŠ
4) ᴵSipad-zi

5) dumu Ur-^{d}Ištaran
6) ^{I}Ur-GAR
7) dumu Ur-dingir-ra
8) ^{I}Ne-sag
9) dumu Úr-bi-šè
10) ^{I}⸢Si⸣pad-uru-na
11) dumu Nin$_{9}$-gissu
12) ^{I}Ur-^{d}Utu
13) dumu Ur-^{d}Nin-ildum$_{3}$
14) ^{I}Lugal-^{giš}kiri$_{6}$
15) dumu Ba-al-NI
16) šeš-U-me
17) ^{I}Ur-na-dù-a
18) ugula Ab-ba LÚ.ŠIM
19) ^{I}Da-da má-laḫ$_{4}$
20) ugula Lú-dingir-⸢ra⸣
21) ^{I}Ur-^{d}Ištaran kug-dím
22) [x] Ur-^{d}Lama
23) [^{I}Du]g$_{4}$-ga-ni
24) [ara]d$_{2}$(?) Nanna^{na}
25) [^{I}X-x]-NI

ii 1) ^{I}Šeš-še[š]
2) arad$_{2}$ dub-sar-maḫ
3) ugula Lugal(!)-šilig-e
4) ^{I}Ur-^{d}Nin-ME ugula
5) ^{I}É-šag$_{5}$-ga
6) ^{I}Dingir-mu-daḫ
7) arad$_{2}$ ensi$_{2}$-ka-me
8) ^{I}Lugal-gaba
9) arad$_{2}$ Me-lám
10) ^{Id}Nin-šubur-an-dùl
11) arad$_{2}$ Lugal(!)-kalam túg-du$_{8}$
12) ^{Id}Šara$_{2}$-bí-dug$_{4}$
13) arad$_{2}$ Lugal-gú dam-gàr
14) ^{I}Gub-ba-ni
15) arad$_{2}$ Da-da dam-gàr
16) ^{I}Lú-^{d}Utu
17) arad$_{2}$ Lú-sipad
18) ^{I}Amar-GIR
19) arad$_{2}$ Ad-da sipad
20) ^{I}Ur-^{d}TUR
21) arad$_{2}$ Ur-^{d}TAG.NUN
22) ^{I}Lugal-nir-gál
23) dumu Níg-^{d}En-líl-li
24) ^{I}Lú-DU.DU

Reverse

iii 1) šeš Da-d[a]
2) ^{I}Ur-^{d}Šara$_2$
3) dumu Ur-⌜x⌝-[x]
4) ^{I}Ur-^{d}Nin-⌜x⌝-[(x)]
5) lú Lugal-[. . .]
6) ^{I}Šubur
7) lú Ne-sag
8) ^{I}[U]r(?)-GAR
9) [x L]ú-^{d}Šara$_2$ šu-ḫa
(rest destroyed)

iv (uninscribed)

A roster of conscripted workers, divided into gangs under foremen (ugula). At least four separate gangs were involved: i 1–18, under Abba; i 19–20, under Lu-dingira; i 21–ii 3, under Lugal-šilige; ii 4–iii 9 (name not preserved). The conscripted men included a number of slaves, whose owners were the chief scribe (ii 1–2), the governor (ii 4–7), a felter (túg-du$_8$; ii 10–11), two merchants (ii 12–15), a shepherd (ii 18–19), and three unidentified individuals (ii 8–9, 16–17, 20–21). Note also the presence of workers identified as lú PN 'man of PN (i.e., member of the household of PN)' (iii 4–7).

As shown by its structure, formulary, and physical characteristics, this text belongs to the Umma rosters classified by Foster, *USP*, pp. 124–26, as group C.5.

i 16. The designation šeš-U, perhaps to be interpreted as šeš-10 '"brother" of the group of 10 men (*eširtu*)', also occurs in the roster CT 50 66:30, where it describes inclusively the personnel classified as guruš, šeš, and engar. The classification šeš (lit.: 'brother'), which is common in Foster's group B.5 texts, probably denotes a junior worker/assistant. It occurs either by itself or with the qualification kaskal '(military or corvée) expedition'. Cf. Foster, *USP*, p. 125.

i 18. For LÚ.ŠIM, probably to be interpreted as ^{lú}lunga(ŠIM), see most recently Steinkeller, *Sale Documents*, p. 91 commentary to no. 98:4.

i 24. Nanna^{na} represents /Nanna-ak/ 'The-One-of-Nanna'.

ii 2. Slaves of the chief scribe are also mentioned in the roster published in *USP* no. 48:16′ ([arad$_2$ du]b-sar-maḫ-me).

ii 21. The Sargonic Umma deity ^{d}TAG.NUN appears in Ur III Umma sources as ^{d}TÚG.NUN (e.g., Kang, *SACT* 2 106:5), ^{d}TÚG.AN (e.g., *SACT* 2 191:6), or ^{d}TÚG.AN.NUN (Nikolski 2 141:19). Note especially *SACT* 2 30:6, 8 and Nikolski 2 150:7, 9, mentioning the scribe Lú-^{d}TÚG.NUN-ka, who in the inscription of his seal (impressed on these two documents) is identified as Lú-^{d}TÚG.AN-ka; and Sigrist, *Syracuse* 196:9, 10, where the two spellings interchange in the same text. In all probability, the deity in question is Uttu(TAG.TÚG), the goddess of weaving; see Sjöberg, in *Studien Falkenstein*, p. 209; Steible, FAOS 5/2, p. 268; and Krebernik, ZA 76 (1986) 202–3. As suggested by the Ur III names Lú-^{d}TÚG.NUN/AN-ka and Ur-^{d}TÚG.NUN-ka (e.g., *SACT* 2 106:5; Sigrist, *Syracuse* 291:9 and seal), the divine name was actually /uttuk/.

No. 31. IM 5592/6 Pl. 17

Obverse

1) [x šu-si] a gi$_6$	[x fingers] of water (rose) at midnight,
2) [x] šu-si a an-bar$_7$	[x] fingers of water (rose) at noon,
3) [1] ud-a-k[am]	[1] day (= 1st day);
4) ⅓ šu-si a gi$_6$	⅓ finger of water (rose) at midnight,
5) (blank) šu-si a an-bar$_7$	0 fingers of water (rose) at noon,
6) 1 ud-a-kam	1 day (= 2d day);
7) 3 šu-si a gi$_6$	3 fingers of water (rose) at midnight,
8) 2 šu-si a an-bar$_7$	2 fingers of water (rose) at noon,
9) 1 ud-a-kam	1 day (= 3d day);
10) 2 šu-si a g[i$_6$]	2 fingers of water (rose) at mid[night],
11) 1 [šu-si a an-b]ar$_7$	1 [finger of water (rose) at no]on,
12) 1 ud-a-kam	1 day (= 4th day);
13) 3 šu-si a gi$_6$	3 fingers of water (rose) at midnight,
14) 10 šu-si a an-b[ar$_7$]	10 fingers of water (rose) at noo[n],
15) 1 ud-a-[kam]	1 day (= 5th day);
16) 4 šu-si a [gi$_6$]	4 fingers of water (rose) at [midnight],
17) 7 šu-si a [an-bar$_7$]	7 fingers of water (rose) at [noon],
18) 1 ud-a-[kam]	1 day (= 6th day);

Reverse

19) 11 šu-si a [gi$_6$]	11 fingers of water (rose) at [midnight],
20) 22 šu-si a an-bar$_7$	22 fingers of water (rose) at noon,
21) 1 ud-a-kam	1 day (= 7th day);
22) (blank) šu-si a gi$_6$	0 fingers of water (rose) at midnight,
23) 20 šu-si a an-bar$_7$	20 fingers of water (rose) at noon,
24) 1 ud-a-kam	1 day (= 8th day);
25) 22 šu-si a gi$_6$	22 fingers of water (rose) at midnight,
26) 5 šu-si a an-bar$_7$	5 fingers of water (rose) at noon,
27) 1 ud-a-kam	1 day (= 9th day);
28) (blank) šu-si a gi$_6$	0 fingers of water (rose) at midnight,
29) (blank) šu-si a an-bar$_7$	0 fingers of water (rose) at noon,
30) 1 ud-a-kam	1 day (= 10th day);
31) (blank) šu-si a gi$_6$	0 fingers of water (rose) at midnight,
32) (blank) šu-si a an-bar$_7$	0 fingers of water (rose) at noon,
33) 1 ud-a-kam	1 day (= 11th day);
(space)	
34) šu-nigin$_2$ ⸢4⸣ kuš lá 6 šu-si	the total of 114 fingers of

35) [a z]i-ga	[ri]sing [water],
36) [11] ud	[(in) 11] days.
37) [(x iti) x] mu	[(x month) x] year.

Measurements of the rising floodwater (probably in the Euphrates or one of its branches), made over a period of eleven days. The readings were taken twice each day: at midnight and at noon. Each measurement appears to represent the difference between the unknown point zero and the current water level, with the total (114 fingers = ca. 190 cm) being a tally of individual readings. A detailed discussion of this unique document is offered in *BSA* 4 (1988) 83–87 (note that the total of floodwater given there on pp. 85–86 is to be corrected from 115 fingers to 114 fingers).

The text comes almost certainly from Umma. This is shown by the fact that all other Sargonic tablets that share the primary accession number IM 5592 (nos. 22–30) are assuredly of Umma provenience.

1. Based on the total (line 34), the figures for the first day may be jointly restored as 1⅓ fingers; their exact breakdown, is, of course, unknown.

2, etc. For an-bar$_7$ (to be read alternatively an-bir$_7$; Akk. ***muṣlalu***) 'noon, midday', see CAD M/2, pp. 243–45. Among the occurrences cited there, note the numerous examples where ***muṣlalu*** is contrasted (as in the present text) with ***mūšu*** (GI$_6$) 'midnight, night'.

37. Since the date formula x iti x mu would be highly unusual (the standard form is x mu x iti), the line should probably be reconstructed [x] mu.

No. 32. IM 55101 — no copy

Tablet cannot be found. Read according to Gelb's transliteration.

Obverse

1) 160 dug-K[A.ZI]	160 ***kā[su*** bowls],
2) 60 dug-níg-lugud$_2$-da	60 ***kupputtu*** pots,
3) Da-ḪI(?)	(from?) Da-ḪI(?),
4) A-šag$_4$-ildum$_3$	(for) the field Ildum;
5) [x] dug-KA.ZI	[x] ***kāsu*** bowls,

Reverse

6) [. . .]-⌜si(?)⌝	[(from?) . . .]-⌜si(?)⌝,
7) [x dug]-⌜KA.ZI⌝	[x] ⌜***kāsu*** bowls⌝,
8) 10 dug-gur$_8$-gur$_8$	10 ***kurkurru*** pots,
9) Da-ḪI(?)	(from?) Da-ḪI(?),
10) Zabalam(AB.INANNA)^{ki}	(to) Zabalam,

Left Edge

11) ^{giš}gigir$_2$ ^{d}Ni[n- . . .]	(for) the chariot of Ni[n- . . .].

This tablet appears to record three expenditures of pots for two different destinations. For the text type, cf. no. 26. Da-ḪI(?) (lines 3, 9) and [. . .]-⌜si(?)⌝ (line 6) were possibly the producers of pots.

1. For dug-KA.ZI, see commentary to no. 26 i 7.

2. dug-níg-lugud$_2$-da = Akk. ***kupputtu***, a type of pot (see CAD K, p. 552). This pot is frequent in Sargonic texts, where it usually serves as a container for animal fats (see, e.g., BIN 8 267 i 2′, 276 i 2, 10, 280 i 1′, 304:2, 312:2; and no. 40 rev. 10′ in this volume). In Ur III sources, it is spelled dug-lugud$_2$-da (see Waetzoldt, *WO* 6 [1971] 19 and n. 139); the same writing appears in the Sargonic text UM 43-3-2:5, 18 (unpubl., courtesy of D. I. Owen) and in lexical sources (see CAD K, p. 552). Since the meaning of lugud$_2$ (Akk. ***karû***) is 'to be short', dug-níg-lugud$_2$-da was probably a short, stocky jar. In this connection, note that another equivalent of ***kupputtu*** is dug-nu-gíd-da (Hh. X 199; Nabnitu IV 114), possibly to be translated 'jar that is not long/tall' (unless it is simply a syllabic rendering of lugud$_2$-da).

3, 9. Gelb copies the second sign as ◇.

8. For dug-gur$_8$-gur$_8$, see commentary to no. 26 i 2.

No. 33. IM 11053/118 Pl. 17

Obverse

1) [x(bùr)] gana$_2$ ŠUKU
2) [M]e-ság
3) 5(bùr) gana$_2$ ŠUKU
4) DINGIR-mu-[d]a
5) [x(iku) I(?)]-sar-⌜$^{d(?)}$EN(?).ZU(?)⌝
6) [x(iku)] ⌜X-x-da⌝
7) [x] ⌜x⌝ [. . .]
8) [x(iku) D]a(?)-d[a(?)]
9) 9(iku) ⌜Ur⌝-sipad-[da]
10) 9(iku) ⌜X⌝-[. . .]
11) 9(iku) ⌜É⌝-^{d}En-líl-⌜e(?)⌝
12) 9(iku) KAL-⌜x⌝
13) sag-apin-me
14) 2(iku) dub-sar-a-šag$_4$-gud(?) [(x)]
15) 9(iku) Lugal-uru sipad-an[še]
16) 9(iku) Gala

Reverse

17) 9(iku) En-mu
18) unud$_x$(ÁB.KU)-me

19) 12(iku) Lugal-ezen
20) 9(iku) Šeš-TUR
21) 9(iku) Dingir-ki-ág
22) 6(iku) Az
23) ⸢sipad⸣-udu-m[e]
(space)
24) šu-nigin$_2$ 24(bùr) 1(eše) 3+[x(iku) gana$_2$] ŠUKU
25) ⸢x x⸣ MU

A record of the prebend land (ŠUKU) held by the governor(?) Mesag (line 2) and his various dependents. The latter include the chief scribe Ilum-mūdâ (line 4), eight(?) heads of plow teams (lines 5–13), a field scribe (line 14), an assherd (line 15), two cowherds (lines 16–18), and four shepherds (lines 19–23). For parallel texts, see Foster, ***Institutional Land***, pp. 53–57.

1. The word ŠUKU 'prebend, subsistence (land)' is read by Sumerologists either as the nonexistent "kur$_6$" (derived artificially from kurum$_6$ = ***kurummatu***) or šuku or šuku-(r). Since in Pre-Sargonic Lagaš sources this term consistently takes the complement -rá (see, e.g., VAS 14 10 i 2, 39 i 2), it appears likely that, at least in the instances where the complements -rá or -ra (as in Ur III texts) are used, its reading is simply pad. For pad /padr/ 'to break, to break off', corresponding to ***kasāpu***, and probably to ***šebēru***, see Steinkeller, *JNES* 46 (1987) 57; *WZKM* 77 (1987) 191. Accordingly, pad, or perhaps better pada$_x$ /padr-a/, could be translated as 'allotment' (lit.: 'a broken-off part'). Cf. here pad, níg-pad-rá 'bite, small repast', corresponding to the Akk. ***kusāpu***. Since lexical texts assign to PAD = ***kurummatu*** the pronunciation šuku (see CAD K, p. 573b), we would have to assume that PAD stands for two separate words, pad and šuku, whose meanings, though similar, differ in some respect.

4. Ilum-mūdâ is identified as dub-sar-maḫ 'chief scribe' in BIN 8 196:20.

12. Possibly to be read Giš(!)-⸢šag$_4$⸣.

20–22. The shepherds Šeš-TUR, Dingir-kiag, and Az occur also in no. 44 and BIN 8 196:29–31. For Az, see also BIN 8 146:3 and 274:2.

No. 34. IM 11053/21? no copy

Tablet cannot be located. Read according to Gelb's transliteration.

Obverse

1) 1½(iku) gana$_2$ [gú-g]ú
2) Ur-íd-[a-da]
3) 1½(iku) ga[na$_2$ . . .]
4) sag-[du$_5$]
5) 1(iku) ga[na$_2$ . . .]
6) nu-[kiri$_6$]
7) udu á [ki-sá-a(?)]

8) 1(iku) g[ana$_2$ . . .]
9) lú-⸢ERIN$_2$⸣

Reverse

10) udu á a-zi-a

A list of field plots and their holders(?). Related texts are BIN 8 185–87, 197, 328, and 342. The meaning of the phrases udu á ki-sá-a (line 7) and udu á a-zi-a (line 10) is obscure. The first phrase also occurs in BIN 8 185:9, 328:5′, and 342:12. The latter phrase, possibly meaning 'sheep of the fee for the rising/flood water', is spelled udu á a-zi in BIN 8 328:8′ (interpreted by Foster, *Institutional Land*, p. 62, as udu á *a-ṣí* "rental sheep forthcoming"). Other tablets belonging to this group use in addition the phrases udu á UD.UD (BIN 8 197:5), ⸢udu⸣ á KA-NI-NI (BIN 8 197:8), and udu á KA (BIN 8 187:3). Foster's suggestion (*Institutional Land*, pp. 62, 68–69) that these phrases are "rental terms" may be correct, but his respective translations are only guesses.

The four persons named in the present text also occur in BIN 8 186:1–8.

1. Reconstructed after BIN 8 187:1.

No. 35. IM 10630 Pl. 18

Obverse

1) 24(gur) še gur-sa[g] še-numun še gud-e kú
2) 2(gur) zíz gur-sag
3) 1(pi) 4(bán) gig
4) Ur-é
5) 12(gur) še gur-sag
6) 1(gur) zíz gur-sag
7) 5(bán) gig
8) I-lu$_5$-lu$_5$
9) 24(gur) še gur-sag
10) 2(gur) zíz ⸢gur⸣-sag
11) 1(pi) 4(bán) gig
12) Ur-sipad-da
13) 12(gur) še gur-sag
14) 1(gur) zíz gur-sag
15) 5(bán) gig

Reverse

16) Da-du
17) 12(gur) še gur-sag
18) 1(gur) zíz gur-sag

19) 5(bán) gig
20) Da-da
21) 12(gur) še gur-sag
22) 1(gur) zíz gur-sag
23) 5(bán) gig
24) Giš-šag$_4$
(space)
25) šu-nigin$_2$ 96(gur) še gur-sag
26) šu-nigin$_2$ 8(gur) zíz gur-sag
27) šu-nigin$_2$ 1(gur) 2(pi) 4(bán) gur-sag gig
28) *a-na* še-numun *ù* gud ⸢kú⸣
29) *in* Sag-ub$^{\ulcorner ki \urcorner}$

A record of barley, emmer, and wheat which were expended in Sagub for seeding and as fodder for plow oxen (lines 1, 28–29). The six recipients, Ur-e, Ilulu, Ur-sipad, Dadu, Dada, and Giš-šag, were important agricultural functionaries of the Mesag estate. Since Ur-sipad, Dada, and possibly Giš-šag are designated in no. 33 as sag-apin-me 'heads of plow teams', the same identification probably also applies to Ur-e, Ilulu, and Dadu. Among other Sagub tablets mentioning these individuals, note especially NBC 7007 (published in transliteration by Bridges, *Mesag Archive*, p. 466), where Ur-e, Dada, Ur-sipad, Ilulu, and Giš-šag receive plow-oxen (gud-giš) and hides. Lines 28–29 suggest that the text was read in Akkadian (see p. 10).

1. For this line (= line 28), cf. *a-na* še-numun še gud-e kú in BIN 8 123 ii 5 and 230:2, and še-numun še gud kú in BIN 8 182 i 2 and passim there.

No. 36. IM 11053/25 Pl. 18

Obverse

1) 8(gur) zíz gur-sag
2) Nam-ti-la-ni šu ba-ti
3) 20 lá 2(gur) gi-TUKUR$_2$(KA×ŠE)
4) lá 30(gur) še gur-sag
5) ⸢É⸣-giš
6) lá 5(gur) še gur-sag
7) Ur-mes
8) lá 2(gur) še gur-sag
9) Giš-šag$_4$
10) É-igi-íl$^{\ulcorner ki \urcorner}$
11) [b]a(?)-D[U . . .]
(no more than one line missing, if anything)

Reverse

1′) ⌜120⌝+40(gur) [še gur-sag]
2′) É-⌜x⌝-[. . .]
3′) ⌜120⌝+22+[x(?)(gur) še gur-sag]
4′) [. . .]
5′) ⌜x x⌝ [. . .]
6′) ⌜x x⌝ [. . .]
7′) 13+[x(?)(gur) še gur-sag]
8′) še [(x)] ⌜KA⌝-[x-x]-⌜x⌝ ba-DU
9′) 106(gur) š[e gu]r-sag
10′) *šu* ⌜Giš⌝-šag$_4$
11′) šu-nigin$_2$ 348(gur) še gur-sag

A record of barley and emmer which were distributed among several individuals. The presence of *šu* 'of' in line 10′ suggests that the text was read in Akkadian (see p. 10).

3. The same word, spelled gi-TUKUR$_2$-ra, appears in BIN 8 215:3 and 231:6. It probably denotes some type of reed container, used for storing barley. Possibly to be read gi-gur$_x$(TUKUR$_2$)-ra, and to be connected with gi-gur 'basket'.

No. 37. IM 11053/44 Pl. 19

Obverse

1) 20 lá 1(gur) še gur-sag-maḫ
2) Lú-^{d}Nanše unud$_x$(ÁB.KU)
3) 10(gur) lá 2(pi) 2(bán) še gur-sag
4) [U]r-ù-kal-l[a]
5) [*š*]*u* Da-da ⌜engar⌝
6) 14(gur) 2(pi) še gur-sag
7) Lú-^{d}Nanše unud$_x$(ÁB.KU)
8) 30(gur) 2(pi) še gur-sag
9) Dingir-a-zu sipad
10) 7(gur) 3(pi) še ⌜gur⌝-sag
11) ⌜Ur-ù-kal⌝-[la]
(rest destroyed)

Reverse

(beginning destroyed)
1′) *šu* ⌜Da(?)-da(?)⌝
2′) 7(gur) 1(pi) 2(bán) Ba-za unud$_x$(ÁB.KU)
3′) *šu* Gala dumu A-li-li
(space)
4′) šu-nigin$_2$ 103(gur) 2(bán) še gur-sag-gál

5′) apin-lá GANA$_2$-gud
6′) Agar$_2$-gàr-mud

A record of barley, delivered as a rental payment (apin-lá) by several persons. The designation apin-lá GANA$_2$-gud Agar$_2$-gàr-mud 'rental payment of the demesne of the field Agar-garmud' shows that the apin-lá land was a subdivision of the demesne (GANA$_2$-gud). As is suggested by the use of *šu* 'of' (lines 5, 1′, 3′), the text was read in Akkadian (see p. 10).

No. 38. IM 11053/106 Pl. 19

Copied by J. A. Black.

Obverse

1) 4(gur) [(. . .) še gur-sag-gál]
2) DINGIR-⌜AŠ(?)⌝-[(. . .)]
3) [x še] gur ⌜x⌝
4) gug-gud
5) [1]+1(pi) še Nin-šeš-šeš
6) 2(pi) še Ama-a-zu
7) 1(pi) 3(bán) še [Me]-si-tum
8) 1(pi) 3(bán) še Ama-nu
9) 1(pi) še Nin-áb
10) 1(pi) 5 sila$_3$ še Am[a- . . .]

Reverse

(space)
11) šu-nigin$_2$ 7(gur) 3(pi) 5 sila$_3$ ⟨še⟩ gur-sag-gál
12) [z]i-ga
13) Nin-šag$_4$(!)-kam

A record of barley expenditures, made by Nin-šag to seven persons and for oxen (line 4).

7. Cf. Me-si-tum in BIN 8 148:84 and 227:5.

No. 39. IM 10631 no copy

Tablet on display; could not be copied. Read according to Gelb's transliteration. Collated by J. A. Black.

Obverse

1) 1(gur) 3(bán) še gur-sag-gál	1 gsg 30 liters of barley,
2) *šu* 3 iti	a three-month (provision),

3)	Eden-bi-šè	(for) Edenbiše;
4)	2(pi) še *šu* 2 iti	120 liters of barley, a two-month (provision),
5)	Lú-kug	(for) Lu-kug;
6)	1(pi) 3(bán) še *šu* 1 iti	90 liters of barley, a one-month (provision),

Reverse

7)	^{d}Šara$_2$-ì-šag$_5$	(for) Šara-išag;
8)	sipad-anše-me	they are assherds.

A record of barley expenditures to three assherds. Note the use of the Akkadian *šu* 'of', which may indicate that the text was read in Akkadian (see p. 10). Šara-išag (line 7) occurs also in BIN 8 249:7, where he is identified as sipad anše-ERIN$_2$ 'shepherd of team-asses'.

No. 40. IM 11053/21 Pl. 20

Obverse

1) [x(gur) níg-àr-r]a g[ur-sag]
2) [x(gur) dabin g]ur-s[ag]
3) [x(gur) img]aga$_3$ gur-sag
4) [x dug] ì-šáḫ
5) [x kuš] gud-⌜giš⌝ ù si sa
6) [x] ^{kuš}esir$_x$(LAK-173)
7) [x]+2 ^{kuš}dám-ga
8) Ur-mes
9) 4(gur) níg-àr-ra gur-sag
10) 6(gur) dabin gur-sag
11) 4(gur) imgaga$_3$ gur-sag
12) 2 dug ì-šáḫ
13) 2 ^{kuš}esir$_x$
14) 4 ^{kuš}dám-ga
15) Da-da engar
16) 2(gur) níg-àr-ra gur-sag
17) 3(gur) dabin gur-s[ag]
18) [x(gur) imgaga$_3$] gur-s[ag]

(rest destroyed)

Reverse

(beginning destroyed)

1′) [x(gur)] níg-à[r-ra gur-sag]
2′) [x]+1(gur) dabin g[ur-sag]

3′) [x]+2(gur) imgaga$_3$ [gur-sag]
4′) [x] dug ì-š[áḫ]
5′) [x] ^{kuš}esir$_x$
6′) [x]+1 ^{kuš}dám-ga
7′) Ur-^{d}En-líl-[li/e]
8′) 1 kuš gud-giš ù s[i sa]
9′) Ur-lú
10′) 3 dug-níg-lugud$_2$-da ì ⸢BA(?) RU(?) A⸣
(space)
11′) [x e]ngar-engar

An expenditure of foodstuffs and various leather goods to five(?) farmers (engar). Related texts are BIN 8 266–67, 269, and 276.

1. For níg-àr-ra (Akk. *mundu*) 'groats', see Hallo, *HUCA* 38 (1967) 56; Postgate, *BSA* 1 (1984) 108.

2. For dabin (Akk. *tappinnu*), a type of flour, see *AHw*, p. 1321a.

3. For imgaga$_3$, see commentary to no. 27 i 9.

5. 'Hides of plow oxen, horns (si), and guts (sa)' (also in rev. 8′). For kuš gud-giš, see also BIN 8 267 i 4′, 269:1, 3, 5, 7, 9, 11, 276 i 12–13, 16. For si sa, see si sa gud (BIN 8 267 i 5′), si áb (BIN 8 276 i 7), and sa áb (BIN 8 276 i 6). For the meaning 'gut' for sa (Akk. *irrū*), see now Kraus, *Verfügungen*, pp. 351–53, 365.

6. For esir$_x$(LAK-173), see Steinkeller, *AfO* 28 (1981–82) 140–41. Add now ^{e}esir$_x$(GI$_4$×GI$_4$) = *sa-na* (= *šānā*(*n*), dual) 'sandals' in VE 1323′ (MEE 4, p. 335). Cf. Civil, in Cagni, *Bilinguismo*, p. 78. Note that the form *šānu* (against the standard Akk. *šēnu*) is also attested in a post-Ur III tablet from Mari (ARM 19 300:2).

7. ^{kuš}dám-ga appears to have been a leather thong or strap. Note especially *USP* no. 15:1–4: 10 ^{kuš}dám-⸢ga⸣ PN dub-sar-e IGI giš-gíd-da-ka(?) si-si-dè šu ba-ti 'PN, the scribe, received 10 dám-ga to attach blades to the spears'. Other occurrences of dám-ga come from MAD 4 41:8 (among the plow equipment: ^{giš}⸢šu⸣-kár šu-du$_7$-a gud-apin), 64:8, 69:8; *STTI* 26 i 4′. Note also the occupation lú-^{kuš}dám-ga in ITT 1 1397:5. I owe the reading dám-ga to M. Civil, who furnishes the following lexical and literary references: éš dam-ga (OIP 99 33+35+225 x 14) = d[am]-ga (MEE 3 45+46 xiii 6); ^{giš}dam-ga apin = *pu-uq-du* (Hh. V 160); ^{giš}da-an-ga (3 NT 354 iii 9′, unpubl. forerunner to Hh. V); ^{giš}da-an-ga ^{giš}šudun-šè ba-ši-in-lá-lá ("Lipit-Ištar and the Plow" line 36; Civil's manuscript).

15. Probably the same Dada (though not described as engar) receives ox hides in BIN 8 276 i 13.

10′. For dug-níg-lugud$_2$-da, see commentary to no. 32:2. The reading of the remainder of the line is uncertain.

11′. The beginning of the line probably contained some term for 'provisions' or the like.

No. 41. IM 11053/333 Pl. 20

Obverse

1) igi-4-gál ⌈kug⌉-[babbar]
2) [x(gur)] 2(pi) 5(bán) zíd-gu [g]ur(!)
3) [x] 5(bán) bappir
4) [x] imgaga$_3$ gur
5) [x] šáḫ-niga
6) [x] 1(bán) 5 sila$_3$ giš-ì
7) [x] 5 sila$_3$ s[um]
8) [x] 5 sila$_3$ sum-sikil
9) [x] ⌈zu⌉-ḫa-ti-nu
10) [x sila$_3$] É-a-[zu]
11) [x g]ú-gú-[gal-gal]
12) 2(bán) gú-g[ú-TUR-TUR]
13) [x] ⌈2(bán)⌉ ŠE.L[Ú]

Reverse

14) [x] ⌈sila$_3$⌉ ^{ú}ga[mun$_2$(TIR)]
15) 3 sila$_3$ zi-bí-b[í]-a-nu
16) 1(bán) gazi
(space)
17) [*š*]*u* 1 ^{giš}apin

A record of various articles—silver (line 1), a barley-fed pig (line 5), and various agricultural products—which were either delivered by or issued to the members of one plowing team (*šu* 1 ^{giš}apin '(those are goods) of one plowing team'; line 17). The use of *šu* 'of' in line 17 may indicate that the text was read in Akkadian (see above p. 10). A parallel text is NBC 10196 (published by Bridges, *Mesag Archive*, p. 475, transliteration only).

2. For zíd-gu, a type of flour, see Edzard, *Tell ed-Dēr*, p. 164.

3. For bappir (Akk. *bappiru*) 'beer-bread', see CAD B, pp. 95–97.

7. For sum (Akk. *šūmu*) 'garlic', see Bottéro, *RLA* 6, pp. 39–41 (under "Knoblauch"), and the more recent discussions by Stol, *BSA* 3 (1987) 57–58; and Waetzoldt, *BSA* 3 (1987) 38–39.

8. For sum-sikil (Akk. *šamaškillu*), see most recently Stol, *BSA* 3 (1987) 59–62; and Waetzoldt, *BSA* 2 (1987) 34–35. Stol argues convincingly for the meaning 'onion', though I fail to understand his reasons for doubting that *šamaškillu* is a loanword from sum-sikil (p. 61); *šamaškillu* must be viewed as a direct loan from sum-sikil, with the pronunciation of the loanword reflecting the "etymology" of sum- as *šammu* (such etymologizing borrowings are common, e.g., among the Akkadian loanwords in Sumerian, as in sa-gaz . . . ak from *šagāšu* and šu bala . . . ak from *šupêlu*); the plant *sikillu*, which Stol cites as a possible base of *šamaškillu* (p. 61), is obviously a loan from (sum-)sikil, too.

9. For *šuḫatinnu*, a type of alliaceous plant, see Stol, *BSA* 3 (1987) 63; and Waetzoldt, *BSA* 3 (1987) 36–38. Its identification is uncertain. In third-millennium texts this vegetable is written za-ḫa-din or za-ḫa-ti; the present spelling is new—note the use of the sign ZU.

10. Reconstructed after NBC 10196:9′, which according to Bridges (*Mesag Archive*, p. 475), reads 1+[x] $sila_3$ É-za-⸢zu⸣. If in that example "-za-" is in fact -a-, the commodity should probably be read *ʾà-a-zu* and identified as *asu* 'myrtle'. Cf. the spelling ŠIM *a-á-zum* in MAD 1 286:4.

11–12. For gú-gú-gal-gal and gú-gú-TUR-TUR, see commentary to no. 27 iii 8–9.

13. For ŠE.LÚ (also in no. 42 i 9) (Akk. *kisibirru*) 'coriander', see CAD K, pp. 420–21.

14. I assume that Ú.TIR (also in no. 42 i 10) is to be read here $^{ú}gamun_2$, and equated with Akkadian *kamūnu* 'cumin(?)'. The same spelling occurs also in BIN 8 123:10. In other Sargonic and Ur III texts, this spice is written syllabically as ga-mun (e.g., BIN 8 132:40, 271:2) or ku-mul (Snell, *Ledgers*, pp. 227, 266). The same item possibly occurs in VE 1431′ (MEE 4, p. 341): Ú.TIR = *ga-ba-na-na-u_9*, *gáb-na-ne-u_9* (cf. also ŠE.TIR = *ga-ba-na-na-ù* in VE 0392, MEE 4, p. 373), where the Semitic *kabanniʾu* or *kabnaniʾu* may be a dialectical form of *kamūnu*. Note also that the same source equates Ú.TIR with *a-za-mi-tum* (MEE 4, p. 233: VE 303), where the Semitic gloss appears to represent the plant *samīdu* = Ú.KUR.ZI (CAD S, pp. 114–15), in turn probably identical with the Neo-Babylonian *asmīdu* (CAD A/2, p. 337).

15. *zibibiānu* (also in no. 42 i 11), which in later periods is written with the logogram Ú.DIN.TIR, may be 'black cumin' (CAD Z, pp. 102–3). This word is obviously related to *zibû*, which is also represented by Ú.DIN.TIR (CAD Z, pp. 104–5).

16. gazi (Akk. *kasû*) is probably 'wild licorice' (*Glycirriza glabra*). See provisionally my comments in *Labor in the Ancient Near East* (ed. M. A. Powell; AOS 68; New Haven, 1987) p. 91. I hope to discuss this problem in detail elsewhere.

17. According to Foster, *ASJ* 4 (1982) 20–21, 25, ^{giš}apin denotes a subdivision of cultivable land: "In Akkadian administration certain areas of cultivable land could be divided into 'plows' of a certain number of iku each" (p. 20). In another place (*Institutional Land*, p. 67), Foster speculated that these hypothetical land units measured 90–100 iku in size. There is nothing in the evidence, however, which would support this interpretation. In the contexts studied by Foster "plows" denote simply plowing teams to whom land was assigned for cultivation.

No. 42. IM 11053/337 Pl. 21

Copied by J. A. Black.

Obverse

i 1) 450(gur) še gur-⸢maḫ⸣
2) K[A]-⸢X-X⸣
3) *im-[ḫur]*
4) 6(gur) 2(bán) ⸢bappir⸣ gur
5) 7(gur) 2(pi) 3(bán) níg-àr-ra gur

6) 7(gur) 2(pi) 3(bán) dabin gur
7) 4(gur) imgaga$_3$ gur
8) 2(pi) 3(bán) gú-gú
9) 2(pi) 3(bán) ŠE.LÚ
10) 3(bán) ^{ú}gamun$_2$
11) [x] zi-bí-bí-a-nu
(rest destroyed)

ii 1) Ama-barag dub-sar
2) 30(gur) še gur si-sá
3) É-nam sag-du$_5$
4) *im-ḫur*
5) 61 guruš 1(pi)-ta
6) 3 dumu-nita 3(bán)-ta
7) 2 dumu-nita 2(bán)-ta
8) 26 geme$_2$ 3(bán)-ta
9) 3 dumu-nita 3(bán)-ta
10) 2 dumu-nita 1(bán)-ta
11) 2 dumu-SAL 2(bán)-ta
12) 3 dumu-SAL 1(bán)-ta
13) še-ba-bi 15(gur) 3(pi) 4(bán) [gu]r
14) [*šu* 1] iti
(rest destroyed)

Reverse

(destroyed)

A list of grains, grain products, and vegetables, which were distributed among three(?) individuals (i 2, ii 1, 3), and of monthly barley rations intended for a group of workers (ii 5–13). The latter included sixty-one men, twenty-six women, ten boys, and five girls. The rations per each category were: 60 liters for men, 30 liters for women, 30, 20, and 10 liters for boys, and 20 and 10 liters for girls.

The rations add up to 4750 liters of barley, and thus the total (ii 13), recording only 4720 liters, is 30 liters short.

For the commodities listed, see commentaries to nos. 27 and 41.

No. 43. IM 11053/41 Pl. 21

Obverse

(beginning destroyed)
1′) 1 má 4 [gur]
2′) Lugal-ḫa-ma-⸢ti(?)⸣
(space)
3′) [x] ma-na dùg-gan
4′) [2(?)]+2 ma-na ba-lu-ḫum

5′) 2(bán) šim-gig
6′) 2(bán) šim-gam-gam-ma
7′) ⸢2(bán)⸣ šim-ku-ku-ru-u[m]

Reverse

8′) ⸢x⸣ šim-⸢x⸣-[. . .]
(space)
9′) ZÍD/ÉŠ 6 má
10′) Íd-maḫ
11′) 2 má 3 [gu]r
(rest destroyed)

A list of aromatics and leather bags and their recipient(s). The mention of boats in lines 1′ and 9′–11′ probably means that the goods listed were to be transported by boats.

3′. '[x] minas of (leather) bags.' For dùg-gan (Akk. ***tuk*(*k*)*annu***), see *AHw*, p. 1367.

4′. For ***baluḫḫu***, a type of aromatic, see CAD B, pp. 74–75; Snell, *Ledgers*, p. 233. In lexical texts ***baluḫḫu*** is equated with giš-šim-ḪAL and giš-šim-A.KAL.ḪAL. Cf. commentary to no. 27 i 11.

5′. For šim-gig (Akk. ***kanaktu***), a type of aromatic, see GIŠ.ŠIM = *ga-na-ga-tum*, *ga-na-ak*(!)(written SUM)-*tum*, VE 464 (cf. Krebernik, *ZA* 73 [1983] 17); CAD K, pp. 135–36; Snell, *Ledgers*, p. 234. Note also šim-ga-na-BÀD (MCS 9 232:18), where -BÀD is possibly to be interpreted as -bàd or -gad$_x$. In third-millennium texts šim-gig occurs with the qualifications gal and tur. For examples, see CAD K, p. 135b; *STTI* 27:5, 61:5, 7 (-gal(!)).

6′. šim-gam-gam-ma, a type of aromatic, corresponds to Akkadian ***ṣumlalû***. See šim-gam-ma/me = ***ṣu-um-la-lu-ú*** in Hh. III 113. Cf. CAD Ṣ, p. 245; Snell, *Ledgers*, pp. 233–34.

7′. ***kukru*/*kukkuru***, a type of aromatic, is equated in lexical sources with GÚR.GÚR, GÚG.GÚG, and KU_7.KU_7; see CAD K, p. 500; cf. also Snell, *Ledgers*, p. 234. The pronunciation ***kukkuru***, against CAD's ***kukuru***, is indicated by the Ur III spelling ***gúk-ku-ru*** in Snell, *Ledgers*, copy 24:14.

9′–10′. 'The . . . of(?) six boats of the Maḫ canal.' The meaning of ZÍD/ÉŠ in the beginning of the line is unclear. The Maḫ canal appears to have been situated in the Lagaš province. See RGTC 1, pp. 221–22.

No. 44. IM 11053/23 Pl. 22

Obverse

i	1)	336 udu	336 sheep;
	2)	40 lá 1 sila$_4$-bi nu-mu-ku$_4$	their 39 lambs were not brought in;
		(space)	

	3)	šu-nigin$_2$ 375 [udu]	total of 375 [sheep].
	4)	síg-bi 5 gú 40 lá 2 ma-na	Their wool, 338 minas,
	5)	É-li-li	Elili
	6)	mu-de$_6$	delivered.
	7)	lá 5 gú 34 síg ma-na	The balance, 334 minas of wool,
	8)	*al* É-li-li	Elili
	9)	*i-ba-šè u-ba-lam*	owes; he will deliver (it).
		(space)	
		(rest destroyed)	
ii	1)	[síg-bi . . .]	[Their wool, x minas],
	2)	Dingir-⌜ki⌝-[ág]	Dingir-⌜ki⌝[ag]
	3)	mu-[de$_6$]	[delivered].
	4)	lá 5 gú 40+[x síg ma-na]	The balance, 340+[x minas of wool],
	5)	*al* Dingir-ki-ág	Dingir-kiag
	6)	*i-ba-šè u-ba-l*[*am*]	owes; he will deliver (it).
		(space)	
	7)	200 udu lá 60(?)+20 +1(?) [x]	200 sheep; the balance . . . ;
	8)	(blank) sila$_4$ nu-tuku	there are no lambs.
	9)	síg-bi 1 gú	Their wool, 60 minas,
	10)	Šeš-TUR	Šeš-TUR
	11)	mu-de$_6$	delivered.
	12)	lá 4 gú 40 ⟨síg⟩ ma-na	The balance, 280 minas ⟨of wool⟩,
	13)	[*al* Šeš]-⌜TUR⌝	[Šeš]-⌜TUR⌝
	14)	[*i-ba-šè u-ba-lam*]	[owes; he will deliver (it)].
		(rest destroyed	

Reverse

iii		(beginning destroyed)	
	1′)	[síg-bi x]+11(?) [ma-na]	[Their wool, x]+11(?) [minas],
	2′)	[A]z sipad mu-d[e$_6$]	[A]z, the shepherd, deli[vered].
	3′)	lá 1 gú 40 m[a-n]a ⌜síg⌝	The balance, 100 minas of ⌜wool⌝,
	4′)	*al* Az	Az
	5′)	*i-ba-šè* ⌜*u*⌝-[*ba-lam*]	owes; he will deliver (it).
iv		(uninscribed)	

A record of wool which was delivered by the shepherds Elili, Dingir-kiag, Šeš-TUR, and Az. Elili occurs also in BIN 8 196:28 (where he is followed by Šeš-TUR, Dingir-kiag, and Az) and 342:4. For Dingir-kiag, Šeš-TUR, and Az, see commentary to no. 33:20–22.

ii 7. I can offer no plausible explanation of the pointed numbers appearing after the sign LAL. They should represent, as elsewhere in the text, minas of wool, but wool would be out of context in this entry.

No. 45. IM 10628 Pl. 22

Tablet on display; could not be collated.

Obverse

1)	⸢úš⸣ É-ḫa-lu-úb	Dead: E-ḫalub;
2)	AŠ Lugal-DU	. . . : Lugal-DU;
3)	nagar-me	the carpenters;
4)	úš TAG-su muḫaldim	dead: TAG-su, the cook;
5)	má Pù-zu-zu má-laḫ$_4$	(assigned to the) boat: Puzuzu, the boatman;
6)	úš Ka$_5^a$ ad-KID	dead: Ka, the basket weaver;
7)	úš Pù-KUG šu-ḫa	dead: Pu-KUG, the fisherman;
8)	nu Na-ba-LUL ŠIM	not (present): Naba-LUL, the brewer;
9)	tu Ì-lí-dan	sick: Ilī-dan;
10)	nu Lugal-ÉŠ	not (present): Lugal-EŠ;
11)	nu Lugal-KA	not (present): Lugal-KA;
12)	úš É-gi$_4$-a geme$_2$	dead: Egia, the slave woman;
13)	ugula Gala	under the authority of Gala.
14)	še Ur-lú ⸢x⸣	(Assigned to) barley: Ur-lu;
15)	nu DINGIR-na	not (present): DINGIR-na;
16)	úš Gala	dead: Gala;
17)	ugula Da-da	under the authority of Dada.
18)	tu Da-da	Sick: Dada;
19)	nu Lugal-iti-da	not (present): Lugal-itida,
20)	dumu Az	son of Az;
21)	ugula É-^{d}En-líl-e	under the authority of E-Enlile.
22)	nu I-lu$_5$-lu$_5$ engar	Not (present): Ilulu, the farmer;
23)	nu Gala	not present: Gala;
24)	úš Eden-⸢bi⸣-šè dumu Me-lu	dead: Edenbiše, son of Melu;
25)	⸢nu⸣ I-lu$_5$-lu$_5$	⸢not⸣ (present): Ilulu;
26)	⸢nu(!)⸣ Da-da	⸢not⸣ (present): Dada;
27)	ugula Giš-šag$_4$	under the authority of Giš-šag;
28)	nu ⸢Az⸣	not (present): ⸢Az⸣;
29)	[x . . .]	[. . . : PN];

Reverse

30)	⸢nu⸣ [Zabalam^{ki}(-x)]	⸢not⸣ (present): [Zabalam(-x)],
31)	dumu ⸢Lugal⸣-[e-á]-⸢na⸣	son of ⸢Lugal⸣-[ea]-⸢na⸣;
32)	nu Ur-^{d}Bìl dumu Geme$_2$-^{d}Utu	not (present) Ur-Bil, son of Geme-Utu;
33)	úš gaba Da-da túg(!)-du$_8$	dead: the infant of Dada, the felter;
34)	nu(!) Ur-^{d}Nin-a-zu	not (present): Ur-Ninazu,
35)	dumu É-ḫa-lu-úb nagar	son of E-ḫalub, the carpenter;
36)	è Maš dumu Da-da	sent out: Maš, son of Dada;
37)	ama É-kug	mother: E-kug;

38)	AŠ Me-ḫa	. . . : Meḫa;
39)	AŠ Geme$_2$-TAR 1 gaba(!)	. . . : Geme-TAR, (with) one infant;
40)	nu Nin-me-na	not (present): Nin-mena;
41)	AŠ Geme$_2$-^{d}Utu 1 gaba	. . . : Geme-Utu, (with) one infant;
42)	nu Nin-un-gá	not (present): Nin-unga;
43)	nu Nin-šeš-šeš dumu Geme$_2$-TAR	not (present): Nin-šeššeš, daughter of Geme-TAR;
	(space)	
44)	šu-nigin$_2$ 20 lú zàḫ-me	total of twenty absentees;
45)	šu-nigin$_2$ 8 lú úš-a-me	total of eight deceased;
46)	šu-nigin$_2$ 7 lú è-me	total of seven who were sent out.
47)	še(?) Nin-me ⌜šu(?)-ḫa(?)⌝	(Assigned) to barley(?): Ninme, the ⌜fisherman(?)⌝;
48)	ugula Ur-sipad-da	under the authority of Ur-sipad.
49)	ì-du$_8$ Nin-en-nu	(Assigned to the) doorkeeper: Nin-ennu;
50)	gud Lugal-èš ugula É-^{d}En-líl⟨-e⟩	(assigned to) oxen: Lugal-eš; under the authority of E-Enlil⟨e⟩.
51)	gud Pù-pù ugula Gala	(Assigned to) oxen: Pupu; under the authority of Gala.

A roster of individuals who did not show up for work. The persons listed in lines 10–40 reappear, in the same order, in BIN 8 243:1–11, rev. 1′–12′. The two texts differ, however, in that in BIN 8 243 all the designations other than nu 'not (present)' are replaced by nu (with the exception of two instances of úš 'deceased'; BIN 8 243:3, rev. 1′). A similar document is NBC 7008, published by Bridges, *Mesag Archive*, p. 467 (transliteration only).

It appears that the twenty lú zàḫ-me 'absentees', who are totaled in line 44, include the sixteen persons designated as nu '(not) present' (lines 8, 10–11, 15, 19, 22–23, 25–26, 28, 30, 32, 34, 40, 42–43), and the four persons designated as AŠ (lines 2, 38–39, 41). Accordingly, the seven lú è-me 'the ones who were sent out' (line 46) must comprise the persons described as è 'sent out' (line 36), má '(assigned to the) boat' (line 5), tu 'sick' (lines 9, 18), še '(assigned to) barley' (line 14), ama 'mother' (line 37), and the person whose description is not preserved (line 29). The eight úš 'deceased' (line 45) appear in lines 1, 4, 6–7, 12, 16, 24, and 33.

Many of the persons listed in the present text appear also in NBC 12319, published by Bridges, *Mesag Archive*, pp. 481–84.

2. The meaning of the notation AŠ (also lines 38–39 and 41) is unclear.

14. Since BIN 8 243:5 has simply Ur-lú, ⌜x⌝ may be accidental scratches.

24. This person is also attested in BIN 8 152:82–84: Me-lú Eden-bi-šè dumu-nita-ni.

29. One would expect this entry to be identical with úš Lú-k[ug], who is listed in BIN 8 243 rev. 1′ immediately before Zabalam-[(x)] dumu ⌜Lugal⌝-[e-á-na]. However, if Lu-kug was listed in this position, his designation could not have been úš 'deceased', since only eight deceased are named in the text.

30-31. The restoration is based on BIN 8 243 rev. 2′-3′ and NBC 7008:5-6.

32. The divine element ^{d}Bìl, occurring in this name, is probably an abbreviation of ^{d}Bìl-ga-mes. See Steinkeller, *Sale Documents*, p. 244 commentary to no. 64:9.

33. This entry is wanting in BIN 8 243. Dada, the felter, appears also in BIN 8 138:10, 237 rev. 2, 239:2, 245:34, 255:5, NBC 6969 iii 13 (= Bridges, *Mesag Archive*, pp. 455-56), NBC 12319 i 6-7. In the last example this person is designated as ⸢Da⸣-da 1 gaba túg-du$_8$.

39. The notation 1 gaba '(with) one infant' occurs also in NBC 12319 passim, which, in addition, uses a notation 2 gaba '(with) two infants' (ii 26, v 14′).

No. 46. IM 10599 Pl. 23

Obverse

1) 3(gur) 1(pi) še gur-sag-gál	3 gsg 60 liters of barley
2) KA-ba-e A-ga-dè^{ki}	KA-ba-e (for) Akkade
3) má-a bí-si	loaded on the boat.
4) 2(gur) 2(pi) Ur-^{d}En-líl	2 gsg 120 liters: (for) Ur-Enlil,
5) dumu Ama-níg-tu	son of Ama-nigtu;
6) 1(gur) Bar-ra-ni ad-KID	1 gsg: (for) Barani, the basket maker;
7) 1(pi) Du-du dumu Ur-PA	60 liters: (for) Dudu, son of Ur-PA;
8) ⸢2(gur)⸣ 5(bán) Nin-gu-la šu ba-ti	⸢2⸣ gsg 50 liters: Nin-gula received;
9) ⸢1(pi)⸣ lu^{sar} an-sa$_{10}$	⸢60⸣ liters: the turnips were purchased (with this barley by him);

Reverse

10) ⸢2(bán)⸣ Ḫu-la ensi(MAŠ+EN.LI)	⸢20⸣ liters: (for) Ḫula, the dream interpreter;
11) [1(bán)] ⸢Ḫu⸣-la ensi(MAŠ+EN.LI)	[10] liters: (for) ⸢Ḫu⸣la, the dream interpreter;
12) ⸢2(bán) Ḫu⸣-la ensi(MAŠ+EN.LI) (space)	⸢20⸣ liters: (for) ⸢Ḫu⸣la, the dream interpreter;
13) šu-nigin$_2$ 10 lá 1(gur) 2(pi) 4(bán) še gur-sag-gál	total of 9 gsg 160 liters of barley (were expended).

A record of nine separate expenditures of barley. This text is linked by prosopography to BIN 8 171 and 174, and possibly also to BIN 8 167, all three of which appear to come from Isin (see p. 7).

2. KA-ba-e occurs also in BIN 8 174:2.

5. Ama-nigtu, the parent of Ur-Enlil, may be the same person as the Ama-nigtu appearing in BIN 8 167:22.

7. Dudu, son of Ur-PA, is also attested in BIN 8 171:4–5.

9. lu^{sar}, which is common in Pre-Sargonic texts (see Bauer, *Lagasch*, p. 661 under udu-sar), is clearly the same as $lu\text{-}úb^{sar}$ (Akk. *laptu*) 'turnip'; CAD L, p. 96. The form lu^{sar}, which is the earlier of the two, is either to be analyzed as an abbreviated spelling or to be read $lub_x(\text{LU})^{sar}$. If we were to follow the second interpretation, lu-úb could then be explained as $lub_x(\text{LU})^{úb}$. (N.B.: the same explanation may apply to ^{giš}ḫa-lu-úb.) Note that úb is attested as a phonetic indicator in the toponym $Urub_x(\text{URU}\times\text{ÚB})^{ki}$ (cf. Sollberger, *ZA* 54 [1961] 9 no. 22, 45 no. 291).

For the conjugational prefix a-, occurring in an-sa_{10}, see commentary to no. 9 i 8.

10–12. I assume that MAŠ+EN.LI stands for ensi(EN.ME.LI) (Akk. *enšû*, *šā᾽ilu*) 'dream interpreter'. As far as I know, the present spelling is completely unique. Cf. ME+EN.LI, followed by engiz(EN.ME.GI), in Charpin-Durand, *Strasbourg* 43:4 (Sargonic).

No. 47. IM 26175 — Pl. 23

Obverse

1)	15 UDU.NITA	15 rams,
2)	40 U_8.SAL	40 ewes;
3)	⌜ŠU.NIGIN$_2$⌝ 55 UDU	⌜total⌝ of 55 sheep;
4)	3 LAK-20	3 male goats,
5)	45 ÙZ	45 she-goats.
6)	*Ì-lu*$_5$-DINGIR	Ilu-ilī,

Reverse

7)	SIPAD	the shepherd,
8)	È	delivered(?) (them).
9)	LAL 1 UDU.NITA	In arrears: 1 ram.
10)	LAL 2 U_8.SAL	In arrears: 2 ewes.
11)	*Uru-zu*	(The property of) Uruzu.

It appears that this text is a record of the sheep and goats which were consigned by their owner (Uruzu) to a shepherd (Ilu-ilī) as part of a herding agreement. A parallel text is MAD 5 76, stemming from Mukdan, which involves the same shepherd: (1) 61 ÙZ (2) *I-lu*$_5$-DINGIR (3) SIPAD (4) [UD].DU

(5) [*i*]*n* MU ŠUDUN (6) LUGAL *in* ᶜ*À-mar-nu-um* (7) *i-li-ga-am*, 'Ilu-ilī delivered(?) 61 goats; in the year of the campaign (when) the king came to Amarnum'. For other early examples of such "herding contracts," see Steinkeller, *Aula Orientalis* 2 (1984) 138, and no. 9 in this volume.

My translation of the verb È in line 8 assumes that the text concerns the return of animals at the conclusion of the agreement (note that lines 9–10 list the animals in arrears). However, since È can equally well be translated 'to bring out, to take away', the text could also record the expenditure of the flock to the shepherd at the commencement of the agreement.

2. Note U_8.SAL in place of the more common U_8.

4. Attestations of the sign LAK-20 are basically limited to Fara and Abu Salabikh sources. Occasionally, though, this sign also occurs in Sargonic peripheral texts (MDP 14 27:1; HSS 10 171, 178, 180). As far as I know, this is the only occurrence of LAK-20 in a Sargonic text from northern Babylonia. Although it is certain that LAK-20 denotes a type of domestic animal, the question of its identification has not until now been satisfactorily resolved. Bauer (*ZA* 61 [1972] 323) proposed that LAK-20 is an earlier form of megida 'sow'. More recently, Pettinato (MEE 3, p. 69), noting that in the Ebla lexical sources LAK-20 occurs in connection with sheep and goats, identifies it as "tipo di ovino." Given the fact that the present text lists the LAK-20 animals together with she-goats and separately from sheep, it becomes apparent that LAK-20 denotes a type of goat. In this connection note that in Ebla lexical texts LAK-20 consistently figures among the terms for goats: following ùz and preceding máš and áš-gàr (VE 925–28 = MEE 4, pp. 302–3); following ùz and áš-gàr and preceding máš (MEE 3 18 lines 33–41). That LAK-20 is a type of goat can also be deduced from the ovine terms recorded in an economic tablet from Abu Salabikh: šu-nigin$_2$ x udu-nita u$_8$ sila$_4$ ùz LAK-20 áš-gàr 'total of x rams, ewes, lambs, she-goats, . . . , (and) kids' (*Iraq* 40 [1978] 112 no. 519 iii′ 1).

Moreover, if one considers that in the present text the LAK-20 animals represent but a fraction of the number of she-goats, the conclusion becomes unavoidable that LAK-20 is a term for 'male goat' (cf. the ratio of 15 rams to 40 ewes in lines 1–2). This interpretation is also evident from the comparison of the ovine terms appearing in the earlier-cited Abu Salabikh tablet, where LAK-20 is clearly the caprine equivalent of udu-nita 'ram'.

Since megida corresponds to the Akkadian *šaḫītu* 'sow' (see Hh. XIV 181–83), any connection between it and LAK-20 seems impossible. The reading of LAK-20 remains, therefore, unknown.

In summary, LAK-20 is to be analyzed as an early Sumerian word for 'male goat'. Already by the end of the ED period, this term appears to have been replaced by máš-nita and máš-gal, though in northern Babylonia (Mukdan) and in the peripheral zone (Gasur, Susa) its usage continued into the Sargonic period.

[For the meaning and reading of LAK-20, see now Pomponio, *RA* 80 (1986) 187–88, whose conclusions coincide partly with ours. Pomponio too considers LAK-20 to be the counterpart of ùz—his translation of LAK-20 as 'she-goat' is obviously a *lapsus linguae* for 'he-goat'. However, his suggestion that LAK-20 is to be read bala$_x$ is highly unlikely, since the sign is distinguished from bala as late as the Sargonic period (see the evidence cited above).]

6. The spelling Ì-lu$_5$-DINGIR, as contrasted with I-lu$_5$-DINGIR in MAD 5 76:2, demonstrates that I-lu$_5$-DINGIR is to be interpreted as */ilu(m)-ilī/* (against Gelb, MAD 3, p. 40, who interpreted it as I-lul-DINGIR and connected with *alālu* 'to rejoice'). The same name, spelled I-lu-DINGIR, appears in *JCS* 10 (1956) 26 no. 2 vi 13 and CT 50 74:5′.

No. 48. IM 43612 Pl. 23

Obverse

1)	6½ GÍN KUG.BABBAR	6½ shekels of silver,
2)	*a-na* SÁM-*me*	as the price of
3)	*Da-áš*-LUL-*tum*	Taš-LUL-tum,
4)	*É-a-sa-tu*	Ea-šadû,
5)	*Um-mi*-DÙG DAM-*zu*	Ummī-ṭābat, his wife,
6)	*I-ti-É-a*	Iddin-Ea
7)	*Ba-sa-aḫ*-DINGIR	(and) Pašaḫ-ilum,
8)	2 DUMU-*su*	his two sons,
9)	KUG.BABBAR *im-ḫu-ru*	received (this) silver.
10)	*Tu-tu*	Tutu
11)	*ù Íl-e-mu-bí*	and Ilʾe-mūpi
12)	Ì.LAL	weighed (it) out.

Reverse

13)	^{I}*Im$_4$-da-lik*	Imtalik,
14)	DUMU *Ba-bi-na-at*	son of Babinat;
15)	^{I}⸢*Ì*⸣-*lí*-TAB.BA DUMU-*su*	Ilī-tappê, his son;
16)	^{I}*Ì-lí*-⸢TAB⸣.BA DUMU DINGIR-*ma*	Ilī-tappê, son of Iluma;
17)	^{I}LAGAB-DINGIR DUMU-*su*	LAGAB-DINGIR, his son;
18)	^{I}*Su-mu-ḫum* DUMU *Nin-tu-a*	Šummuḫum, son of Ninituʾa;
19)	^{I}*Ag-rí-rí* MAR.TU	Agriri, the Amorite,
20)	DUMU DINGIR-*mu-da*	son of Ilum-mūdâ;
21)	^{I}DINGIR-*ba-ni* DUMU DINGIR-*mu-da*	Ilum-bāni, son of Ilum-mūdâ;
	(space)	
22)	ŠU.NIGIN$_2$ 7 AB×ÁŠ	total of seven witnesses.

The origin of this sale document is almost certainly Umm el-Jir (ancient Mukdan). This is indicated by the fact that the buyers Tutu and Ilʾe-mūpi (probably brothers) seem to occur in other Mukdan texts. For Tutu, see BIN 8 160:42–43, which mentions a *Tu-tu šu* DUMU *Be-lu-lu* 'Tutu, (the man) of the son of Belulu', and cf. also no. 49:3–4 in this volume. For Ilʾe-mūpi, see no. 49:1 and *ASJ* 4 (1982) 45–46 no. 14 iv 22 (read *Íl-e-*⸢*mu*⸣*-bí*, against Foster, *ASJ* 4 [1982] 13, who reads *Íl-e-*⸢*li*⸣?-NE). Furthermore, note that the present text and no. 49, which definitely comes from Mukdan, bear adjacent accession numbers. This suggests that both tablets were acquired from the same source.

Given that the sellers are members of a nuclear family (a husband, his wife, and two sons), the sold woman (or girl) probably was their daughter and sister.

3. The reading of the sign LUL in this name is uncertain. See Steinkeller, *SEL* 1 (1984) 16 n. 30.

17. The reading of LAGAB in this name, which is common in Sargonic texts (see, e.g., MAD 1, p. 210; Rasheed, *Himrin* 7 iii 10; and no. 73:13 in this volume), is unknown.

18. Evidently, the same name as the OB Šummuḫum (spelled *Šu*(*-um*)*-mu-ḫu*(*-um*) 'Very-Rich, Abundant' (see *AHw*, p. 1274a). Contrast Gelb, MAD 3, p. 275, who reads this name *Su-mu-núm*, with the analysis Šummunum 'Fat'.

No. 49. IM 43613 Pl. 24

Obverse

1) ^{I}*Íl-e-mu-bí*	Ilʾe-mūpi
2) *ù Gu-lí-zum*	and Kullizum;
3) ^{I}DINGIR-UR.SAG	Ilum-uršān,
4) DUMU *Be-lu-lu*	son of Belulu,
5) *ù ʾÀ-da-mu*	and Adamu,
6) *šu Be-lí-ba-na*	(the man) of Bēlī-bana,

Reverse

7) *Ì-lí-ib*^{ki}	(the citizen of) Ilib;
8) ^{I}*Ip-ḫu-ru-um*	Iphurum
9) *ù I-nin-e-ru-um*	and Inin-erum;
(space)	
10) *Na-me-zi-na*$^{\langle\mathrm{ki}\rangle}$	(they reside? in) Namezina.

A list of six individuals, residing(?) in Namezina. The attribution of this tablet to Mukdan rests on the fact that Adamu, man of Bēlī-bana (lines 5–6), also appears in the Mukdan text BIN 8 160:51–52 (*ʾÀ-da-mu* ⟨*šu*⟩ *Be-lí-ba-na*). It is noteworthy that the latter text lists fields that were held by various people (among them Adamu) in Ilib, thus corroborating the information that Adamu was a citizen of Ilib (see line 7).

1. The same person possibly occurs in no. 48:11 and *ASJ* 4 (1982) 45–46 no. 14 iv 22. Cf. commentary to no. 48.

3–4. Cf. *Tu-tu šu* DUMU *Be-lu-lu* 'Tutu, (the man) of the son of Belulu' (BIN 8 160:42–43), where the unnamed son of Belulu is probably our Ilum-uršān. Note also that the same text lists an Ilum-uršān in line 33. For Tutu, cf. no. 48:10.

5. For this name, see MAD 3, p. 19.

6. For the element *-bana* or *-pana*, see MAD 3, p. 99.

7. For I/Elib (or I/Elip), see RGTC 1, p. 77; 3, p. 71; Charpin, *RA* 72 (1978) 17–22; Steinkeller, *Vicino Oriente* 6 (1986) 37.

9. For the element *-erum*, see MAD 3, p. 59.

10. Possibly the same toponym as *Na-m[e-z]i-ga-na*^{ki}, which appears in the subscript of *ASJ* 4 (1982) 45–46 no. 14 left edge (read by Foster on p. 13 as *Na-zi-ga-na*^{ki}). If so, the pronunciation of the toponym could be reconstructed as Namezig(a)na (by assuming that the present occurrence is to be read *Na-me-zìg-na*).

No. 50. IM 2886/D Pl. 24

Obverse

1)	11 GIŠ.ŠID 2 KÙŠ	11 GIŠ.ŠID (and) 2 cubits
2)	IM.MIR	(is the length of) the northern (side);
3)	13 GIŠ⸢.ŠID⸣ 1 KÙŠ 1(?) ŠÚ.BAD	13 GIŠ.ŠID, 1 cubit, (and) 1(?) ŠÚ.BAD
4)	IM.U$_5$	(is the length of) the southern (side);
5)	6 GIŠ.ŠID 1 KÙ[Š]	6 GIŠ.ŠID (and) 1 cubit
6)	IM.MAR.TU	(is the length of) the western (side);
7)	⸢7 GIŠ.ŠID⸣ 1 KÙŠ	⸢7 GIŠ.ŠID⸣ (and) 1 cubit

Lower Edge

8)	[I]M.KUR	(is the length of) the eastern (side).

Reverse

9)	2 ⟨GIŠ.⟩ŠID *a-na*	2 ⟨GIŠ.⟩ŠID times
10)	6 GIŠ.ŠID	6 GIŠ.ŠID.
11)	1 GIŠ.ŠID *a-na*	1 GIŠ.ŠID times
12)	10 GIŠ.ŠID	10 GIŠ.ŠID.
	(space)	
13)	ŠU.NIGIN$_2$ 10 GIŠ.IŠ.NE	Total of 10 "chairs" (of land),
14)	É *Da-ba-lum*	the house-lot (which) Dabalum
15)	*a-na Ku-ku i-din*$_x$(GIM)	sold (lit.: gave) to Kuku.

The present text is related to MAD 1 336 and Gelb, *OAIC* 2, which likewise deal with house-lots and involve the same Dabalum. In MAD 1 336 Dabalu, together with U-KA-KA and Tašqitum, measures out (*iš-du-tu*, line 12)

4 "chairs" of a house-lot (É GIŠ.GU.ZA) to a certain Ummimi. In Gelb, *OAIC* 2, Dabalum (identified as Idā-pî-ilī, line 2) and *Da-bi-lum* (line 16) measure out (*iš-du-ud*, line 3) 1½ "chairs" of a house-lot (GIŠ.IŠ.NE É) to Bēlī-bāni. A similar text is YBC 12310 (unpubl.), which records the dimensions of a field belonging to certain *I-te*(?)-DINGIR and Mašum, and lists four witnesses, identified as AB×ÁŠ *si-da-ti* GANA_2 'witnesses of the measuring of the field'.

Although it is clear that the above documents concern the transfer of real property, it is uncertain whether they should be analyzed as outright sale documents or as records of the preliminary procedure of measuring and evaluating the property that preceded the actual sale transaction. The fact that no. 50, MAD 1 336, and Gelb, *OAIC* 2 seem to come from the archive of Dabalum, who was the seller of the houses in question, supports the second solution, since sale documents are always prepared for the buyer. Cf. also *ELTS*, p. 209.

The house-lot described in the text comprised three (separate?) areas: the main area (lines 1–8) and two additional areas (lines 9–12). Since the additional areas amount to 22 square GIŠ.ŠID, it can be established on the basis of the total (10 GIŠ.IŠ.NE = 100 square ŠID) that the main area, forming a trapezoid, was computed according to the approximative formula

$$A = \frac{a1 + a2}{2} \times \frac{b1 + b2}{2}$$

In applying this formula, the surveyor used only the measurements in GIŠ.ŠID, disregarding the smaller length-units. The resulting calculation is

$$\frac{11 + 13}{2} \times \frac{6 + 7}{2} = 78 \text{ square GIŠ.ŠID}$$

Since, as demonstrated by the present text, 1 GIŠ.IŠ.NE = 10 square GIŠ.ŠID, it becomes clear that GIŠ.IŠ.NE is identical with the surface-measure GIŠ.GU.ZA, which is attested in the Sargonic, Ur III, and Early OB texts from the Diyala Region. That 1 GIŠ.GU.ZA equals 10 square GIŠ.ŠID is shown by MAD 1 336 (collated), recording a house-lot of the dimensions 7 ŠID x 9 ŠID x 5 ŠID x 5 ŠID, with a total area of 4 GIŠ.GU.ZA. The measure GIŠ.GU.ZA appears also in Gelb, *OAIC* 8:18 (spelled GU.ZÉ), Steinkeller, *Sale Documents* no. 75:1 ([g]u-za), and Early OB sale documents from Ešnunna (courtesy of R. M. Whiting). For the translation of GIŠ.IŠ.NE as 'chair', see commentary to line 13.

The length of (GIŠ.)ŠID is unknown, though, as shown by line 1, it must have been more than 2 kùš. M. A. Powell (personal communication) suggests that (GIŠ.)ŠID is a logogram for *nikkas* (= *purīdu* = 3 kùš), "an inference made likely by the semantic and graphic connections between ŠID and *nikkassu*." If so, 1 GIŠ.IŠ.NE/GIŠ.GU.ZA would measure 90 square kùš = 22.5 m^2.

3. ŠÚ.BAD appears to be a "syllabic" variant of the logogram ŠU.BAD, for which phenomenon cf. the Old Assyrian spelling KUG.KI for KUG.GI. The pronunciation of ŠU.BAD is probably zipaḫ; see Landsberger, *WZKM* 56 (1960) 109–10.

13. The meaning 'chair' of GIŠ.IŠ.NE is indicated, apart from its identity with the surface-measure GIŠ.GU.ZA, by the fact that a piece of furniture so named is otherwise attested in Pre-Sargonic and Sargonic texts. See 1 IŠ.NE ^{giš}taskarin (Foxvog, in Alster, *Death*, p. 68 ii 3, following 1 ná ^{giš}taskarin); 2 ^{giš}IŠ.NE (ITT 2 4508:1, 4, 6; delivered by the carpenters); 4 ^{giš}IŠ.NE 1 ^{giš}IŠ.NE barag 'chair of the dais' (ITT 2 4646:15–16); oil ^{giš}IŠ(!).NE barag íb-ak 'was used to anoint a chair of the dais' (ITT 2 5742:3–5); 1 ^{giš}IŠ.NE ḫašḫur (ITT 5 9273:3′); x GIŠ.IŠ.NE (Rasheed, *Himrin* 43:1, 3, 5, 7). Note also PN *šu* GIŠ.IŠ.NE ENSI$_2$ in no. 73:1–2, for which compare *šu-ut/ša* GIŠ.GU.ZA (MAD 1 226, 233 iii 9). Quite likely, IŠ.NE is to be read iš-dè and analyzed as a variant spelling of aš-te (Akk. *kussû, aštû*) 'chair, throne'. In this connection, it is of interest that aš-te was thought by the Babylonian lexicographers to be an Emesal form of gu-za (see [mu-a]š-te = giš-gu-za = *ku-*[*us-su-ú*] in MSL 4, p. 21 line 144).

14. For Dabalum, see also *JCS* 26 (1974) 80 no. 8:8.

15. For the spelling of *iddin* with the sign GIM/DÍM, cf. 10(GUR) PN *a-na* PN$_2$ BAḪAR$_2$ *i-din*$_x$(GIM) '10 gur (of barley) PN gave to PN$_2$, the potter' (Gelb, *OAIC* 36:5; cf. ibid., p. 288).

No. 51. IM 11053/277 Pl. 24

Obverse

i (beginning destroyed)
1′) 5 *Šu-Eš*$_4$*-dar*
2′) [1]+4 *Ì-lí-lí*
3′) *šu-ut* ^{d}*Tišpak-kùn*
4′) 5 *Ga-at-núm*
5′) 5 *Zu-zu*
6′) 5 *Da-da*
7′) X *I-sa-ru-um*
8′) [. . .] ⸢x⸣
(rest destroyed)

ii (beginning destroyed)
1′) 5 *Bí-za-núm*
2′) 1 TÚG *Pù-su-su*
3′) 1 TÚG *Ì-lí*-NE
4′) 1 TÚG *Ú-zu-ur-ba-su*
5′) X *Šu-Dur-ùl*
6′) X *A-li-a-ḫu*
7′) *šu-ut* I-NE-NE
8′) 3 ⸢x⸣ [. . .]
(rest destroyed)

Reverse

(destroyed)

An account of garments and their recipients. Column i and the beginning of column ii may have concerned the disbursement of another article or commodity.

The Diyala origin of the present text is indicated by the presence of the personal name Tišpak-kūn (i 3′), which invokes Tišpak, the chief god of Ešnunna. As a matter of fact, all of the names appearing here are listed in the index to MAD 1.

i 7′. X (also in ii 5′ and 6′) is a scribal check mark.

No. 52. IM 10604 Pl. 25

Obverse

1)	[x] gín kug-babbar	["(Concerning) x] shekels of silver
2)	[X]-^{d}Nin-šubur-ka	[which X]-Ninšubur,
3)	[šu]-⸢ḫa⸣-e ma-lá-a-a	[the fish]erman, had weighed out to me
4)	[mu] á arad$_{2}$-gá-šè	as the wages of my slave—
5)	ud-ba 1 gín kug-babbar 10 še-ka	at that time, (for) 1 shekel (and) 10 grains of silver
6)	še-bi 1(gur) 4(bán) še gur	1 gur (and) 40 liters of barley
7)	al-ág	were measured out,"
8)	Uru-^{d}Utu^{ki} dam-gàr	Uru-Utu, the merchant,
9)	na-bi-a	thus continues (lit.: says),
10)	arad$_{2}$-zu ki kin ba-⸢x⸣	"'Your slave has ⸢abandoned(?)⸣ the place of work!'—

Reverse

11)	ma-dug$_{4}$	he (i.e., [X]-Ninšubur) (later) told me."
12)	^{I}Gìr-ni ⸢nu-èš⸣	Girni, the ⸢***nêšakku*** priest⸣;
13)	^{I}nin-dingir ^{d}Nin-šubur-ka	the ***ēnu*** priest(ess) of the goddess Ninšubur;
14)	^{I}Ur-^{d}En-líl-lá SIG-da-um	Ur-Enlila, the . . . ;
15)	^{I}Du-du sipad	Dudu, the shepherd;
16)	^{I}Lugal-iti-da nu-èš	Lugal-itida, the ***nêšakku*** priest;
17)	^{I}Ur-é-maḫ	Ur-emaḫ;
	(space)	
18)	[lú]-ki-inim-ma-me	(these) are the witnesses.
19)	[X-^{d}]Nin-mug-ra-ke$_{4}$	[X]-Ninmug
20)	[maškim(?)] gál-la-àm	was the [bailiff?].

I assume that this text is a witnessed declaration of the merchant Uru-Utu, concerning a claim raised by the fisherman [X]-Ninšubur. It appears that [X]-Ninšubur had hired a slave from Uru-Utu, but the slave later abandoned his place of work. Consequently, [X]-Ninšubur demanded the return of the wages.

The unusual feature of the text is that the phrase 'Uru-Utu, the merchant, thus says' (lines 8–9), rather than preceding Uru-Utu's declaration, is placed in the middle of it. This particular formulation seems to be due to the fact that the second half of the declaration quotes [X]-Ninšubur's words; by moving the introductory formula closer to the statement 'he told me (this)' (line 11), the scribe probably wanted to make it clear that the intervening words are a quotation.

5–7. Since one expects only 1 shekel in a tariff statement, the *Winkelhacken* (= 10) in line 5 should possibly be ignored. If so, 1 gín kug-babbar še-ka could be interpreted as an inverted genitive: 'of 1 shekel of silver of the barley (tariff), (its barley etc.)'.

8. The personal name Uru-Utu 'Town-of-Utu' is unusual, but note the parallel name Uru-Iškur^{ki} (or Āl-Adad^{ki}), appearing in the Sargonic sale document *JCS* 35 (1983) 169 no. 4:3.

10. Possibly to be restored ba-⸢šub(!)⸣ 'he has abandoned', but the traces of the sign are inconclusive.

14. The meaning of the title/occupation SIG-da-um (to be read se$_{11}$-da-um?) is unknown. The same word is attested in BIN 8 196:21 (*Gi-šum* SIG-*da*-[*um*]) and the Sargonic seal Buchanan, *Ashmolean* no. 367b: AN.GIŠ.GAG, SIG-da-um (cf. Edzard, *AfO* 22 [1968–69] 17 6.1). Note also ^{I}É-gud si-da-um SI.X.DU$_7$.NI (*WO* 13 [1982] 15–16 no. 1:9–10; Sargonic, transliteration only), 10(guruš) si-da-um (Charpin-Durand, *Strasbourg* 83:5; Sargonic), [P]N si-da-um (*STTI* 168 i 5′; Sargonic), and Ur-mes su-da-um (A 825:4; Sargonic, edited by Zhi Yang, *A Study of the Sargonic Archive from Adab* [Ph.D. diss., University of Chicago, 1986], pp. 349, 468 [photograph]). One might consider that SIG-da-um is a *parrās* formation from *šatû* 'to weave', that is, **šettāʾum*, assuming, of course, that the Old Akkadian infinitive could be reconstructed as **šetû*.

19. Since the DN ^{d}Nin-mug takes the complement -ga (see Ur-^{d}Nin-mug-ga in Limet, *Anthroponymie*, p. 555), the spelling with -ra, occurring here, is unexplainable. Perhaps MUG is a scribal mistake for UR$_4$ (i.e., for ^{d}Nin-ur$_4$-ra).

No. 53. IM 10613 — Pl. 25

Obverse

1) 1½(iku) gana$_2$ giš-ì	1½ iku of sesame land:
2) Lú-tukul engar	Lu-tukul, the farmer;
3) 1¼(iku) Lugal-iti-d[a] ni-is-[ku]	1¼ iku of land: Lugal-itid[a], the . . . ;
4) 1(iku) Lugal-⸢sukud(?)⸣-[rá(?)]	1 iku of land: Lugal-⸢sukud(?)⸣-[ra];

Reverse

5) $1\frac{1}{2}+\frac{1}{8}$(iku) ⌜X⌝-[. . .]	$1\frac{5}{8}$ iku of land: ⌜X⌝-[. . .],
6) ašla[g_4(GIŠ.TÚG. KAR.[DU]))]	the fuller of
7) Lugal-KU-⌜e⌝	Lugal-KU-e;
8) $1\frac{1}{8}$(iku) Amar-bàd ⌜nu⌝-èš	$1\frac{1}{8}$ iku of land: Amar-bad, the ***nêšakku*** priest.

A record of five land allotments(?).

3. For ni-is-ku, a type of dependent or retainer, see most recently Foster, *USP*, p. 85. The same term occurs also in no. 56:14.

No. 54. IM 23457/21 Pl. 25

Obverse

1) ^{I}Mug-gi_4	Mugi,
2) dumu Ur-^{d}Nin-mug	son of Ur-Ninmug;
3) ugula Ur-^{d}Nin-pirig	(his) foreman (is) Ur-Ninpirig;
4) nu-[ba]nda_3 Lú-$šag_5$	(his) supervisor (is) Lu-šag;

Reverse

5) $gurum_2$ nu im dagal daḫ-ḫi-dam	there was no inspection (or: he was not present at the inspection); (his name) is to be added to the "broad" tablet.

A record concerning the worker Mugi. The fact that the goddess Ninmug (line 2) is at home at Umma suggests that this tablet comes from Umma.

5. $gurum_2$ nu is probably an abbreviation for $gurum_2$ nu-ak. Alternatively, one could see in nu the negative enclitic copula -nu 'is not', for which see commentary to no. 5:12′.

No. 55. IM 23459 Pl. 25

Obverse

1) 74 guruš sig_4	74 men, the brick(-makers),
2) 16 ugula	16 foremen,
3) 7 lú a	7 water(-drawers?),
4) 10 tu-ra	10 sick,
5) 7 gir-ba-núm	7 clod(-pickers?),

6) 3 ì-du$_8$	3 doorkeepers,
7) 4 zi-ga	4 conscripted,

Reverse

8) 20 lá 3 šu šidim	17 under the charge of the mason.

A roster of workers. The question of the language of this text depends on whether šu in line 8 is to be interpreted as the Sumerian šu X-ak 'the authority of X', or the Akkadian relative/determinative pronoun *šu* 'he of'. The latter possibility may be supported by the mention of the Akkadian word *kirbānu* 'clod (of earth)' in line 5 (but see the commentary below). Since this question cannot be satisfactorily resolved, I have classified the text as Sumerian, following the safer avenue.

5. The context suggests that gir-ba-núm represents the noun *kirbānu* 'clod (of earth)', rather than the personal name Kirbānu, for which see MAD 3, p. 150. The picking of earth-clods (Sum. lag . . . ri-ri-(g); Akk. *kirbāna laqātu*) was a standard type of agricultural work. See *Eames Collection*, pp. 161–62.

No. 56. IM 30350 Pl. 26

Obverse

1) [1(bùr) 1(eše)] gana$_2$ [15 sar(?)]
2) [11(gur)] 1(pi) 4(bán) še gur-sag-⌜gál⌝
3) Ad-da nu-banda$_3$
4) 3(iku) gana$_2$ lá 25 sar 1(gur) 3(bán) gur-sag
5) Ù-ku-za-at
6) 1(iku) gana$_2$ 40 sar
7) 1(gur) 1(pi) 3(bán) gur-sag
8) Puzur$_4$-Ma-ma ad-KID
9) 2(iku) gana$_2$ 1(gur) 3(pi) gur-sag
10) Ìr-a-mu-um
11) 3(iku) gana$_2$ 4(gur) 2(pi) gur-sag
12) Ì-la-ak-nu-id(DA)
13) 3(iku) gana$_2$ 1(gur) 2(pi) gur-sag
14) Ì-lí-dan ni-is-ku
15) 3(iku) gana$_2$ 1(gur) 2(pi) gur-sag
16) Ì-la-la dub-sar
17) ⌜1(eše)⌝ 3(iku) (erasure) gana$_2$

Reverse

18) 5(gur) gur-sag
19) DINGIR-dan
(space)
20) šu-nigin$_2$ 2(bùr) 2(eše) gana$_2$ 30 sar
21) šu-nigin$_2$ 28(gur) 4(bán) še gur-sag-gál
22) apin-lá
23) 1(eše) Mu-mu-sa-tu
24) 1(eše) SI.A-um
25) ⸢1(eše)(?)⸣ Li-bur
26) [1(eše)(?) Ì]-lí-dan
27) [1(eše)(?) . . .]-li

A list of leased fields, their renters, and the corresponding rental payments (apin-lá). Individual entries have the following pattern: x(iku) gana$_2$ x(gur) še gur-sag-gál PN 'x iku of land; (its rent is) x gsg of barley; (the renter is) PN'. Lines 20–21 give the totals of the leased fields and the rent. The following five lines probably list the renters who failed to make the payment.

The total of 48 iku and 30 sar (line 20) can only be obtained if one reconstructs [15 sar] at the end of line 1. However, the break following the sign GANA$_2$ appears to be too small to accommodate such a reconstruction.

Since the first renter listed is an overseer (Ad-da nu-banda$_3$), renting the largest field, it is possible that the text lists members of the same corvée team, with Adda representing their supervisor. Note also that, whereas the overseer has a good Sumerian name, all of his subordinates bear Akkadian names.

5. For this name, see MAD 3, p. 26, under ***ukkuṣum***.

14. For ni-is-ku, see commentary to no. 53:3.

No. 57. IM 43431 Pl. 26

Obverse

1) ⸢6(?)⸣ igi-6 gín kug-babbar	⸢6(?)⸣ (and) 1/6 shekels of silver
2) níg-sám Me-Unug^{ki}-kam	is the price of Me-Unug.
3) Ur-níg-túl-la dam-⸢gàr(?)⸣	Ur-nigtula, the mer⸢chant(?)⸣,
4) É-maḫ sagi	E-maḫ, the cupbearer,
5) Bi-bi dam Giš nar	(and) Bibi, wife of Giš, the singer,
6) kug-bi šu-ne-ne ab-si	their (i.e., the preceding three persons) hands were filled (with) this silver.
7) Lugal-giš sagi	Lugal-giš, the cupbearer;
8) Ur-ur ⸢zadim⸣	Ur-ur, the ⸢lapidary⸣;

9)	Bar-ra-ni-šè ⌜zadim⌝	Baraniše, the ⌜lapidary⌝;
10)	Šag$_4$-kug-gi zadim	Šag-kuge, the lapidary;

Reverse

11)	Mu-ni-[(x)]	Muni-[(x)];
12)	Nin-é	Nin-e;
	(space)	
13)	lú-ki-inim-ma-bi-me	these are the witnesses.

The main question raised by this sale document is the identity of the sellers and the buyer. My translation assumes that the text names only the sellers, and that the name of the buyer is omitted, due, apparently, to the scribe's oversight. This interpretation rests primarily on the fact that in the Sargonic sale documents using the operative section with the construction kug šu-a . . . si 'to fill someone's hand with silver' (see, e.g., no. 61; MAD 4 77–78, 81, 150), the name of the buyer is never included in the operative section. Further evidence in support of this assumption is provided by the fact that the present text appears to belong to the Dagula archive (see nos. 58–60); note that the lapidary Ur-ur (line 8) is attested as a witness also in no. 58:14. In view of this provenience, the person who would be expected to act as buyer in the present text is either Dagula or his son Dada (see no. 58), neither of whom, however, is mentioned. This corroborates the assumption that the name of the buyer is wanting in the text.

Since the three sellers are clearly unrelated to each other, it is possible that they were creditors of Me-Unug. In that arrangement, the "price" paid for Me-Unug would constitute the sum of the debts owed by him/her to his/her three creditors. As such, the transaction would amount, for all practical purposes, to a self-sale. Cf. Nikolski 1 17, discussed by Steinkeller, *JESHO* 24 (1981) 144 n. 84, which also deals with the sale of a debtor by his creditors.

A similar text is the sale document no. 61, where the sellers of the person sold are his mother and two other persons, a fuller and his wife, who very likely were the mother's creditors. Virtually identical sale transactions are recorded in MAD 4 81 and 150. In the latter two texts the recipients of the purchase price are, in each case, the person sold, his mother, and another, unrelated, individual, who appears have been the mother's creditor. Since no. 61, MAD 4 81, and MAD 4 150 all use, like no. 57, the construction kug šu-a . . . si, it is tempting to consider that this type of operative section was specifically reserved for the sale transactions in which the purchase price was intended to compensate the seller's creditors.

3. The traces of the last sign are inconclusive. If the sign is NI (so the copy, but not confirmed by the collation), Ur-nigtula would be the husband (dam-⌜ni⌝) of Me-Unug, and, accordingly, E-maḫ and Bibi would be his creditors.

No. 58. IM 43451 Pl. 27

Obverse

1)	[x gín kug-babbar]	[x shekels of silver],
2)	níg-sám	the price of
3)	Nin-[x]-kam	Nin-[x],
4)	Da-⌜da⌝	Da⌜da⌝,
5)	⌜dumu⌝ Da-gu-[l]a-k[e$_4$(?)]	⌜son⌝ of Dagula,
6)	in-lá	weighed out.
7)	⌜Kur⌝-ni-šè	⌜Kur⌝niše
8)	⌜ù⌝ En-ku-li	⌜and⌝ En-kuli
9)	[da]m(?)-⌜gàr(?)⌝ sag-gá-me	are the ⌜dealers(?)⌝ of the slave.
10)	^{I}UD.UD nar	UD.UD, the singer;
11)	^{I}Bí-za-za	Bizaza,

Reverse

12)	dam Ma-ḫa-NI-a	wife of Maḫa-NI-a;
13)	^{I}Ur-maḫ nagar	Ur-maḫ, the carpenter;
14)	^{I}Ur-ur zadim	Ur-ur, the lapidary;
15)	^{I}É-ni-gara$_2$	Eni-gara;
16)	^{I}Lú-⌜ùz(?)⌝	Lu-⌜uz(?)⌝;
17)	^{I}Lugal-èn-tar na[gar(?)]	Lugal-entar, the car[penter(?)];
18)	^{I}Ur-^{d}Išt[aran]	Ur-Išt[aran],
19)	dub-s[ar]	the scri[be];
	(space)	
20)	lú-ki-in[im-ma(-bi)-me]	[(these) are] the wit[nesses].

Dada, son of Dagula, who is the buyer in the present text, should be connected with the Dagula of nos. 59–60. These three documents evidently come from the archive of Dagula's family. Another text which appears to belong to the same archive is no. 57.

9. The reconstruction [da]m(?)-⌜gàr(?)⌝, though not entirely satisfactory, is supported by the traces of the signs; cf. GÀR in no. 59:9, which stems from the same archive. However, the use of the term dam-gàr in the sense of 'seller', required by context, seems to be completely unique.

14. Attested as a witness also in no. 57:8.

No. 59. IM 43741 Pl. 27

Obverse

1)	10 ⌜lá⌝ [1(?)] ⌜gín kug-babbar⌝	⌜9(?) shekels of silver⌝

2) Da-gu-la	Dagula,
3) níg-sám Ki-tuš-dùg-šè	as the price of Kituš-dug,
4) Ur-si$_4$(?)	(to) Ur-si(?)
5) e-na-sum	gave.
6) kug-kug è	The . . .

Reverse

7) TUR-TUR è-àm	. . .
8) ^{I}Gìr-ni	Girni,
9) dam-gàr	the merchant;
10) UD-dib(?)	Ur-dib(?);
11) Lugal-giš	Lugal-giš;
12) lú-ki-inim-ma-bi-me	these are the witnesses.

This sale document belongs to the Dagula archive, which includes nos. 58 and 60, and probably also no. 57.

6–7. I am unable to offer a plausible translation of these lines. The expression kug-kug è 'the silver was issued(?)' is also attested in two Ur III texts, but its meaning there is equally obscure: 59 gín k[ug-babbar] kug-kug è PN ba-a-DU ki PN$_2$-ta PN$_3$ ù PN$_4$ šu ba-ti mu lugal-bi in-pàd-dè-eš, '59 shekels of sil[ver], the . . . , PN . . . ; PN$_3$ and PN$_4$ received (it) from PN$_2$; they swore by the name of the king' (ITT 4 7116:1–8 = MVN 6 115); 2 gín kug-babbar PN kug-kug è BIR(?) IM ki PN$_2$-ta PN$_3$ šu ba-ti, '2 shekels of silver, PN . . . ; PN$_3$ received (it) from PN$_2$' (YOS 4 13:1–6).

No. 60. IM 43759 Pl. 27

Obverse

1) 1(bùr) gana$_2$	18 iku of land,
2) ŠUKU A-zu-zu engar	the prebend of Azuzu, the farmer,
3) Da-gu-la	Dagula
4) šu ba-ti	received.
5) Lugal-šùd	Lugal-šud
6) in-na-sum	gave (it) to him (i.e., to Dagula).

Reverse

7) 15(gur) še gur	15 gur of barley,
8) še Da-gu-la	the barley of Dagula,
9) A-zu-zu engar	Azuzu, the farmer,
10) šu ba-ti	received.
11) ^{I}⌜Sag⌝-apin	⌜Sag⌝-apin;

12) ^{I}Lugal-zi	Lugal-zi;
13) lú-ki-inim-ma-bi-me	these are the witnesses.

Left Edge

14) ^{I}É-maḫ nagar-gal	E-maḫ, the chief carpenter;

Right Edge

15) ^{I}Lugal-KA arad$_{2}$ É-RU.DUG	Lugal-KA, the servant of E-RU.DUG;

Lower Edge

16) ^{I}Ur-ki-sag	Ur-kisag (are also the witnesses).

Azuzu, the farmer, transfers his prebend field to Dagula, in exchange for a fee. The transfer was carried out (or supervised) by a certain Lugal-šud, who appears to have been an official in charge of prebend land. For Dagula, see nos. 58–59.

There survive three other texts, one Sargonic and two dating to the Ur III period, which likewise deal with the transfer of prebend land. Because of their bearing on the interpretation of the present text, I cite their pertinent sections in full.

1. MDP 14 19 (Sargonic)

ki Lú-^{d}Šara$_{2}$ ensi$_{2}$ Umma^{ki}-ka-ta Di-^{d}Utu dub-sar-ke$_{4}$ ⅓ ŠA kug-babbar šu ba-ti Na-na dam Lugal-si-ra [i]n-na-[lá] ŠUKU a-šag$_{4}$ 12(bùr) gana$_{2}$-šè Agar$_{2}$-da-^{giš}pèš é-gal ^{giš}erin-KU.ÉŠ-ka šu ba-ti

Di-Utu, the scribe, received 20 shekels of silver from Lu-Šara, the governor of Umma, and (then) weighed it out to Nana, wife of Lugal-si; she received (it) for 216 iku of prebend land, (located) in the field Agar-da-peš, at the palace of Erin-KU.EŠ (lines 1–11); witnesses (lines 12–35).

Nana transferred her prebend field (which she had probably inherited from her dead husband) to the governor of Umma. In exchange, she received 20 shekels of silver, which had been delivered to her by the scribe Di-Utu, the governor's representative. The field in question was located in the vicinity of Umma, as shown by the fact that the field-name Da-^{giš}pèš is well attested in Umma texts (see, e.g., BIN 8 86:94). If, as it appears quite likely, the text was written at Susa, Nana was probably a resident of Susa; this, in turn, would explain the use of an intermediary in conveying the silver.

2. *NATN* 258 (Ur III)

1(eše) 3(iku) gana$_{2}$ ŠUKU Lugal-KA-gi-na-ka Geme$_{2}$-^{d}EN.ZU dam-ni ù Péš-TUR-TUR dumu-SAL-ni Lugal-ḫé-gál-ra igi-ne-ne in-ši-gar-ru-éš ŠUKU-gá ÍL-bi íl-ba-ab in-na-an-dug$_{4}$ Lugal-ḫé-gál-e mu ŠUKU-ra-šè 5 gín kug-babbar Geme$_{2}$-^{d}EN.ZU dam Lugal-KA-gi-na-ra ù Péš-TUR-TUR dumu-SAL-a-ni-ir in-na-an-sum

(Concerning) 9 iku of land, the prebend of Lugal-KA-gina, Geme-Sin, his wife, and Peš-TUR-TUR, his daughter, approached Lugal-ḫegal; she (i.e., Geme-Sin) told him: "Take over the obligation of my prebend!"; on account of the prebend, Lugal-ḫegal gave 5 shekels of silver to Geme-Sin, wife of Lugal-KA-gina, and Peš-TUR-TUR, his daughter (lines 1–13); no-contest clause and witnesses (lines 14–27).

Geme-Sin, wife of Lugal-KA-gina (who was presumably deceased), and his daughter Peš-TUR-TUR, approached a certain Lugal-ḫegal with an offer that he take over Lugal-KA-gina's prebend field and its corvée obligation. In exchange for the field, Lugal-ḫegal paid them 5 shekels of silver.

3. YOS 4 21 (Ur III)

5 gín kug-babbar mu a-šag$_{4}$ a-gàr-gu-la Urim$_{2}^{ki}$-da gub-ba ŠUKU nam-10-na-šè ki Ur-^{d}Ba-ú-ta Am-ma-mu šu ba-ti

Ammamu received from Ur-Bau 5 shekels of silver, on account of his tithe prebend, located in the field Agar-gula, toward Ur (lines 1–6); oath (line 7).

Ammamu transferred his prebend field to Ur-Bau in exchange for 5 shekels of silver.

The combined evidence of no. 60 and the latter three texts demonstrates quite clearly that in the Sargonic and Ur III periods the title to prebend land could, at least in some cases, be alienated. Moreover, MDP 14 19 and *NATN* 258 show that the wife of a prebend-holder could inherit her husband's field, and that she was free to dispose of it. However, due to the paucity of pertinent information, the question whether these practices constituted the norm or an exception is difficult to answer. Here I note that in the Old Babylonian period the law distinguished between the land allotments held by dependents of the crown and those in possession of other types of dependents: while the former could neither be alienated (CH §36) nor passed on to the prebender's wife or daughter (CH §38), the latter could be alienated, on the condition that the purchaser assume the obligations that were attached to the prebend (CH §40).

14–16. These three entries clearly belong to the list of witnesses. It appears that, once the scribe reached the last line of the reverse, he put down the rubric lú-ki-inim-ma-bi-me, and then wrote the remaining three names on the edges of the tablet.

15. É-RU.DUG may be the same temple as (èš-)DUG.RU of the Pre-Sargonic Lagaš sources. For the occurrences of (èš)-DUG.RU, see Behrens and Steible, FAOS 6, p. 409; Bauer, *Lagasch*, p. 569 (sanga DUG.RU).

No. 61. IM 43453 Pl. 28

Previously published by van Dijk, *Sumer* 13 (1957) 133 A (copy); idem, TIM 9 99 (copy); Krecher, *ZA* 63 (1974) 242–45 no. 19 (transliteration and translation). Recopied.

Obverse

1) [x g]ín kug-babbar	[x she]kels of silver,
2) [níg-sám] ^{I}⌈En⌉-níg-kas$_{4}$-kam	is the [price] of ⌈En⌉-nigkas.

3)	[X]-⌜x⌝ ama-ni	[X]-⌜x⌝, his mother,
4)	Kar-GAG ašlag$_4$(GIŠ.TÚG.KAR.DU)-gada	Kar-GAG, the fuller of linens,
5)	Geme$_2$-é	(and) Geme-e,
6)	[d]am Kar-GAG	[w]ife of Kar-GAG,
7)	kug-bi šu-ne-ne-a	their hands (with) this silver
8)	ab-si	were filled.
9)	giš-gan-na íb-ta-bala-e-éš	They made him (i.e., En-nigkas) cross over the pestle.
10)	En-za-ra dam-gàr	En-zara, the merchant,
11)	lú giš-erin$_2$ dab$_5$-ba-àm	was the weigher of silver (lit.: the one who held the balance).

Reverse

12)	Ur-^{d}A-ba-ba	Ur-Ababa
13)	lú sag sa$_{10}$-àm	is the one who bought the "head."
14)	^{I}Ur-šag$_5$ dub-sar	(Before) Ur-šag, the scribe,
15)	^{I}Lú-kal-la ašgab	Lu-kala, the leatherworker,
16)	šeš Lú-šag$_5$ ašgab	brother of Lu-šag, the leatherworker,
17)	[^{I}X]-NAM nu-èš	(and) [X]-NAM, the ***nêšakku*** priest,
18)	dam sanga-ke$_4$	the wife of the temple administrator
19)	mu-gi$_4$	replied:
20)	níg-na-me nu-da-tuku	"There are no claims on him (i.e., on En-nigkas);
21)	[in]im-mu-ta ḫé-[s]a$_{10}$-sa$_{10}$ bí-dug$_4$	with my consent/authorization he (i.e., Ur-Ababa) may buy him"—she declared.
22)	[l]ú-ki-inim-ma-bi-me	These are the witnesses.

Kar-GAG and his wife Geme-e, who share in the proceeds from En-nigkas's sale, possibly were the creditors of En-nigkas's mother. See the discussion of no. 57.

2. The reading ⌜En⌝-, already considered by Krecher (*ZA* 63 [1974] 242), is quite certain.

4. The personal name Kar-GAG is also attested in the Umma text Foster, *USP* no. 7:9 (misread by Foster on p. 21, as ⌜Ašlag⌝).

There is a clear GADA after ašlag$_4$. Krecher (*ZA* 63 [1974] 242) reads ašlag$_x$(GIŠ.TÚG.KAR.DU!).

9. For this clause, see commentary to no. 73:15–18.

17. In contrast to Krecher (ZA 63 [1974] 242), who reads this line $^{[I!]}$n[a]m-nu-èš, and sees in it the name of the "wife of the temple administrator" who appears in the following line, I assume that a witness is found here. I base this interpretation on the fact that no other examples of names construed with nu-èš (Akk. ***nêšakku***) are known.

18–19. Krecher (*ZA* 63 [1974] 243) reads: dam saĝĝa(ŠID(!))-ke$_4$ mu gi$_4$ "die Ehefrau des Verwaltungsleiters (hat) den Eid (beim König o.ä.) geleistet dafür, daß sie auf die verkaufte Person nicht) zurückkommen (werde)." This interpretation assumes that mu gi$_4$ is an abbreviation of mu lugal-bi nu-ba-gi$_4$-gi$_4$-dè in-pàd (or the like). A simpler and more likely solution is to analyze these two signs as a finite verbal form: mu-gi$_4$ 'she replied (in answer to the query about the status of the sold person)'.

No. 62. IM 43483 no copy

Previously published by van Dijk, TIM 9 95 (copy).

Obverse

1)	na-bi-[a]	What he (i.e., the sender) says
2)	Šeš-šeš-mu	(to) Šeš-šešmu
3)	ù-na-dug$_4$	say.
4)	12 gud-giš	12 plow-oxen
5)	1 áb	(and) 1 cow
6)	⸢a⸣-na-lá	were harnessed for him (i.e., Šeš-šešmu) (by the sender).

Reverse

(uninscribed)

The address formula used in this letter is standard for the period (see Sollberger, TCS 1, p. 3), except for the omission of the sender's name.

6. For lá (Akk. *ṣamādu*) 'to yoke, to harness', see CAD Ṣ, p. 90 lexical section of *ṣamādu*. For the conjugational prefix a-, see commentary to no. 9 i 8.

No. 63. IM 43702 Pl. 28

Obverse

1)	135(gur) 1(pi) 1(bán) še gur-sag-gál	135 gsg 70 liters of barley
2)	A-da-gal	(for) Adagal;
3)	40 lá 1(gur) še gur	39 gsg of barley
4)	Lú-^{d}Inanna	(for) Lu-Inanna;
5)	90+[21]+3(gur) lá 1(bán) še gur	⸢113⸣ gsg 230 liters of barley,
6)	[še] ensi$_2$-kam	[the barley] of the governor;

Reverse

7)	26(gur) še gur	26 gsg of barley,
8)	Lugal-ušur$_3$(LÁL×LAGAB)	(received by) Lugal-ušur

9)	A-bum(KA)-⌜ma⌝-šè	for Abuma;
10)	20(gur) še gur	20 gsg of barley
11)	Lú-^{d}Inanna	(for) Lu-Inanna;
12)	40(gur) še gur	40 gsg of barley,
13)	še ensi$_2$-kam	the barley of the governor;
14)	šu-nigin$_2$ 374(gur) 1(pi) še gur	total of 374 gsg 60 liters of barley.

A record of six expenditures of barley; note that Lu-Inanna and the governor made two withdrawals each. Adagal, listed in line 2, seems to occur also in nos. 64-65. These three documents thus probably come from the same archive. Its origin could be E-malza (see no. 65).

No. 64. IM 43706 Pl. 29

Obverse

1)	5(gur) še gur	5 gur of barley
2)	DINGIR-ba-ni	(for) Ilum-bāni;
3)	1(gur) še gur	1 gur of barley
4)	Mu-ni-da	(for) Munida;

Reverse

5)	8(gur) še gur	8 gur of barley
6)	Lugal-a	(for) Lugal-a;
7)	A-da-gal	Adagal
8)	ì-zi	issued (it).

A record of three expenditures of barley made by Adagal, for whom see nos. 63 and 65.

No. 65. IM 44026 Pl. 29

Obverse

1)	95(gur) še gur GIR-ri	95 gur of barley, the . . . ,
2)	še Lugal-níg-zu-kam	the barley of Lugal-nigzu,

Reverse

3)	A-da-gal	Adagal
4)	šu ba-ti	received.
5)	É-ma-al-za^{ki}	(In) E-malza.

A receipt of barley. The recipient was Adagal, for whom see nos. 63–64.

1. There is a *Winkelhacken* between GIR and RI, which probably should be ignored. The meaning of GIR-ri is unclear.

5. The toponym É-ma-al-za^{ki} is not otherwise attested. Perhaps one should see in it a syllabic spelling of É-mar-za^{ki}, for which see RGTC 1, p. 47; 2, p. 46.

No. 66. IM 43726 Pl. 29

Obverse

1)	3(gur) lá 2(bán) gur	2 gur 280 liters (of barley):
2)	A-ba-da	Abada;
3)	1(gur) 2(pi) 5(bán) še è gur	1 gur 170 liters of issued(?) barley,
4)	1(gur) 2(bán) 4 sila$_3$ gur	1 gur 24 liters (of barley):

Reverse

5)	Ma-ma	Mama.
	(space)	
6)	šu-nigin$_2$ 5(gur) 1(pi) lá 2 sila$_3$ še gur	Total of 5 gur 58 liters of barley.

This text concerns either a delivery or an expenditure of barley by two persons. For the designation è 'expended, issued', which describes the barley listed in line 3, cf. the term še è-a, discussed in the commentary to no. 3.

The total, amounting to 1558 liters, is 116 liters short. The difference cannot be represented by the entry designated as è (line 3), since the latter amounts to 470 liters.

No. 67. IM 43765 Pl. 30

Obverse

1) 2(pi) ^{d}Li-si$_4$
2) 2(pi) $^{d⌜}$En$^{⌝}$-ki
3) 2(pi) $^{d⌜}$Ìr(?)-x$^{⌝}$
4) 2(pi) ^{d}Nin-mug
5) ⌜2(pi)⌝ ^{d}Utu

Reverse

(uninscribed)

A record of unidentified foodstuff (probably barley) allotted to five different deities. The mention of Lisi and Ninmug suggests that the text comes from Umma.

3. The second sign definitely is not RA, which excludes the reading ^{d}⸢Ìr-ra⸣.

No. 68. IM 44018 Pl. 30

Copied and collated by J. A. Black.

Obverse

1)	4(gur) še gur	4 gur of barley
2)	Nita-e	Nita
3)	^{giš}Kul-ab$_4$^{ki}	(to?) Kulˀaba
4)	ì-de$_6$	took.
5)	1(gur) še gur	1 gur of barley
6)	Lugal-⸢x⸣	(for) Lugal-⸢x⸣.

Reverse

7)	4(bán) lá igi-4-gál	39 3/4 liters of barley,
8)	sám ^{túg}TUM-*gunû*	(is) the price of the . . . garment.

A record of three expenditures of barley.

3. The Kulˀaba mentioned here is either the famous district of Uruk or its northern Babylonian namesake. The question of the existence of a northern Babylonian Kulˀaba, raised by Steinkeller in *Vicino Oriente* 6 (1986) 40 nn. 64 and 66, can be answered in the affirmative. See BÀD ^{uru}*Gu-la-ba*$_8$(BÀD)^{ki} in Samsuiluna A (*BAL* 3 pl. 31 iii 2 = CT 21 49 iii 5), which was one of the six fortresses built by Sumulael (and later restored by Samsuiluna). For the reading, see already Gelb, MAD 2^2, p. 210 add. to p. 72 no. 114.

8. The reading of ^{túg}TUM-*gunû* is uncertain. For other occurrences of this garment, see ITT 1 1091:7; MVN 3 74:5; BIN 8 290:4 (síg(!)), 7 (gada); BE 1 11:7 (*ˀà-dam-mu*), 8 (*ḫi-šè-lu-ḫi-na*), 9 (*ˀà-dam-m⟨u⟩* LIBIR); CT 50 78 left edge. The sign TUM-*gunû* may be a graphic variant of TUM×KÁR (possibly egir$_x$), which appears in the PN TUM×KÁR-ra (Nikolski 1 89 i 4).

No. 69. IM 44019 Pl. 30

Obverse

1)	1½ gín kug-bab[bar]
2)	Ur-^{d}Nin-⸢šubur(?)⸣
3)	½ gín k[ug-babbar]
4)	Ma-⸢BÀD(?)⸣

Reverse

5) [ig]i-4-gá[l]
6) dumu Im-⸢x⸣
7) ig[i(!)-6-g]ál
8) ⸢Engar⸣
(space)
9) šu-nigin$_2$ 2 gín igi-3-gál 15 še

An account of silver which was either delivered or received by four different persons.

No. 70. IM 44021 Pl. 31

Obverse

1) 2(gur) 1(pi) še gur
2) Ur-TUR
3) 1(gur) 3(bán) še gur
4) Ur-gá

Reverse

5) 1(gur) 1(pi) še gur
6) ^{d}En-líl-sipad
(space)
7) šu-nigin$_2$ 4(gur) 2(pi) 3(bán) še gur-sag-gál
8) Ur-gá

This text records either an expenditure or a delivery of barley. Note that Urga, one of the three recipients(?) of barley, is also named following the total.

Foster (*USP*, p. 97) connects the present text with the mu-iti tablet MCS 9 263, on the assumption that they both mention a certain Ur-gú. In our text, however, the name is clearly Ur-gá.

No. 71. IM 44025 Pl. 31

Obverse

1) 12(gur) 2(pi) še gur
2) Ur-ki-ni
3) 6(gur) 2(pi) še gur
4) Ad-da
5) 10 lá 1(gur) še gur

Reverse

6) Dingir-AB-gu
7) 5(gur) še gur
8) Šu-Eš$_4$-dar
9) 5(gur) še gur
10) Lugal-šag$_5$
11) 10(gur) še gur

Upper Edge

12) [U]r-^{d}Nin-tu

A record of barley which was either received or delivered by six different persons.

No. 72. IM 43381 Pl. 31

Obverse

1) 2(BÁN) ŠE *Ša-a*	20 liters of barley: Šaʾa;
2) 1(BÁN) *I-ti-É-a*	10 liters: Iddin-Ea;
3) 1(BÁN) *Ḫa-la-lum*	10 liters: Ḫalalum;
4) 1(BÁN) *Puzur$_4$-Eš$_4$-dar*	10 liters: Puzur-Eštar;
5) 1(BÁN) *I-lu$_5$*-DINGIR	10 liters: Ilu-ilī;
6) 2(BÁN) *Ga-la-ab-É-a*	20 liters: Kalab-Ea;
7) 1(BÁN) *Su$_4$*(?)*-be-lum*	10 liters: Šu(?)-bēlum;
8) 2(BÁN) 4 SILA$_3$ *Mu-mu*	24 liters: Mumu;

Reverse

9) 2(BÁN) *Zi-gur-ra*	20 liters: Sikkūra;
10) 2(BÁN) *Pù-⸢su⸣*-GI	20 liters: Pû⸢šu⸣-kīn;
11) 2(BÁN) 4 SILA$_3$ *Máš*(?)-*zu*	24 liters: Massu(?);
12) 2(BÁN) 4(SILA$_3$) PAB.ŠEŠ	24 liters: Pašīšum;
13) 2(BÁN) 4(SILA$_3$) DINGIR-A.ZU	24 liters: Ilum-asu;
14) 2(BÁN) *Be-lu-u*	20 liters: Beluʾu;
15) 2(BÁN) *Ku-ku*	20 liters: Kuku;
16) 2(BÁN) *Lu-lu*	20 liters: Lulu;
17) ŠU.NIGIN$_2$ 1(GUR) LAL 1(BÁN) 4(SILA$_3$) GUR	total of 286 liters of barley,

---

Left Edge

18) *u-ḫur-ra-um*	the remainder
19) ŠU.DÙ *Ì-la-la*	(of ?) the . . . of Ilala.

The interpretation of this text hinges on the meaning of lines 18–19. The term ***uḫurrāʾu***, hitherto unattested, is evidently a ***purussāʾu*** formation of the verb ***aḫāru*** 'to be late, to remain behind' (see *AHw*, p. 18). For other examples of the formation ***purussāʾu*** in Old Akkadian, see Gelb, MAD 2^2, p. 155. Given the range of the meanings of ***aḫāru*** (note also the noun ***uḫḫuru*** 'left behind?, left over?', listed in *AHw*, p. 1404a), ***uḫurrāʾu*** should probably be translated 'remainder, arrears'. Following this interpretation, in the present text ***uḫurrāʾu*** could denote either a remainder of barley allotments, due to the sixteen individuals listed in the text, or the outstanding balance of unpaid loans. The small sizes of the amounts involved (10, 20, and 24 liters), as well as their uniformity, seem to favor the first possibility. The meaning of the following phrase, ŠU.DÙ Ì-la-la, is less clear. Although ŠU.DÙ can quite confidently be connected with the verb šu . . . dù/du$_8$ 'to take possession of, to hold', it is uncertain whether it should be analyzed as the noun šu-dù/du$_8$-a 'pledge' or as a finite verbal form. For the latter usage of šu . . . dù/du$_8$, see the Sargonic texts MAD 1 152 and Rasheed, *Himrin* 8 (cf. also MAD 5 25 and 26), dealing with the transfer of animals to shepherds for herding, which end with the following note: PN (SIPAD) ŠU.DU$_8$ 'PN (the shepherd) took hold of / received (the animals)'.

5. For the interpretation of this name, see commentary to no. 47:6.
9. For this name, see MAD 3, p. 239 under *sikkūrum*.

No. 73. IM 43488 Pl. 32

Obverse

1) ^{I}DINGIR-*ba-ni*	Ilum-bāni,
2) *šu* GIŠ.IŠ.NE ENSI$_2$	(the man) of the governor's chair;
3) ^{I}*Ra-bí*-DINGIR	Rabi-ilum;
4) ^{I}*Zu-zu* DUMU DINGIR-*nu-id*	Zuzu, son of Ilum-nuʾid;
5) ^{I}*Íl-e-mu-bí*	Ilʾe-mūpi;
6) ^{I}*I-ti*-DINGIR *šu Bu*(!)-ga-ni	Iddin-ilum, (the man) of Bugani;
7) ^{I}*Da-da* ⸢UŠ.KU(?!)⸣ *Eš$_4$-dar*	Dada, the ⸢lamentation priest(?)⸣ of Ištar;
8) ^{I}*Tu-tu* DUMU DINGIR-*me-sar*	Tutu, son of Ilum-mēšar;
9) ^{I}*Gur-ru-um* MAR.TU	Gurrum, the Amorite;
10) [^{I}X].⸢MU⸣-GI	[X].⸢MU⸣-GI;
11) [^{I} . . . -*s*]*ag*	[. . . -s]ag,

Reverse

12) [DUB].SAR	[the scr]ibe;
13) ^{I}LAGAB-DINGIR DUMU PÙ.⸢ŠA⸣-^{d}*Irḫan$_x$*(MUŠ)	LAGAB-DINGIR, son of Puzur-Irḫan;
(space)	

14) ŠU.NIGIN$_2$ 11 AB×ÁŠ *šu-ut*	total of eleven witnesses (to the fact) that
15) PÙ.⸢ŠA⸣-^{d}*Nu-mu*[*š-d*]*a*	Puzur-Numu[šd]a
16) ⸢*Ì*⸣-[*l*]*í-be-lí a-na áš-rí*	made I[l]ī-bēlī cross over the pestle
17) ⸢*x*⸣-*gi-im* GIŠ.GANA	for/in the place of . . . ;
18) [*u-š*]*a-ti-gu-ni*	
19) ⸢*a*⸣-*na Pù-pù*	For Pupu,
20) DUMU URU-*puzur*$_4$-*šu-ni*	son of Ālī-puzuršuni,
21) *Ì-lí-ra-bí*	Ilī-rabi
22) [PA].KAS$_4$	(was) the bailiff.

Left Edge

23) *Gi-šum ti-nam*	Qīšum gave the judgment.
24) *i-*⸢*ti*⸣*-in*	

This text appears to deal with the litigation concerning an earlier slave sale. The litigants were Puzur-Numušda and Pupu. It appears that the slave Ilī-bēlī had originally been sold by Puzur-Numušda to Pupu, but Puzur-Numušda later contested the sale and took Pupu to court. During the court proceedings, which were conducted by a certain Qīšum (possibly a governor, see below and note to lines 23–24), the witnesses to the original transaction testified that Puzur-Numušda had transferred the slave to Pupu, by performing the *bukāna šūtuqu* rite. Although the text does not state it, the case was apparently decided in Pupu's favor.

The origin of the present text is possibly Mukdan. Note that the Mukdan tablet MAD 5 69 i 5′–6′ mentions a governor Qīšum, who may be the same person as the judge Qīšum, appearing in line 23. In favor of the Mukdan attribution may also be the occurrences of Ilʾe-mūpi (line 5) and Tutu (line 8), possibly identical with their namesakes in no. 48.

1–2. Ilum-bāni was probably a chair-carrier. For GIŠ.IŠ.NE 'chair', see commentary to no. 50:13.

6. *Bu-ga-ni* may be a genitive of the name *Bu-ga-núm /bukānum/* (see, e.g., no. 74:4 in this volume and MVN 3 219:2).

10. This name should possibly be restored [AD].⸢MU⸣-GI */abī-kīn/*.

13. For the reading of the divine element ^{d}MUŠ as Irḫan$_x$, rather than ^{d}Neraḫ, when it appears in Sargonic and Ur III personal names, see Steinkeller, *Sale Documents*, p. 244 note to no. 64:8.

15–18. The form *ušātiquni* 'he made him cross over (the pestle)' lends support to Edzard's assumption (ZA 60 [1969] 11–12) that the grammatical object of the *bukāna šūtuqu*/giš-gana . . . bala clause is the person sold and not the pestle. For a discussion of the significance of this ceremony, see most recently Steinkeller, *Sale Documents* §2.4. I cannot provide a plausible restoration of the first sign in line 17.

19–20. Alternatively, but less likely, these lines could be part of the preceding clause: '(Puzur-Numušda made Ilī-bēlī cross over the pestle . . .) for Pupu, son of Ālī-puzuršuni.'

23–24. Qīšum may be the same person as the governor Qīšum, attested in the Mukdan tablet MAD 5 69 i 5′–6′. The latter official may in turn be identical with the governor of Kazallu of that name, who appears in BIN 8 122:12, 18. Cf. Edzard, in *Kraus AV*, p. 31.

No. 74. IM 43490 Pl. 32

Obverse

1) ^{I}*I-tum-É-a*	Idum-Ea,
2) DUMU *A-bí-sa-tu*	son of Abī-šadû,
3) *Zu-bu-ri*^{ki}	(the citizen of) Ṣup(u)ri;
4) 1 ARAD$_2$ *Bu-ga-núm*	one slave of Bukānum,
5) DUMU *Im-se*$_{11}$*-a-bù-*⸢*ni*(?)⸣	son of Imše-abu⸢ni(?)⸣,
6) *Tar-rí*(= URU×TAR)*-šu-ḫa*^{ki}	(the citizen of) Tarrišuḫa;
7) 1 ARAD$_2$ ⸢*X*⸣-[(*x*)]-⸢*ba*⸣-LUM	one slave of ⸢X⸣-[(x)]-⸢ba⸣-LUM,
8) DUMU *Mu-na*	son of Muna,

Reverse

9) *Ša-ad*-DUMU.[(NITA)^{ki}]	(the citizen of) Šad-mari;
10) ^{I}⸢*Ur-*^{d}X⸣	⸢Ur-X⸣,
11) DUMU-⸢*šu*(?)⸣	⸢his(?)⸣ son.

A memo concerning four individuals. Its origin appears to be northern Babylonia.

3. For this toponym, compare various OB place-names composed with *ṣupru* (RGTC 3, p. 214), and also note UMBIN.DU$_8$^{ki} in MEE 3 56:148. Cf. Steinkeller, *Vicino Oriente* 6 (1986) 35.

5. Perhaps to be analyzed as Imši-abuni 'He-Has-Forgotten-Our-Father'. Cf. CAD M/1, p. 400, for examples of the use of *mašû* in personal names.

6. The same toponym occurs in MEE 3 56:245 as Tar-rí-šu-ḫa^{ki} (Abu Salabikh), Tar-zé-ḫu^{ki} (Ebla). Cf. Steinkeller, *Vicino Oriente* 6 (1986) 36.

9. In all probability, the same toponym as Ša-ad-DUMU.NITA^{ki}, listed in MEE 3 56:137. Probably also identical with the lexical Ša/Sa-ad-ma-ri^{ki}. See Steinkeller, *Vicino Oriente* 6 (1986) 35 and n. 36.

Indexes

Index of Personal Names

A-ba-da 66:2
A-ba-mu-na son of Gissu 28 ii 3
Ab-ba
1. LÚ.ŠIM 30 i 18
2. son of Ur-UM+ME-ga 28 ii 6
3. 24:23
AB.É 2 iii′ 1′
A-bí-sa-tu father of I-tum-É-a 74:2
A-bum-⌜ma⌝ 63:9
Abzu-ki-dùg 1 x 6
A-da-gal 63:2, 64:7, 65:3
ʾÀ-da-mu *šu* Be-lí-ba-na 49:5
Ad-da
1. nu-banda$_3$ 56:3
2. sipad 30 ii 19
3. 9 iii 6, 71:4
Ag-rí-rí MAR.TU son of DINGIR-mu-da 48:19
Á-kal-li 13:17, 17:3
A-li-a-ḫu *šu* I-NE-NE 51 ii 6′
A-li-li father of Gala 37:3′
Al-lú son of Ur-^{d}Saman$_3$ 28 iii 6
Ama-a-zu 38:6
Ama-barag dub-sar 42 ii 1
Ama-bar[ag(-gi)] 25:9′
Ama-IŠ father of Lum-ma 30 i 3
Ama-níg-tu father of Ur-^{d}En-líl 46:5
Ama-nu 38:8
Amar-bàd ⌜nu⌝-èš 53:8
Amar-^{d}Ezinu$_2$
1. father of ⌜Si$_4$-si$_4$⌝, husband of Nin-ur$_x$-ra 4 xvi 8′
2. 3 iii 1
Amar-GIR arad$_2$ Ad-da sipad 30 ii 18
Amar-⌜má⌝ dub-sar 1 vii 9
Amar-si$_4$ 24:23
Am[a-. . .] 38:10
⌜A-pú(?)-lú⌝ son of ⌜UM/MES-x⌝-[x] 6 i 5′
Áš-⌜DUB(?)-SI(?)⌝ 8 iv 2
Az
1. sipad 44 iii 2′
2. ⌜sipad⌝-udu 33:22
3. father of Lugal-iti-da 45:20
4. 44 iii 4′, 45:28
A-zu-zu engar 60:2, 9

Ba-bi-na-at father of Im$_4$-da-lik, grandfather of ⌜Ì⌝-lí-TAB.BA 48:14
Ba-al-NI father of Lugal-^{giš}kiri$_6$ 30 i 15
Bar-ra-ni ad-KID 46:6
Bar-ra-ni-šè ⌜zadim⌝ 57:9
Ba-sa-aḫ-DINGIR brother of I-ti-É-a, son of É-a-sa-tu and Um-mi-DÙG 48:7
^{d}Ba-ú-ig-gal ìr Sig$_4$-zi 2 iv′ 12′
Ba-za unud$_x$ 37:2′
Be-lí-ba-na 49:6
Be-lu-lu father of DINGIR-UR.SAG 49:4
Be-lu-u 72:14
Bi-bi wife of Giš nar 57:5
Bí-za-núm *šu* I-NE-NE 51 ii 1′
Bí-za-za wife of Ma-ḫa-NI-a 58:11
Bu(!)-ga-ni 73:6
Bu-ga-núm son of Im-se$_{11}$-a-bù-⌜ni(?)⌝ 74:4

Da-ba-lum 50:14
Da-da
1. dam-gàr 30 ii 15
2. engar 37:5, 40:15
3. ⌜GALA(?!)⌝ Eš$_4$-dar 73:7
4. má-laḫ$_4$ 30 i 19
5. sag-apin 33:8
6. túg(!)-du$_8$ 45:33
7. brother of Lú-DU.DU 30 iii 1
8. father of Maš 45:36
9. son of Da-gu-[l]a 58:4
10. 35:20, 37:1′, 45:17, 18, 26, 51 i 6′

[L]ú-ʳbarag(?)ꜗ-ab-du   25:24′
Lú(!)-dingir   4 xvii 7′
Lú-dingir-ra
   1. son of Ur-ʳAB.SI₄ꜗ   5:3′
   2. 30 i 20
Lú-DU.DU brother of Da-d[a]   30 ii 24
Lugal-a   64:6
Lugal-an-ni ìr Sig₄-zi   2 iv′ 8′
Lugal-banšur-e ugula   30 i 1
Lugal-DU nagar   45:2
ʳLugalꜗ-[e-á]-ʳnaꜗ father of
   [Zabalamᵏⁱ(-x)]   45:31
Lugal-ég   19:2
Lugal-èn-tar na[gar(?)]   58:17
Lugal-éš   45:10
Lugal-èš
   1. father of KA-ʳkugꜗ   28 ii 18
   2. father of Ur-ᵈA[b-ú]   28 iv 1
   3. 45:50
Lugal-ezen
   1. ʳsipadꜗ-udu   33:19
   2. 3 i 2
Lugal-gaba arad₂ Me-lám   30 ii 8
Lugal-giš
   1. sagi   57:7
   2. 59:11
Lugal-gú dam-gàr   30 ii 13
Lugal-ḫa-ma-ʳti(?)ꜗ   43:2′
Lugal-ḫur-sag   3 iii 2
Lugal-íb-ta-ni-è   3 ii 7
Lugal-iti-da
   1. ni-is-[ku]   53:3
   2. nu-èš   52:16
   3. son of Az   45:19
   4. son of Ur-ʳᵈꜗTUR   10:5′
Lugal-KA
   1. arad₂ É-RU.DUG   60:15
   2. 14:2, 45:11
Lugal(!)-kalam túg-du₈   30 ii 11
Lugal-ᵍⁱˢkiri₆ son of Ba-al-NI   30 i 14
Lugal-KISAL-e son of Úr-ra-ni   5:5′
Lugal-KISAL-si gala   1 v 6
Lugal-KU-ʳeꜗ   53:7
Lugal-kur   15:8
Lugal-lirum   1 vii 1
Lugal-ma-DU-e   5:11′
Lugal-níg-zu
   1. son of Ur-LI nigir   6 i 2′
   2. 5:9′, 6 ii 2′, 8′, 65:2
Lugal-nir-gál son of Níg-ᵈEn-líl-li
   30 ii 22

Lugal-nisag-e   28 iii 9
Lugal-ʳsukud(?)ꜗ-[rá(?)]   53:4
Lugal-šag₅   71:10
Lugal-še   13:11
Lugal(!)-šilig-e   30 ii 3
Lugal-sùd   60:5
Lugal-ur-mu   8 iii 1
Lugal-uru sipad-an[še]   33:15
Lugal-ušur₃   63:8
Lugal-zi   60:12
Lugal-ʳxꜗ   68:6
Lugal-[. . .]   10:7′, 30 iii 5
Lú-ᵈInanna   63:4, 11
Lú-kal-la ašgab brother of Lú-šag₅
   ašgab   61:15
Lú-kug sipad-anše   39:5
Lu-lu   72:16
Lum-ma son of Ama-iš   30 i 2
Lum-[m]a-mu   8 iii 2
Lú-na-NAM dub-sar   1 iv 7
Lú-ᵈ[N]anna   25:20′
Lú-ᵈNanše unudₓ   37:2, 7
Lú-sipad   30 ii 17
Lú-šag₅
   1. ašgab brother of Lú-kal-la
      ašgab   61:16
   2. nu-[ba]nda₃   54:4
Lú-ᵈŠara₂
   1. šu-ḫa   30 iii 9
   2. 24:24
Lú-tukul engar   53:2
Lú-ᵈUtu arad₂ Lú-sipad   30 ii 16
Lú-ʳùz(?)ꜗ   58:16
Lú-ʳxꜗ-ke₄   9 i 2
L[ú-. . .]   25:21′

Ma-ʳBÀD(?)ꜗ   69:4
Ma-ḫa-NI-a husband of Bí-za-za   58:12
Ma-ma   66:5
Maš son of Da-da   45:36
Máš(?)-zu   72:11
Me-gud-e father of Ga-la-su-ni and
   Ur-Ab-zu   4 xvi 18′
Me-ḫa   45:38
Me-lám   30 ii 9
Me-lu father of Eden-ʳbiꜗ-šè   45:24
[M]e-ság   33:2
[Me]-si-tum   38:7
Me-Unugᵏⁱ   57:2
Me-zu   28 ii 4
Me-zu-an-da   4 xviii 6′

Šeš-šag$_{5}$
1. father of DINGIR-ni 28 ii 12
2. son of [. . .]-gú 28 iv 6

Šeš-še[š] arad$_{2}$ dub-sar-maḫ 30 ii 1
Šeš-šeš-mu 62:2
Šeš-TUR
1. ⸢sipad⸣-udu 33:20
2. 44 ii 10, 13

Šubur lú Ne-sag 30 iii 6
Šu-Dur-ùl *šu* I-NE-NE 51 ii 5′
Šu-Eš$_{4}$-dar
1. *šu* ^{d}Tišpak-kùn 51 i 1′
2. 24:14, 71:8

Šu-i 1 vii 4
Šu-na-KU(?)-K[A(?)] 25:7′
Šu-ni-ba-sum 7:10

TAG-su muḫaldim 45:4
^{d}Tišpak-kùn 51 i 3′
Túl-t[a(?)] 25:25′
Tu-Tu
1. son of DINGIR-me-sar 73:8
2. 48:10

TU(?)-⸢X⸣ 25:19′

UD-dib(?) 59:10
UD.UD nar 58:10
Ù-ku-za-at 56:5
⸢UM/MES-X⸣-[x] father of ⸢A-pú(?)-lú⸣ 6 i 6′
Um-mi-DÙG mother of Ba-sa-aḫ-DINGIR and I-ti-É-a, wife of É-a-sa-tu 48:5
Ur-^{d}A-ba-ba 61:12
Ur-⸢AB.SI$_{4}$⸣ father of Lú-dingir-ra 5:3′
Ur-^{d}Ab-ú
1. son of [Lu]gal-èš 28 iii 20
2. 13:5, 31

Ur-Ab-zu brother of Ga-la-su-ni, son of Me-gud-e 4 xvi 17′
Ur-^{d}Alla son of Ur-mes 28 ii 14
Ur-An-tu[m] 9 iv 11
Ur-Ap-ra father of Ur-AŠ.DUN 9 iv 3
Ur-AŠ.DUN
1. son of Ur-Ap-ra 9 iv 2
2. 9 v 3

Ur-^{d}Ba-ú 28 ii 2
Ur-^{d}Bìl son of Geme$_{2}$-^{d}Utu 45:32
Úr-bi-šè father of Ne-sag 30 i 9
Ur-b[i(?)]-⸢x⸣-[(x)] son of [. . .] 2 iii′ 7′
⸢Ur(?)-BU(?)-DU(?)⸣ 1 v 1
Ur-dingir-ra father of Ur-GAR 30 i 7
Ur-DUN 22:4
Ur-é 35:4
Ur-é-maḫ 52:17
Ur-^{d}En-líl son of Ama-níg-tu 46:4
Ur-^{d}En-líl-lá SIG-da-um 52:14
Ur-^{d}En-líl-[li/e] engar 40:7′
Ur-^{d}EN.ZU 19:4, 20:4, 21:15
Ur-é(!)-^{d}Saman$_{3}$ 1 vi 6
Ur-gá 70:4, 8
Ur-GAR
1. son of Ur-dingir-ra 30 i 6
2. 30 iii 8

U[r-^{giš}]gigir$_{2}$ 13:21
[Ur]-^{giš}gigir$_{2}$-e son of [. . .-A]B 28 i 10
⸢Ur⸣-gu 4 xvii 2′
Ur-íd-[a-da] 34:2
Ur-^{d}Iškur father of Ur-ni[gin$_{3}$] 28 iii 16
Ur-^{d}Ištaran
1. dub-s[ar] 58:18
2. kug-dím 30 i 21
3. father of Sipad-zi 30 i 5

⸢Ur⸣-Kèš^{ki} father-in-law of [G]eme$_{2}$-^{d}Ma-[mi] 10:3
Ur-ki 4 xv 15′
Ur-ki-ni 71:2
Ur-ki-sag 60:16
Ur-^{d}Lama 30 i 22
Ur-LI
1. nigir father of [Lu]gal-níg-zu 6 i 3′
2. 5:9′

Ur-lú
1. engar 40:9′
2. ⸢x⸣ 45:14

Ur-maḫ nagar 58:13
Ur-me 2 iii′ 3′
Ur-mes
1. engar 40:8
2. father of Ur-^{d}Alla 28 ii 15
3. 36:7

Ur-⸢MIR(?)⸣ 1 iv 9
Ur-na-dù-a 30 i 17
Ur-ni[gin$_{3}$] son of Ur-^{d}Iškur 28 iii 15
Ur-níg-túl-la dam-⸢gàr(?)⸣ 57:3
Ur-^{d}Nin-a-zu
1. son of É-ḫa-lu-úb nagar 45:34
2. 25:1′

Ur-^{d}Nin-gír-su ì-du$_{8}$ Ti-ra-áš 2 ii′ 4′
Ur-^{d}Nin-ildum$_{3}$
1. ì-du$_{8}$ 3 i 6
2. father of Ur-^{d}Utu 30 i 13

Ur-^{d}Nin-isin$_{x}$ 4 xviii 2′

Ur-^{d}Nin-me ugula 30 ii 4
Ur-^{d}Nin-mug father of Mug-gi$_{4}$ 54:2
Ur-^{d}Nin-pirig ugula 54:3
Ur-^{d}Nin-⸢šubur(?)⸣ 69:2
[U]r-^{d}Nin-tu 71:12
Ur-^{d}Nin-⸢x⸣-[(x)] lú Lugal-[. . .] 30 iii 4
[U]r-^{d}Nu-muš-da father of [. . .]-barag 28 i 3
Ur-PA father of Du-du 46:7
Úr-ra-ni father of Lugal-KISAL-e 5:5′
Ur-sag-dingir 3 i 2
Ur-^{d}Saman$_{3}$ father of Al-lú 28 iii 7
Ur-si$_{4}$(?) 59:4
Ur-sipad-da
  1. sag-apin 33:9
  2. 35:12, 45:48
Ur-šag$_{5}$ dub-sar 61:14
Ur-^{d}Šara$_{2}$
  1. son of Ur-⸢x⸣-[x] 30 iii 2
  2. 18:4, 19:6, 20:2
Ur-^{d}TAG.NUN 30 ii 21
⸢Ur-TAR⸣ 4 xv 7′
Ur-túl-sag ka-guru$_{7}$ 1 iv 3
Ur-^{d}TUR
  1. arad$_{2}$ Ur-^{d}TAG.NUN 30 ii 20
  2. father of Lugal-iti-da 10:6′
  3. 13:23
Ur-TUR 70:2
U[r(?)]-ú ugula 2 iv′ 5′
Ur-UD.BU 9 i 9, ii 5, 10, iv 6, v 2
[Ur]u-KA-gi-na lugal Lagaš^{ki} 2 v′ 5′
[U]r-ù-kal-l[a] 37:4, 11
Ur-UM+ME-ga father of Ab-ba 28 ii 7
URU-puzur$_{4}$-šu-ni father of Pù-pù 73:20
Ur-ur
  1. zadim 57:8, 58:14
  2. father of ⸢X-x-x⸣ 5:2′
  3. 1 iii 6
Ur-^{d}Utu son of Ur-^{d}Nin-ildum$_{3}$ 30 i 12
Uru-^{d}Utu^{ki} dam-gàr 52:8
Uru-zu 47:11
⸢Ur-^{d}X⸣ 74:10
Ur-^{d}⸢X⸣-[. . .] 24:29
Ur-⸢x⸣-[x] father of Ur-^{d}Šara$_{2}$ 30 iii 3
Ur-[. . .] son of [. . .] 4 xiv 7′
U[r-. . .] 2 iv′ 3′
^{d}Utu-mu⟨-gi$_{4}$⟩ 18:2, 20:5
Ú-zu-ur-ba-su *šu* I-NE-NE 51 ii 4′

[Zabalam^{ki}(-x)] son of ⸢Lugal⸣-[e-á]-⸢na⸣ 45:30
Zag-mu 8 ii 2, 24:24
Zag-^{d}Sùd-ta
  1. MAŠ.GAG 1 v 4
  2. unud$_{x}$ 1 x 1
Zi-gur-ra 72:9
Zu-zu
  1. son of DINGIR-nu-id 73:4
  2. 51 i 5′

⸢X⸣-DÙL-kug 26 iv 8
⸢X⸣-LU 6 i 9′
[X].⸢MU⸣-GI 73:10
[X]-NAM nu-èš 61:17
[X-^{d}]Nin-mug 52:19
[X-^{d}Ni]n-pirig father of [. . .]-GAN 28 iv 2
[(X-)]^{d}Nin-sún 4 iv 2′
[X]-^{d}Nin-šubur [šu]-⸢ḫa⸣ 52:2
⸢X-pum(?)⸣ 10:4′
⸢X⸣-[(x)]-⸢ba⸣-LUM son of Mu-na 74:7
⸢X-x-da⸣ sag-apin 33:6
[X-x]-NI 30 i 25
[X(-x)]-šag$_{5}$-[(x)] 2 ii′ 1′
[X]-⸢x⸣ mother of ⸢En⸣-níg-kas$_{4}$ 61:3
⸢X-x-x⸣ son of Ur-ur 5:1′
[X]-⸢x⸣-[x]-⸢x⸣ 15:5
⸢X⸣-[. . .]
  1. ašla[g$_{4}$] 53:5
  2. sag-apin 33:10
  3. son of [. . .] 4 v 1′
  4. 8 iv 4, 26 iv 10
⸢X⸣-[. . .]-⸢x⸣ 8 ii 3

[. . .-A]B
  1. father of G[Á(?)-x]-⸢x⸣-TUR 28 i 6
  2. father of [Ur]-^{giš}gigir$_{2}$-e 28 i 11
[. . .]-barag son of [U]r-^{d}Nu-muš-da 28 i 2
[. . .]-GAN son of [X-^{d}Ni]n-pirig 28 iv 3
[. . .]-gú father of [Šeš(?)]-šag$_{5}$ 28 iv 7
[. . .]-ì-lí 25:15′
[. . .]-li 56:27
[. . .]-NE-⸢x⸣ 8 ii 1
[. . .-s]ag [DUB].SAR 73:11
[. . .]-⸢si(?)⸣ 32:6
[. . .]-⸢šag$_{5}$(?)⸣ 25:13′
[. . .]
  1. father of Ur-b[i(?)]-⸢x⸣-[(x)] 2 iii′ 8′
  2. father of Ur-[. . .] 4 xiv 8′
  3. father of ⸢X⸣-[. . .] 4 v 2′

Index of Divine Names

Index of Geographical and Topographical Names

Index of Words Discussed

Akkadian

Sumerian

Plates

No. 1

Obverse

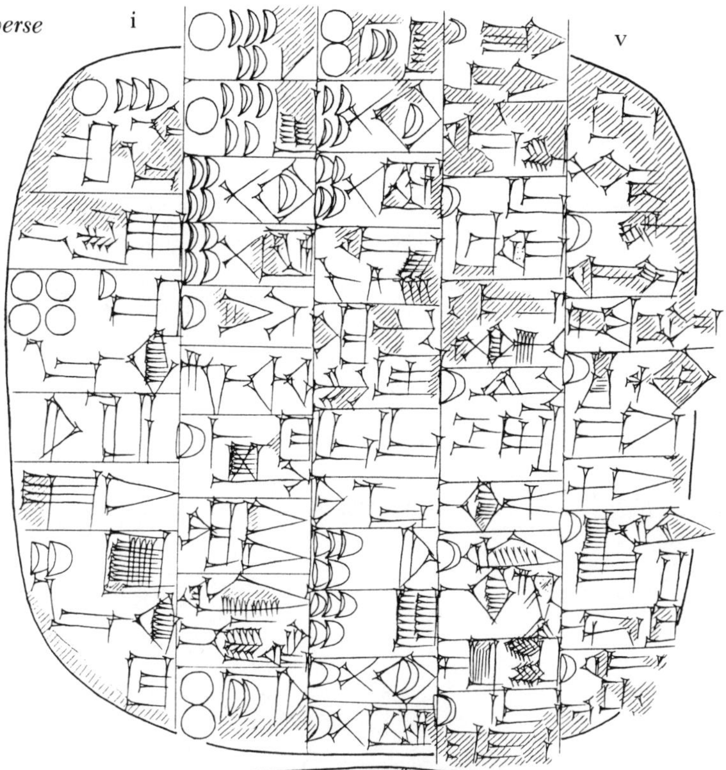

Reverse

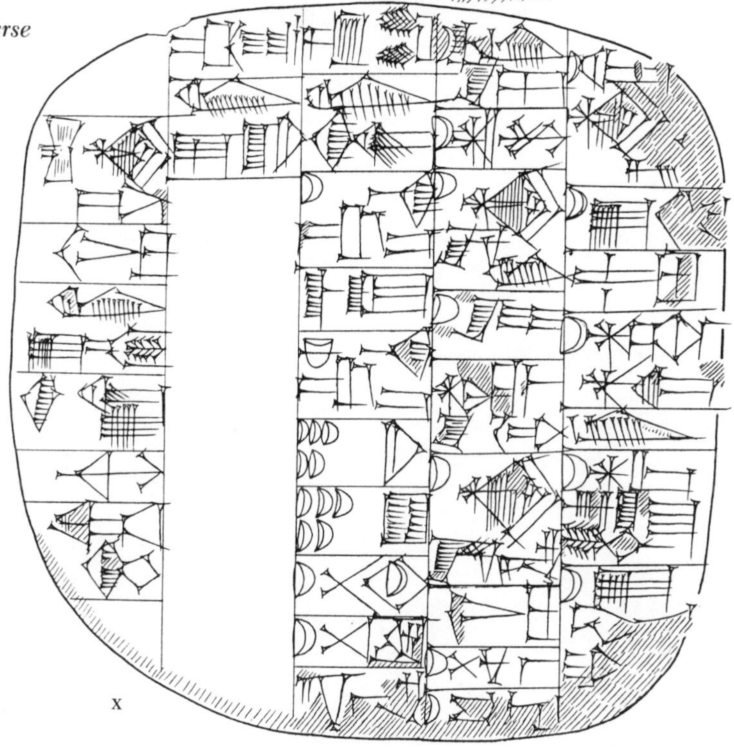

No. 2

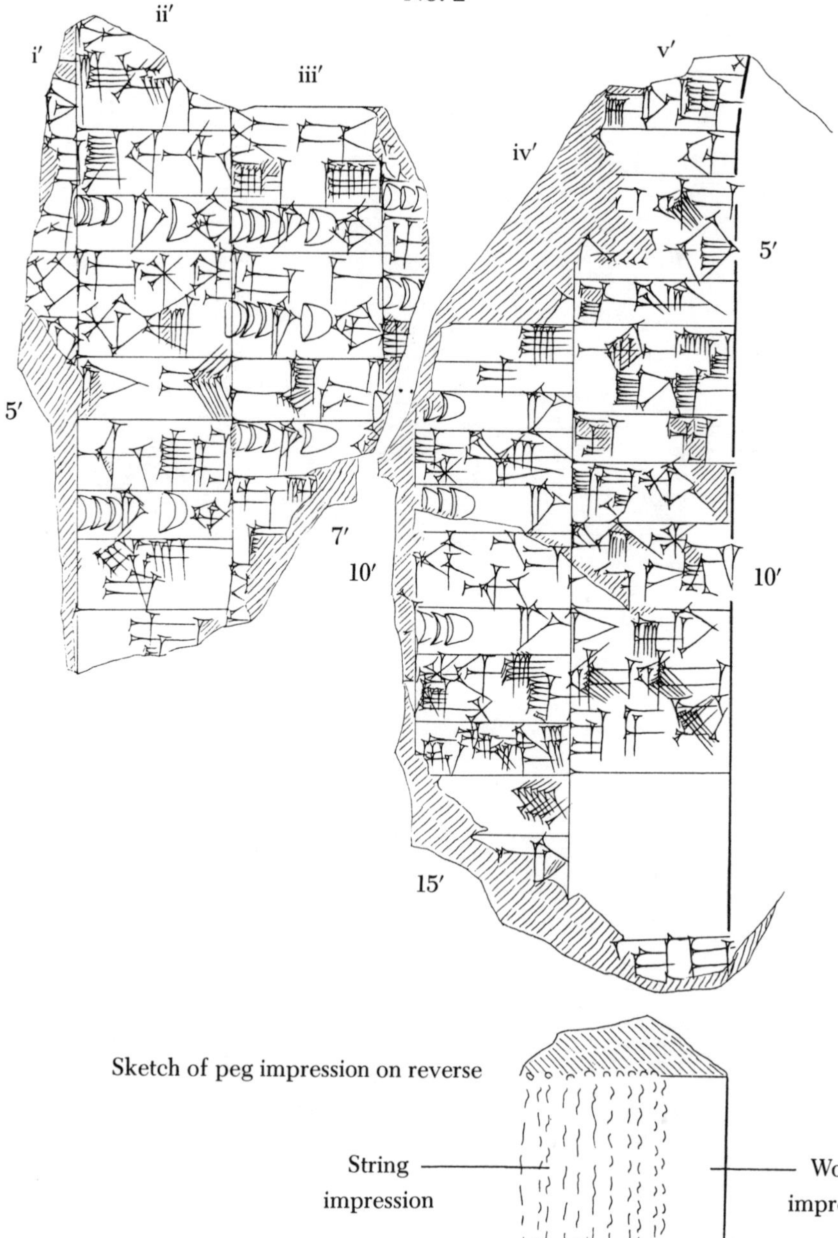

Sketch of peg impression on reverse

No. 3

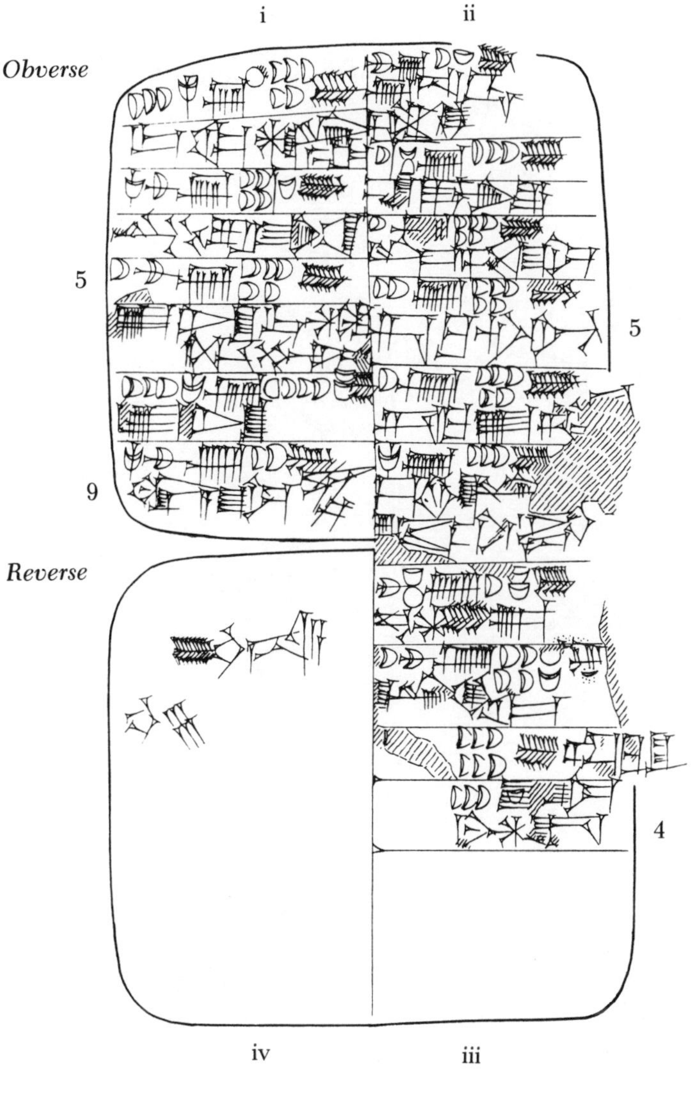

No. 4

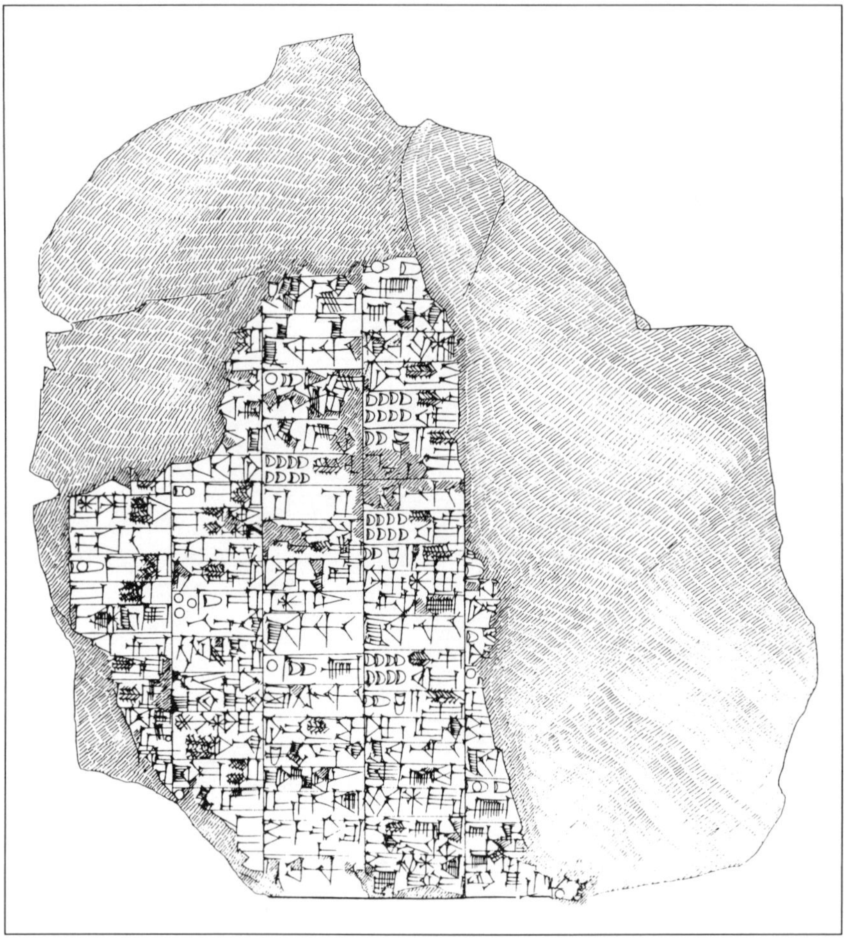

Reproduction of Reverse at 50% to show tablet boundaries (see pl. 5 for full size)

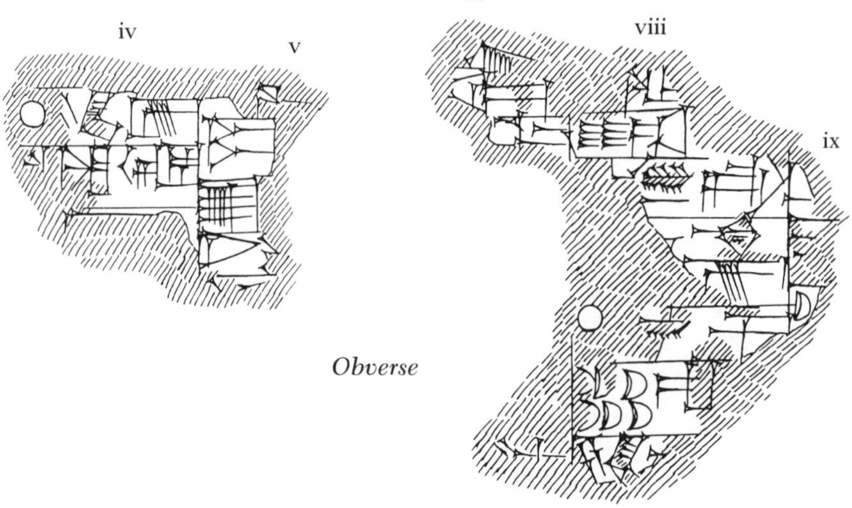

Obverse

No. 4

Reverse

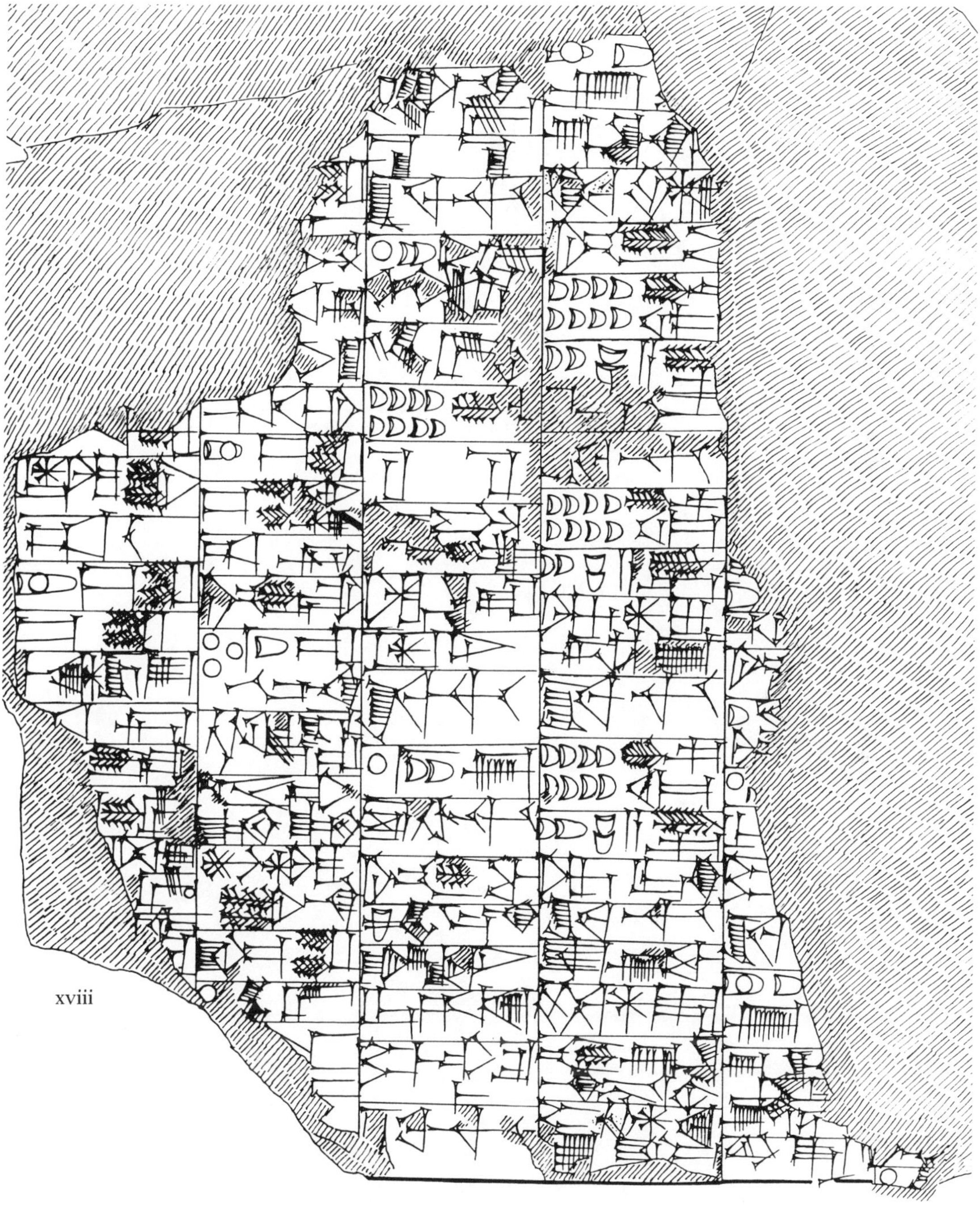
xviii
xvii
xvi
xv
xiv
xiii

Plate 6

Obverse

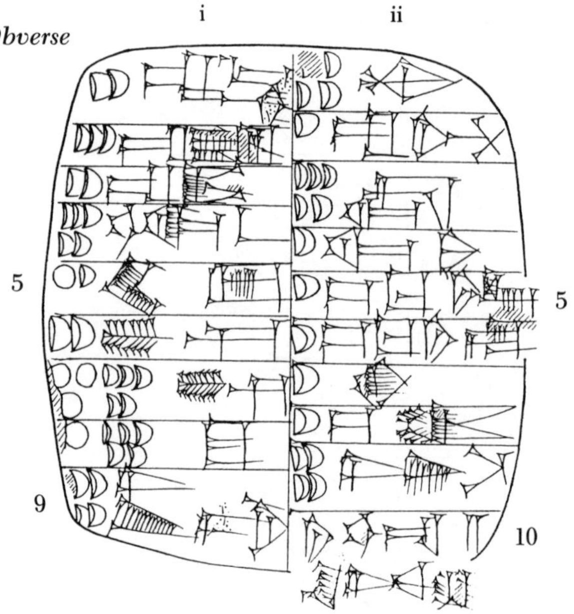

No. 7

Obverse

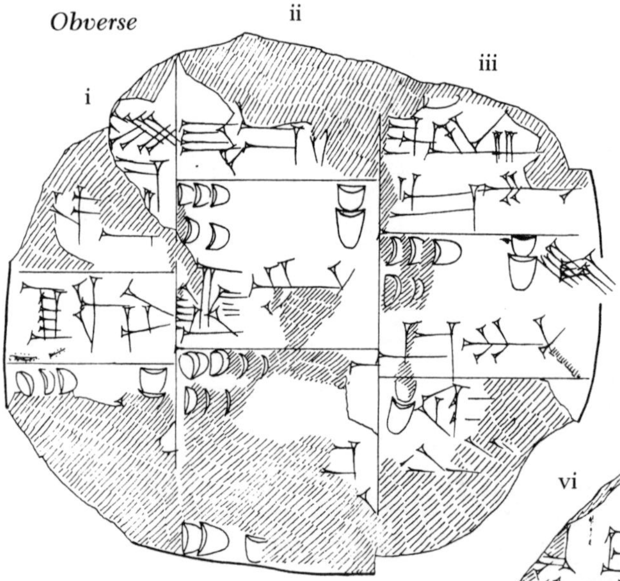

No. 8

Reverse

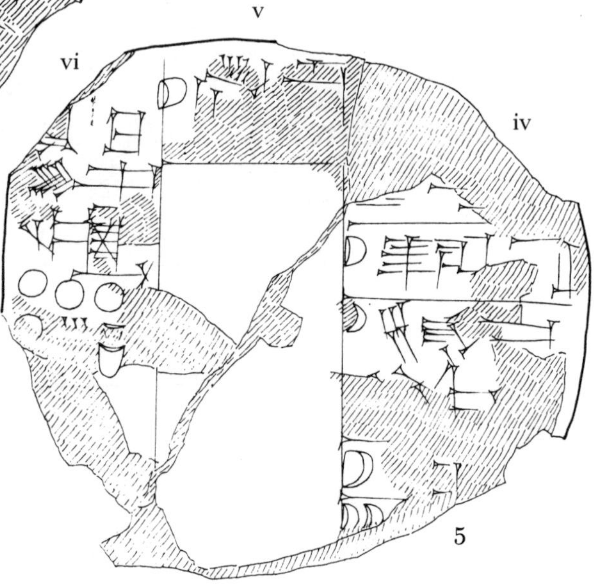

No. 9

Obverse

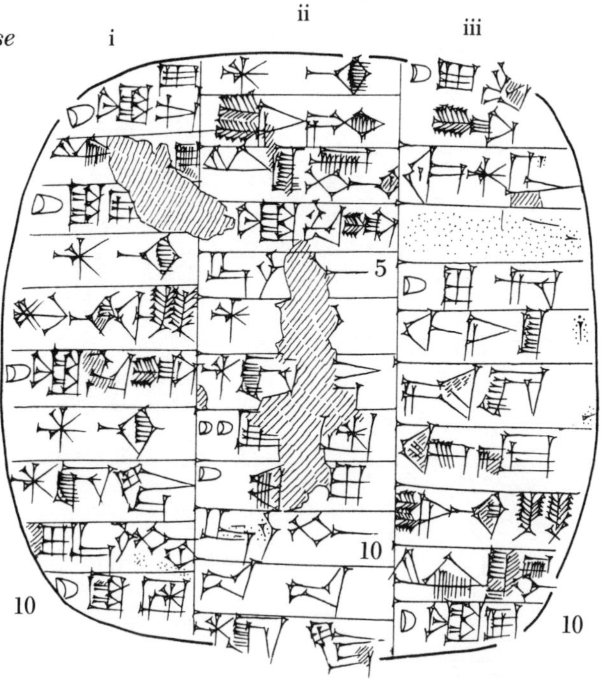

Reverse

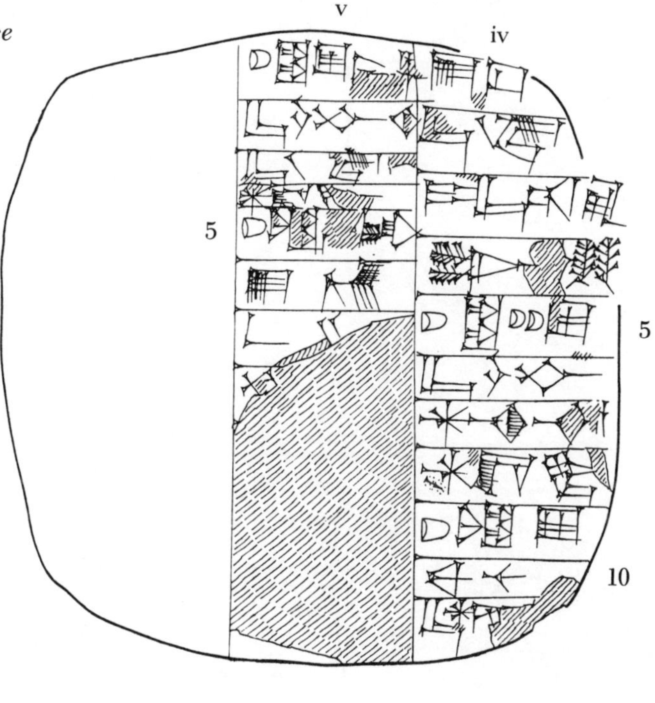

No. 10

Obverse

5

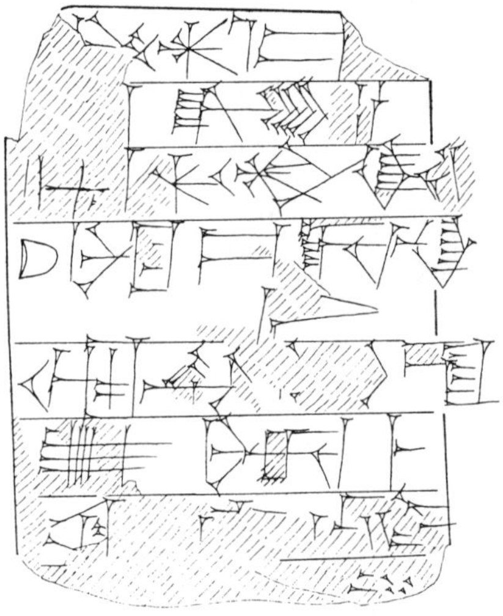

Reverse

5′

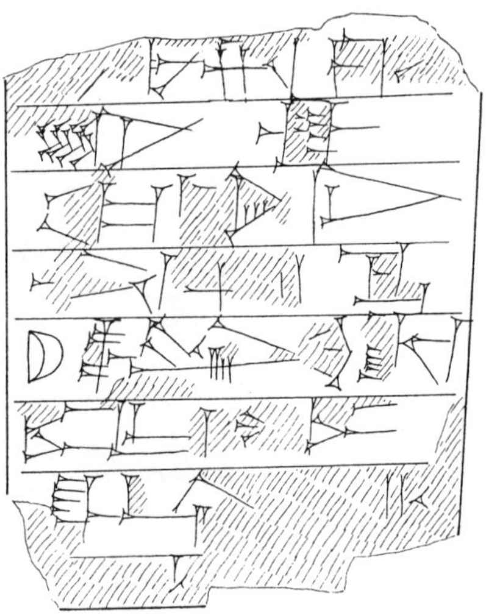

No. 11

Obverse

4

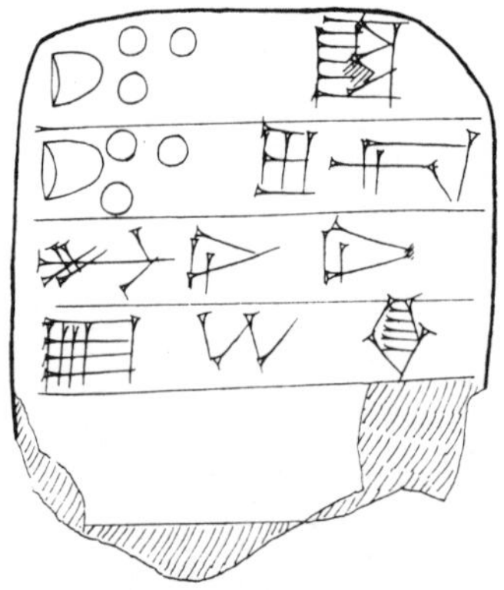

Reverse

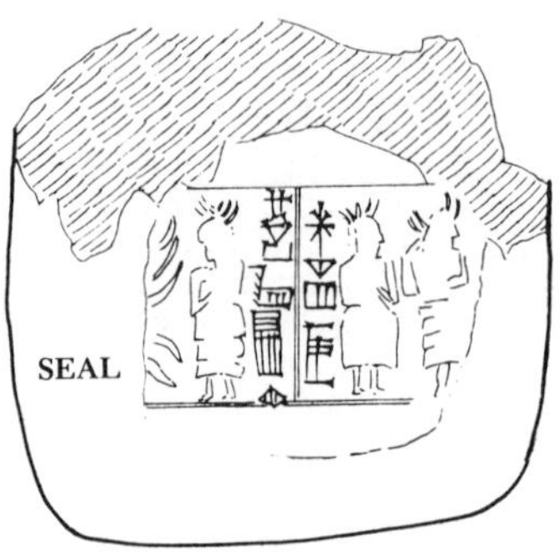

No. 12

Obverse

i ii

4

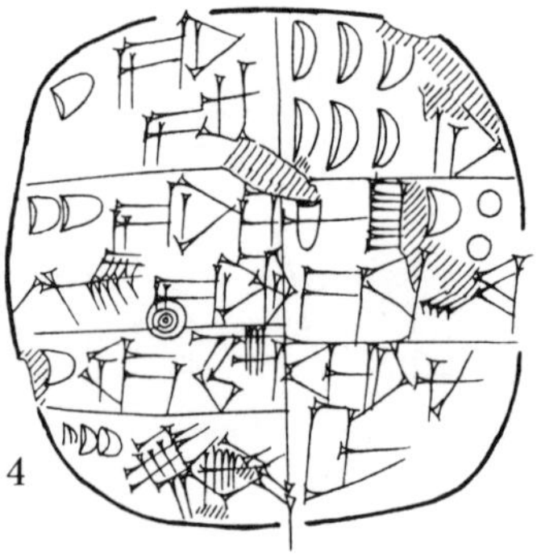

Reverse

iv iii

4

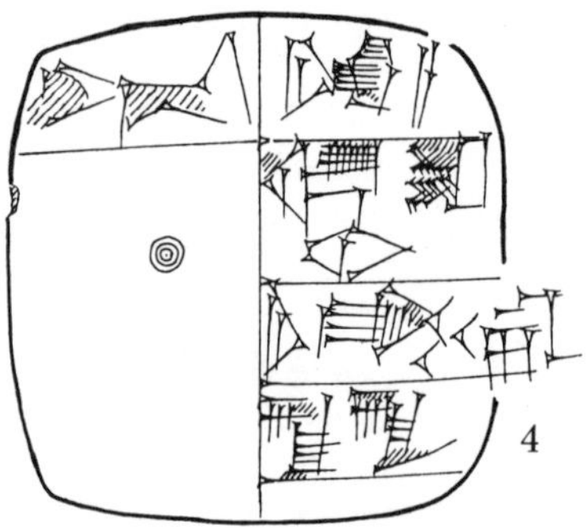

No. 13

Obverse

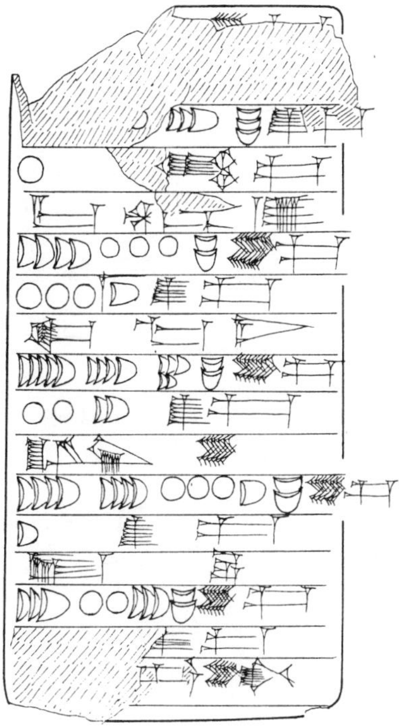

Reverse

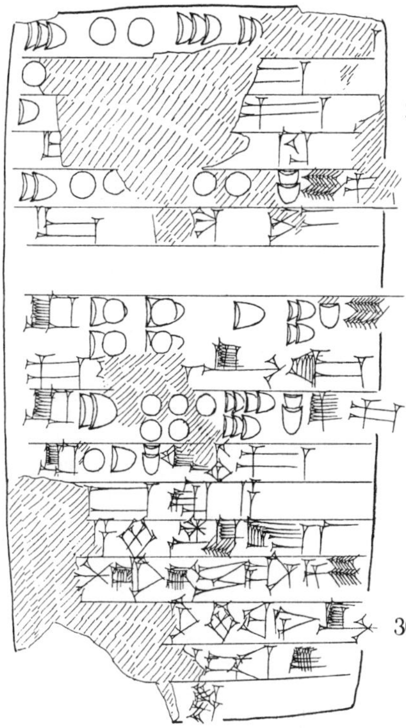

No. 14

Obverse

No. 15

Obverse

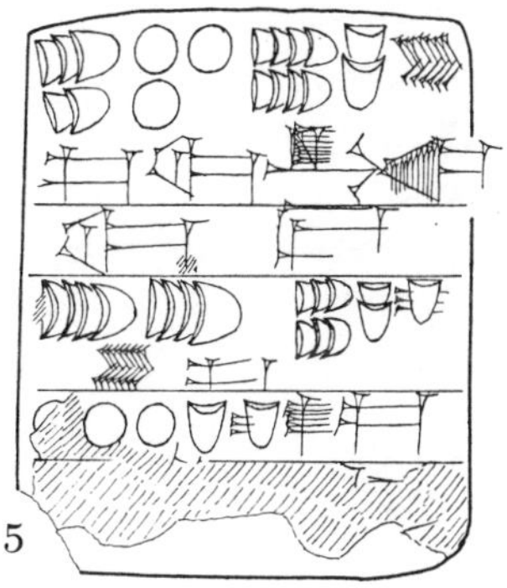

Reverse

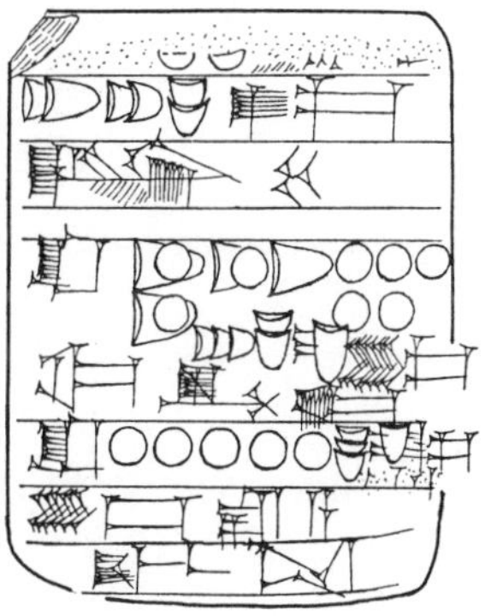

No. 16

Obverse

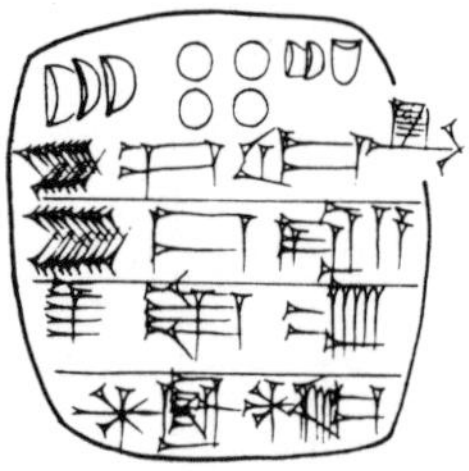

No. 17

Obverse

Reverse

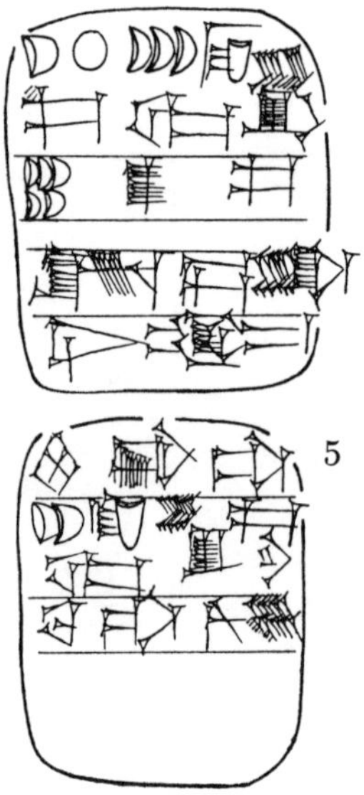

No. 18

Obverse

Reverse

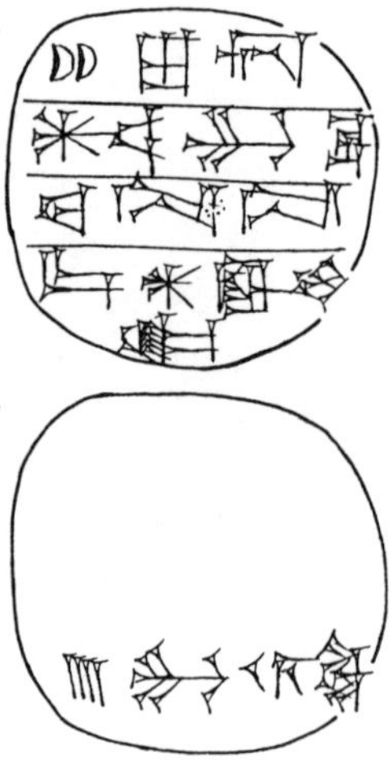

No. 19

Obverse

Reverse

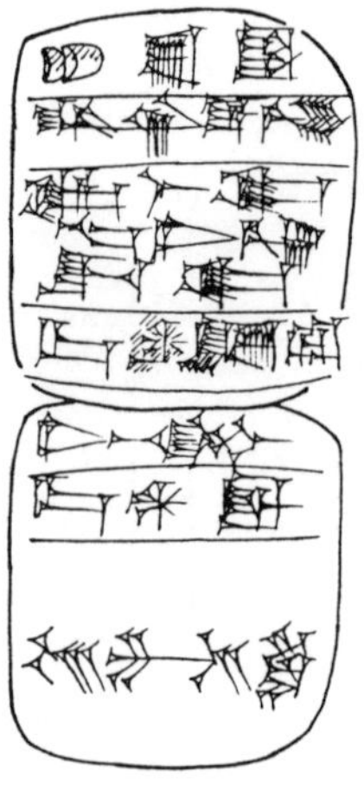

No. 20

Obverse

Reverse

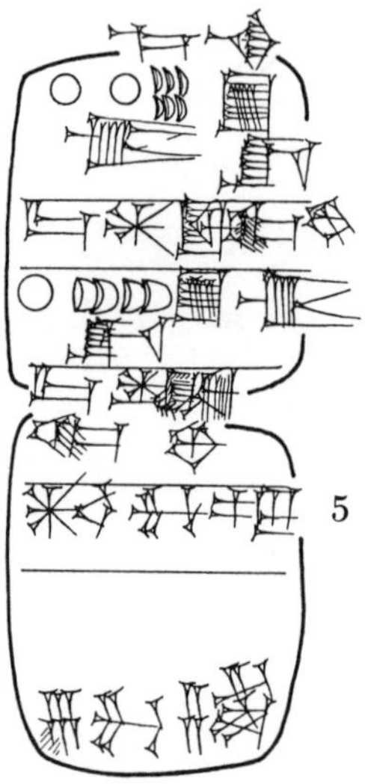

No. 21

Obverse

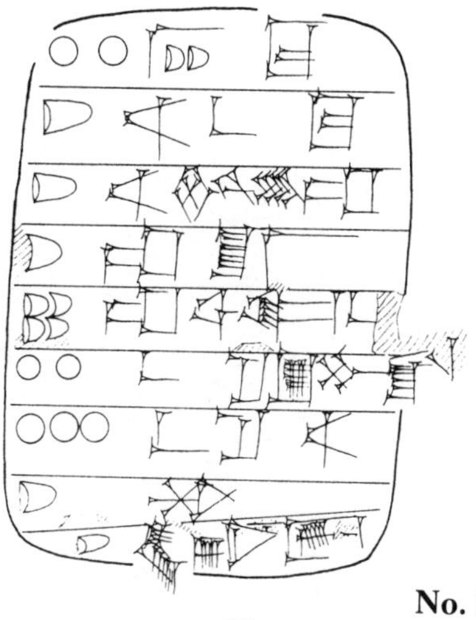

Reverse

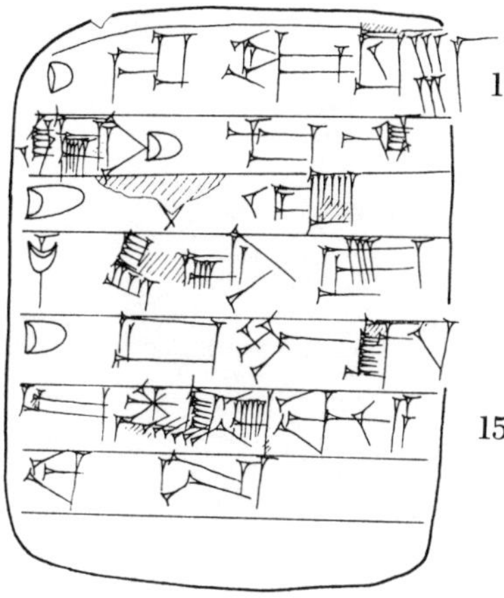

No. 22

Obverse

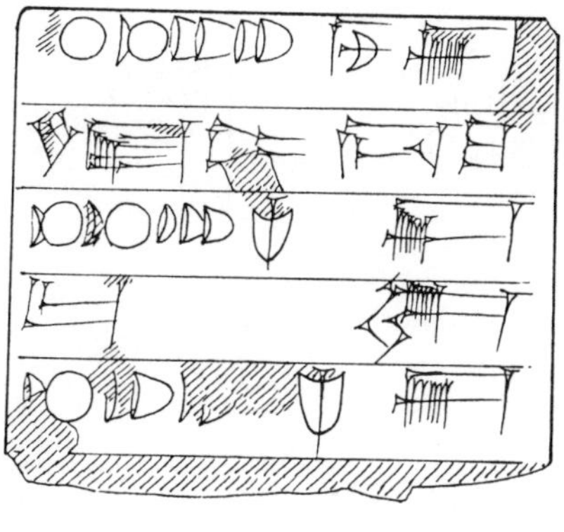

No. 23

Obverse

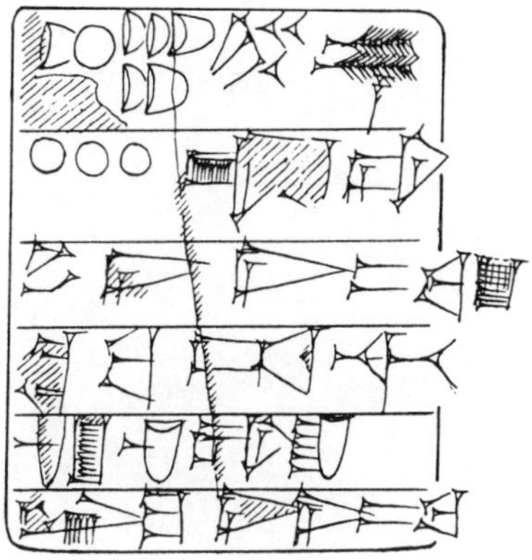

Reverse

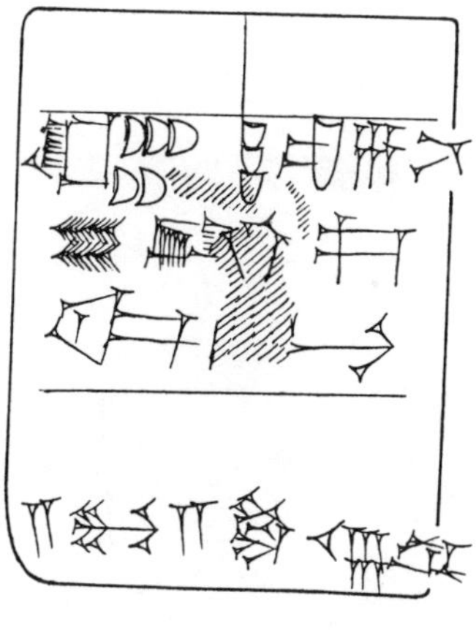

Plate 12

No. 24

Obverse

Left Edge

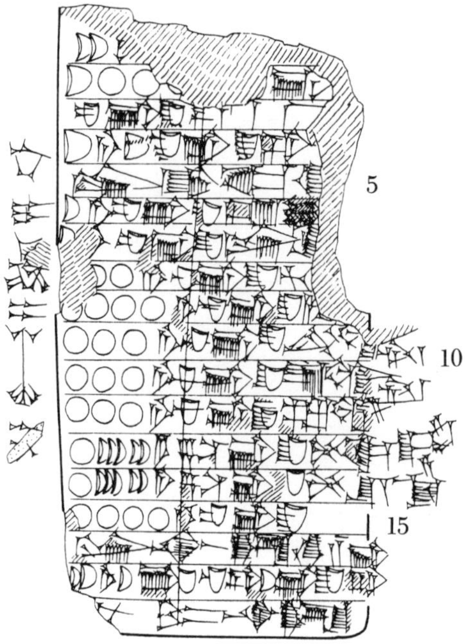

Reverse

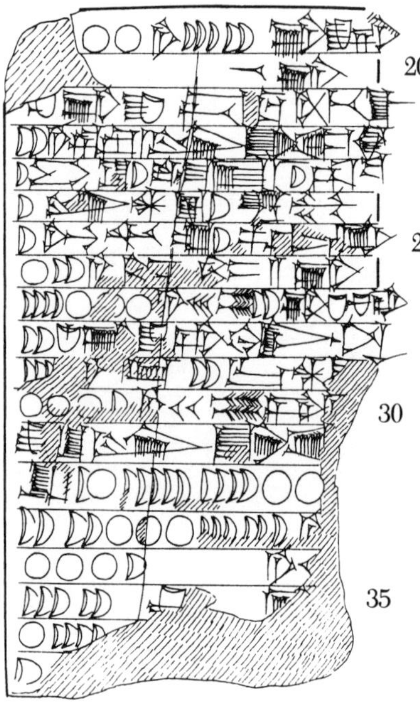

No. 25

Obverse

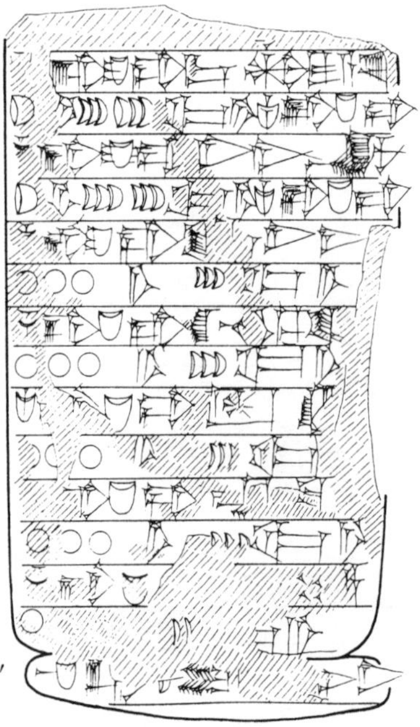

Lower Edge

Reverse

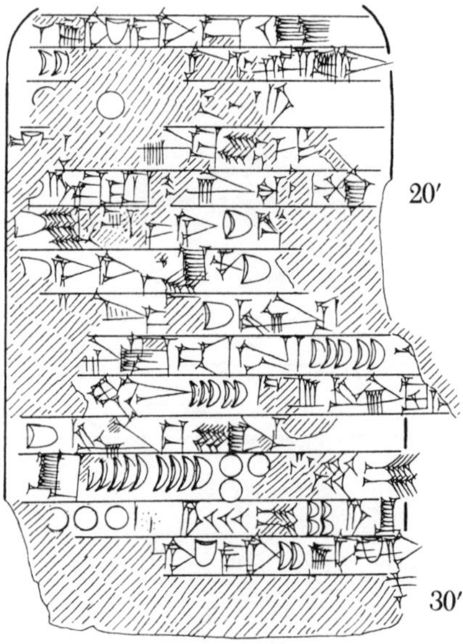

No. 26

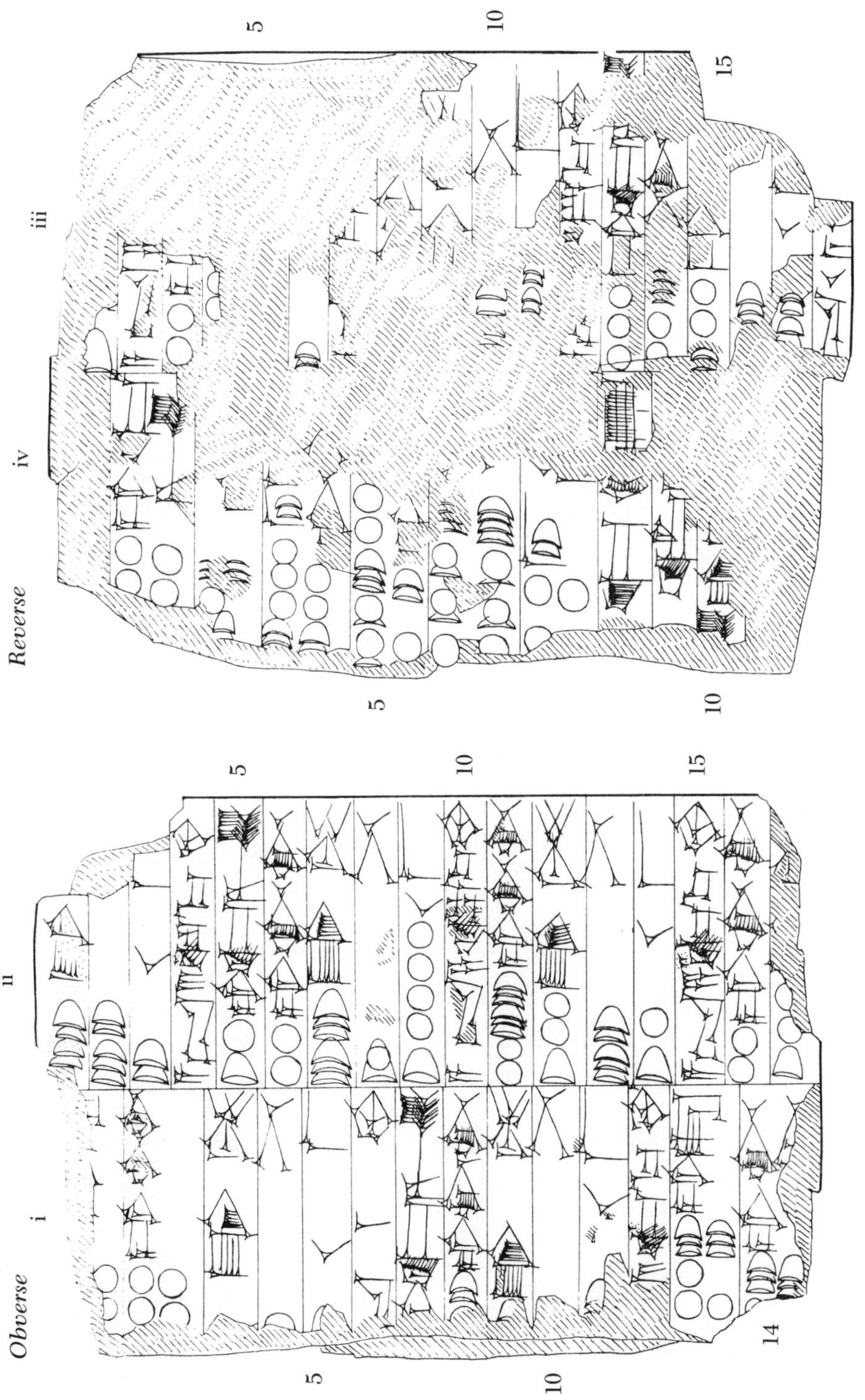

No. 27

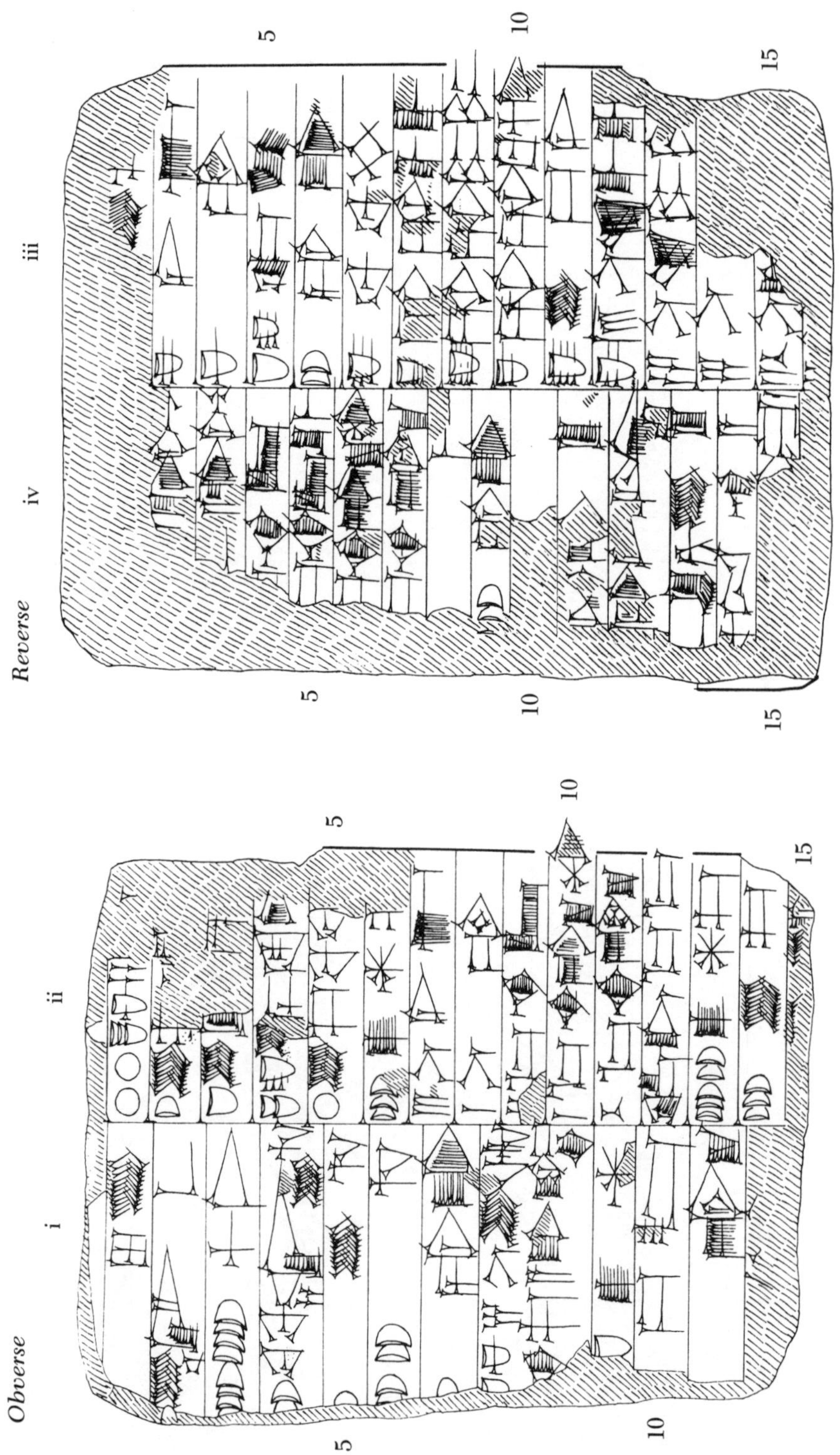

No. 28

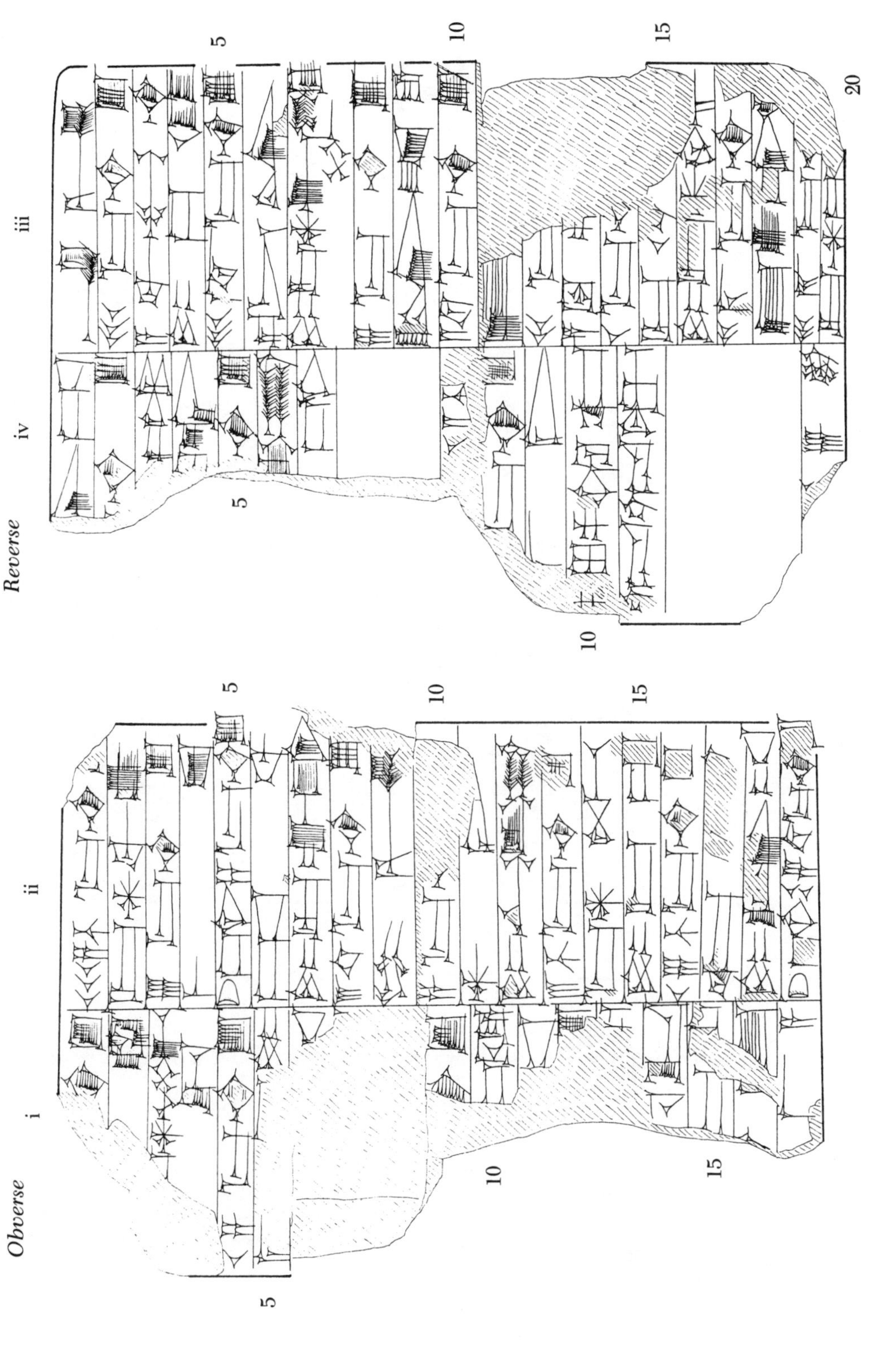

No. 29

Obverse

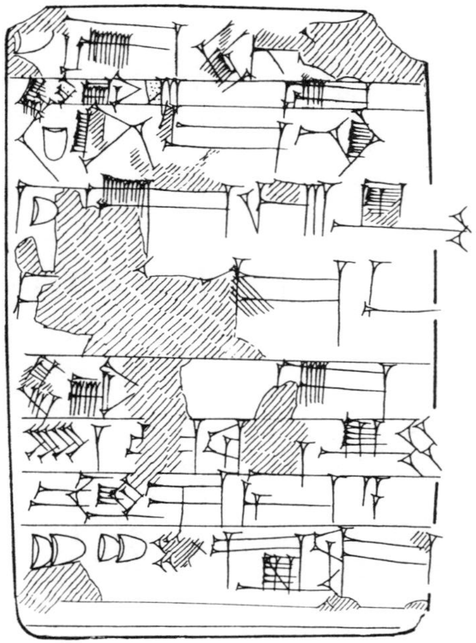

Reverse

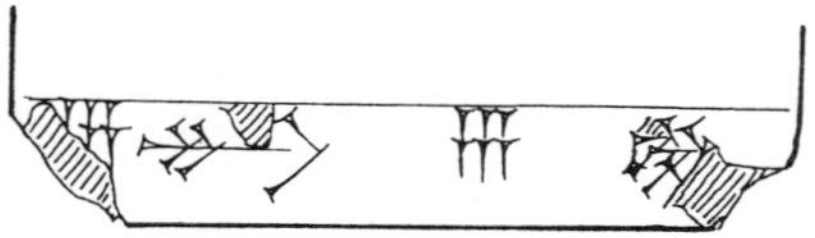

No. 30

Obverse

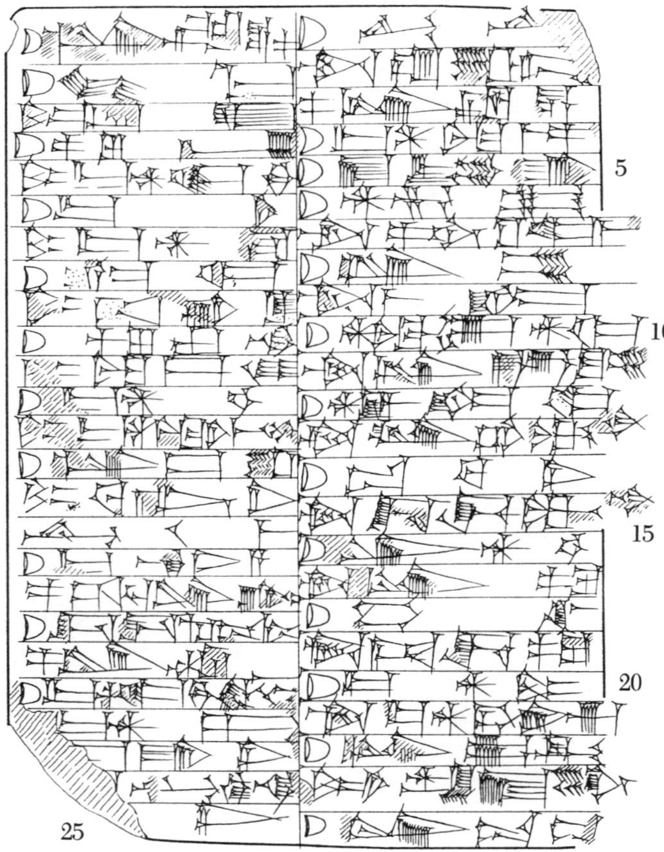

Reverse

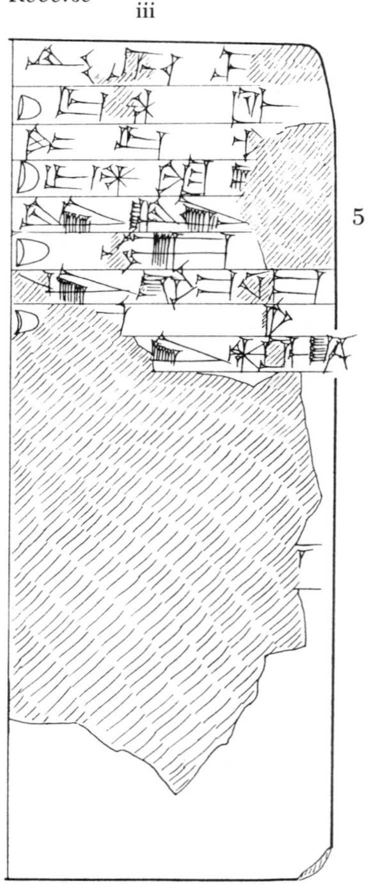

No. 31

Obverse

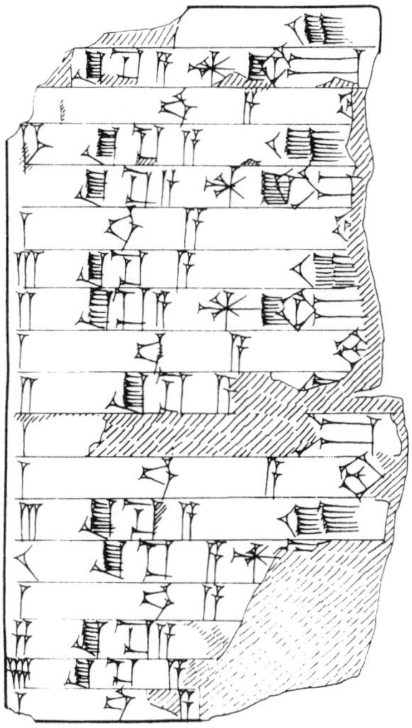

Reverse

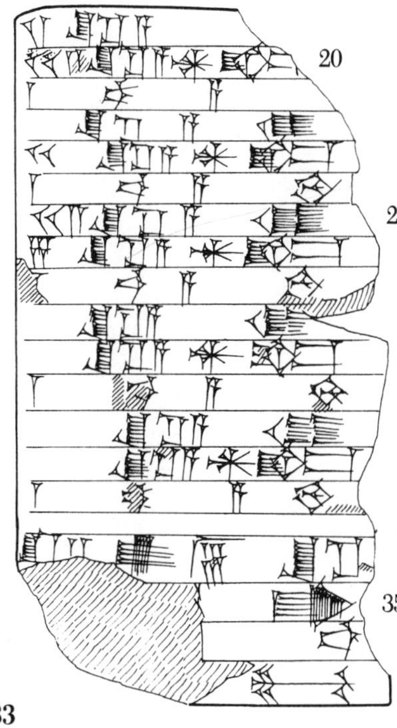

No. 33

Obverse

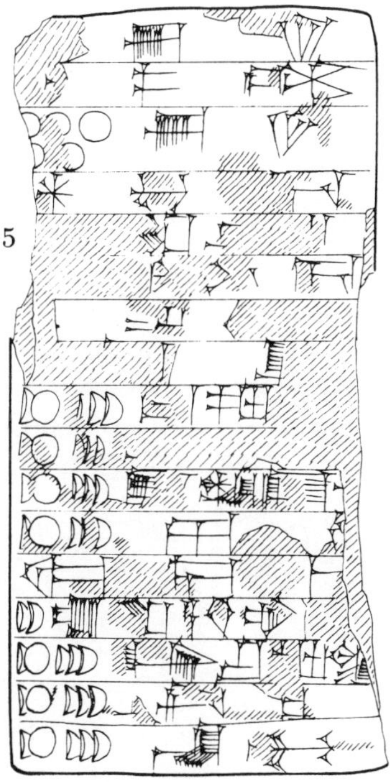

Reverse

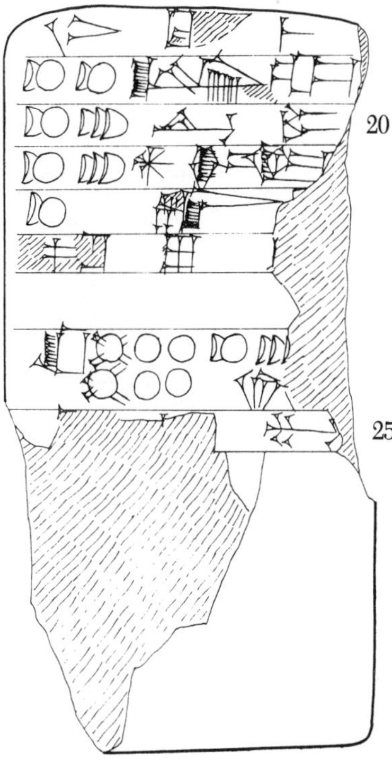

No. 35

Obverse

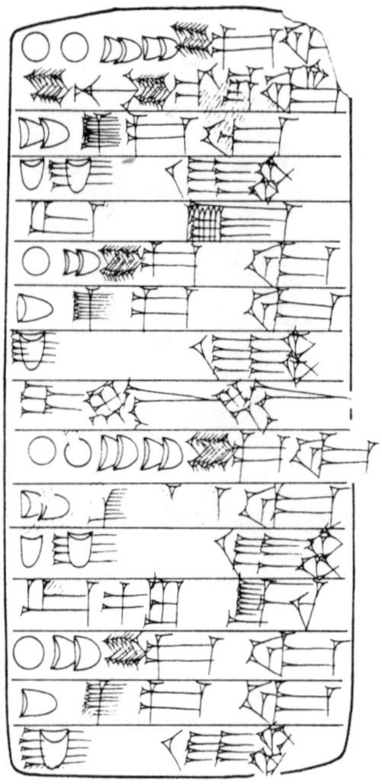

Reverse

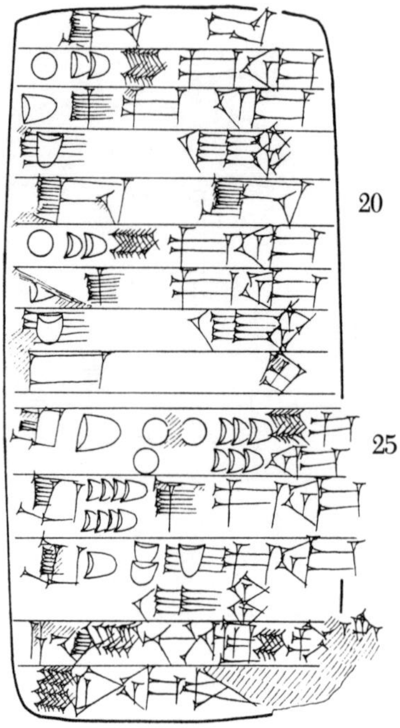

No. 36

Obverse

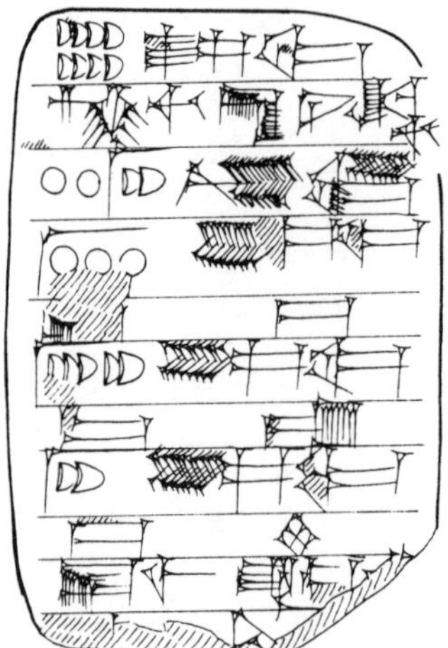

Reverse

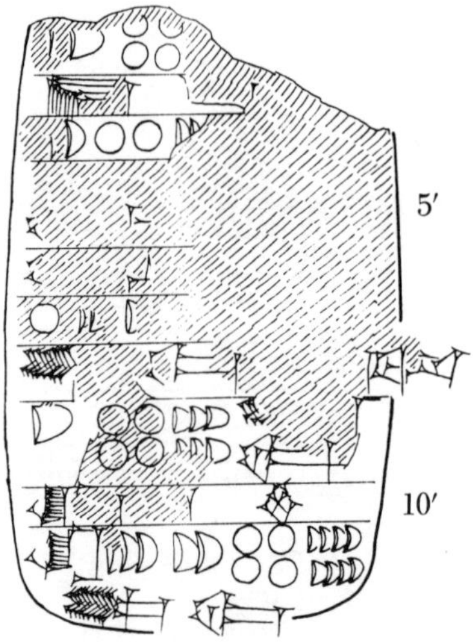

No. 37

Obverse

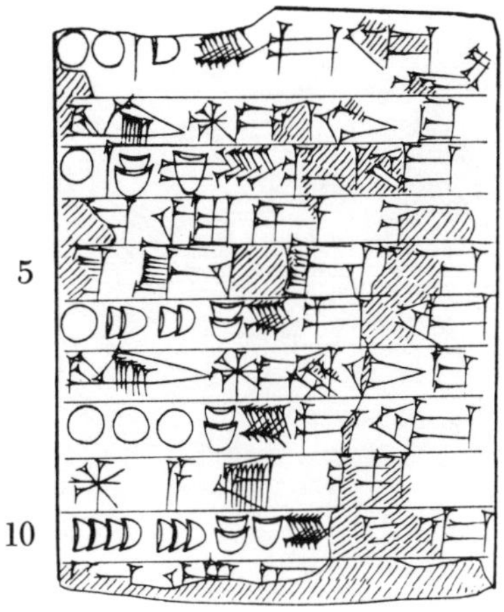

Reverse

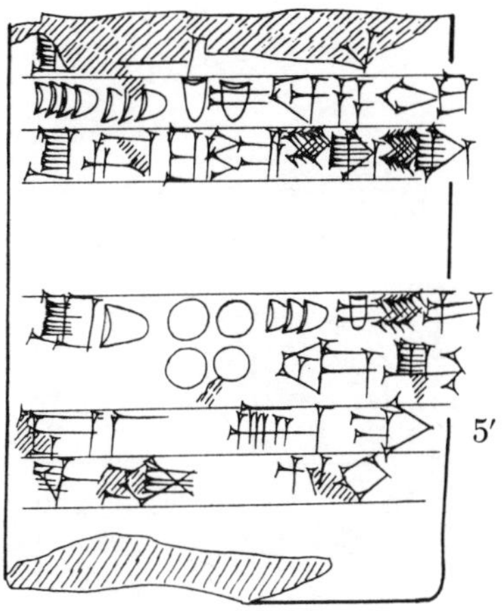

No. 38

Obverse

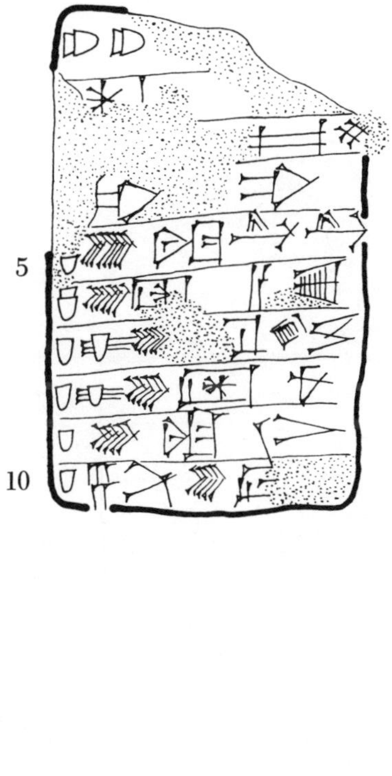

Reverse

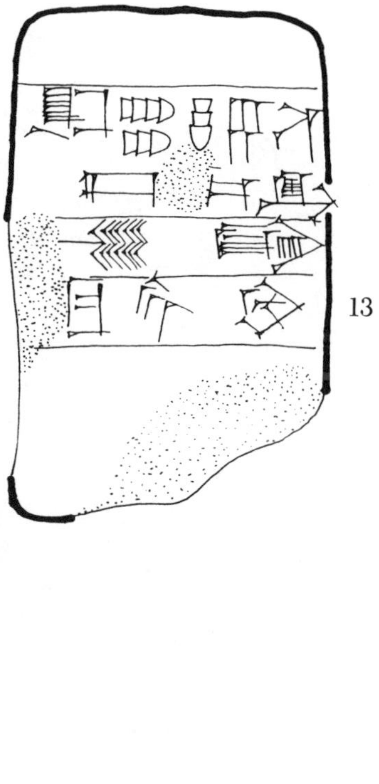

Plate 20

No. 40

Obverse

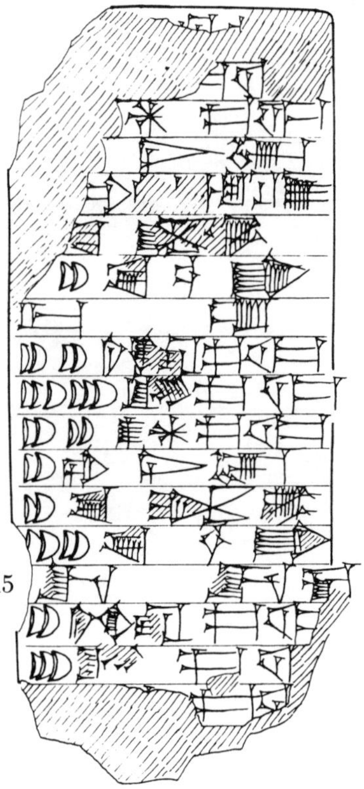

Reverse

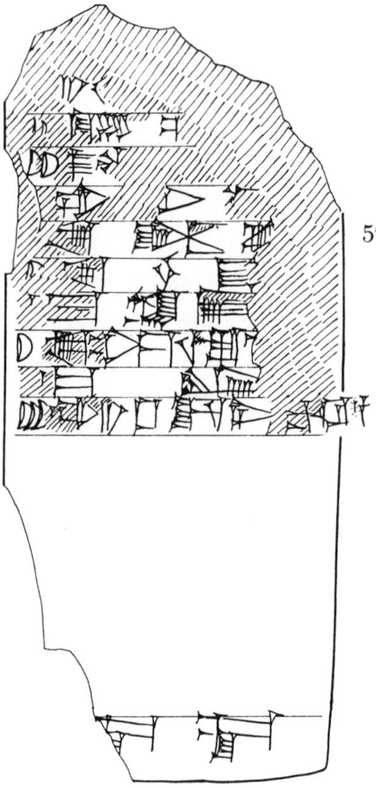

No. 41

Obverse

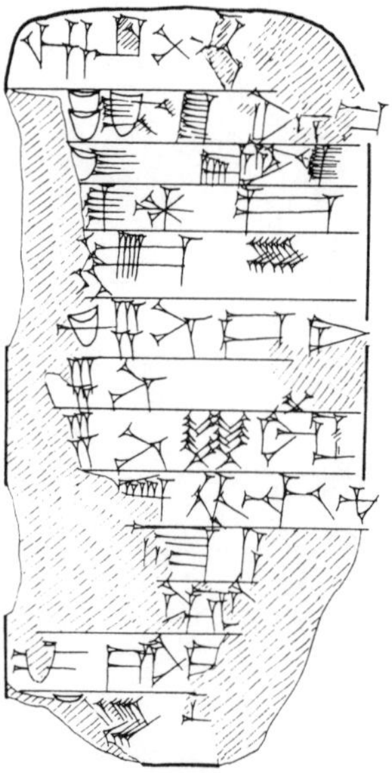

Reverse

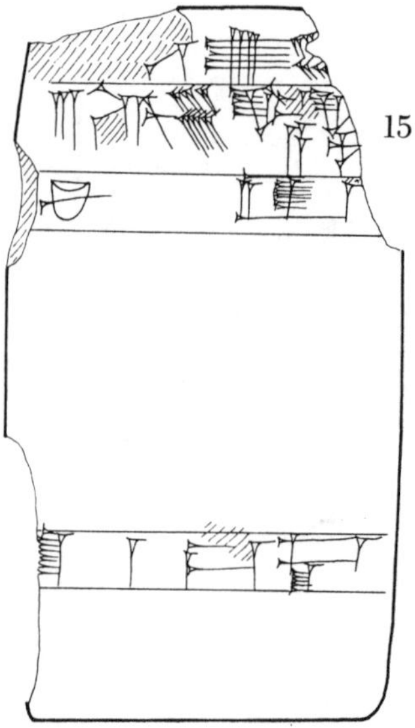

No. 42

Obverse

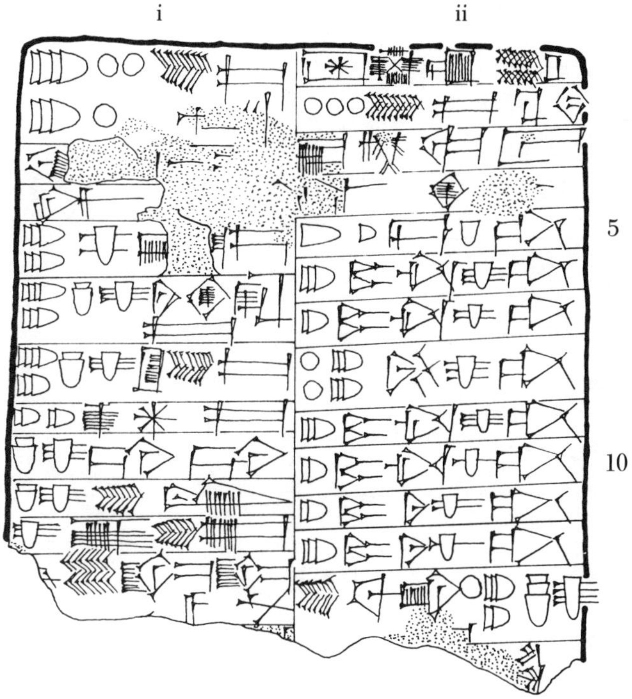

No. 43

Obverse

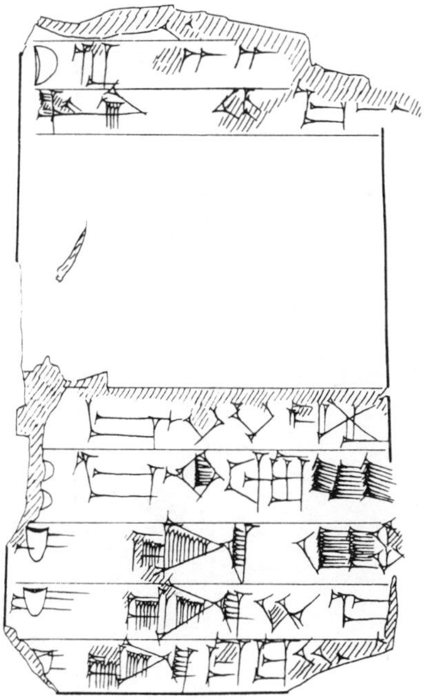

Reverse

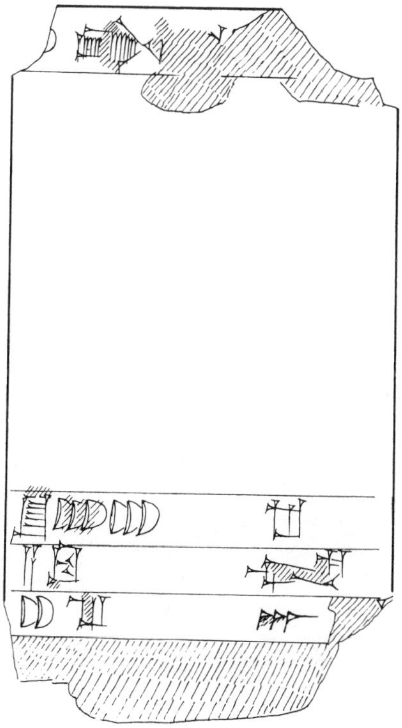

Plate 22

No. 44

Obverse

i ii

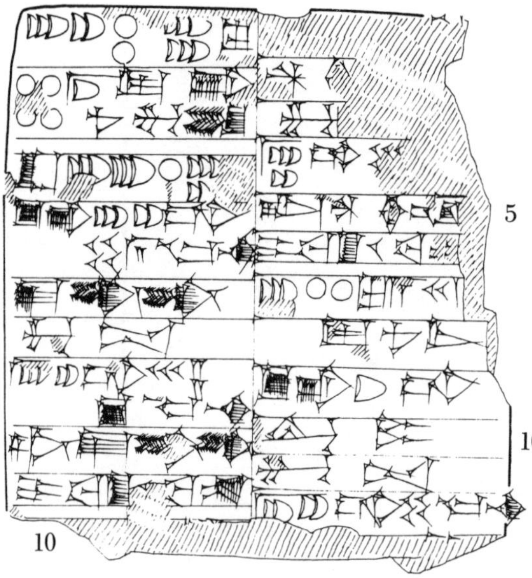

Reverse

iii

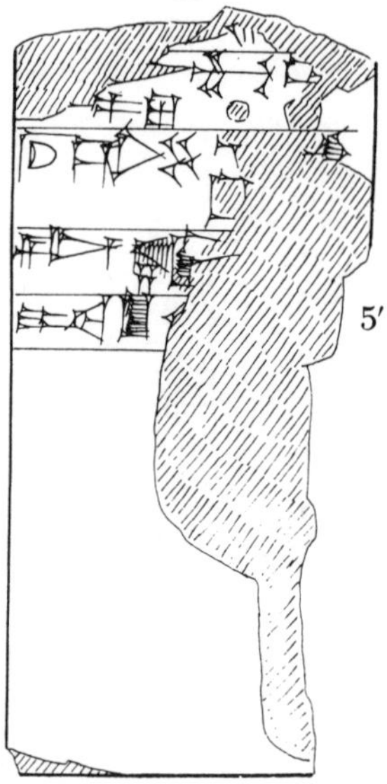

No. 45

Obverse

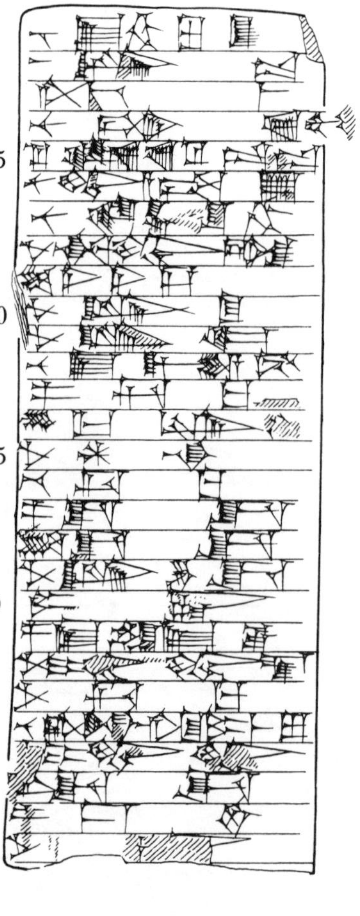

Reverse

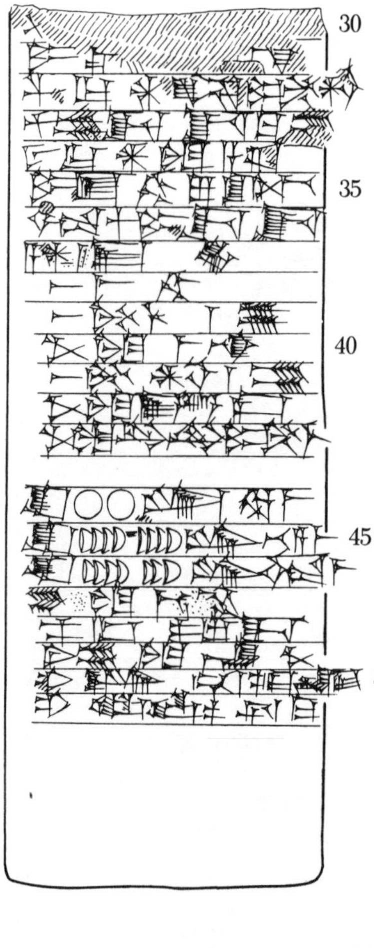

No. 46

Obverse *Reverse*

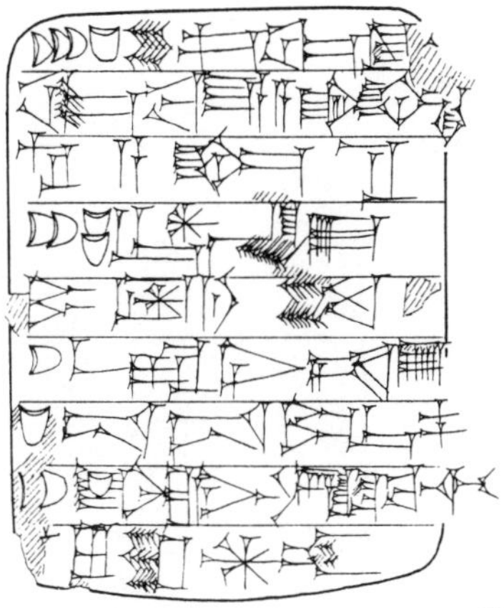

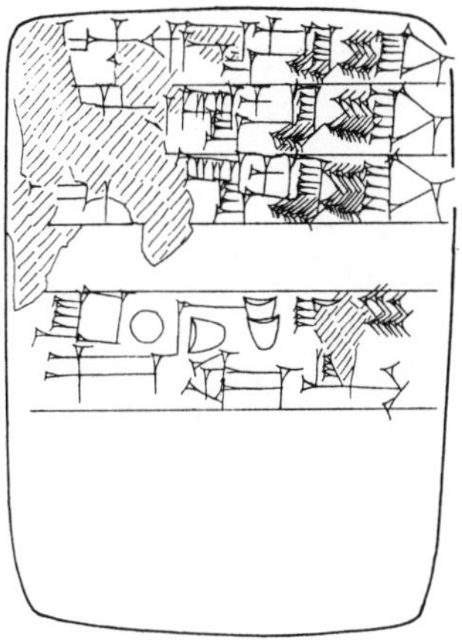

No. 47

Obverse *Reverse*

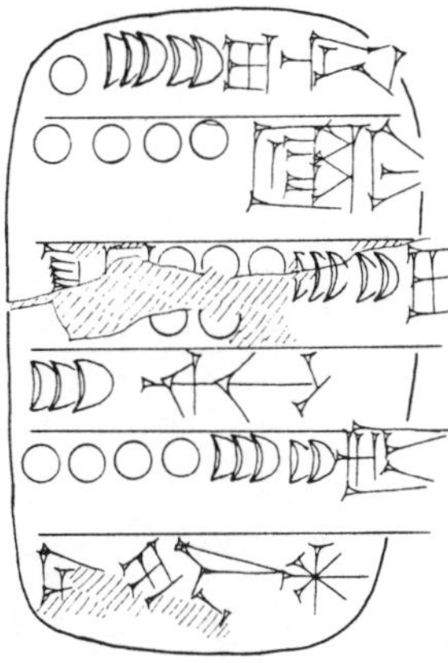

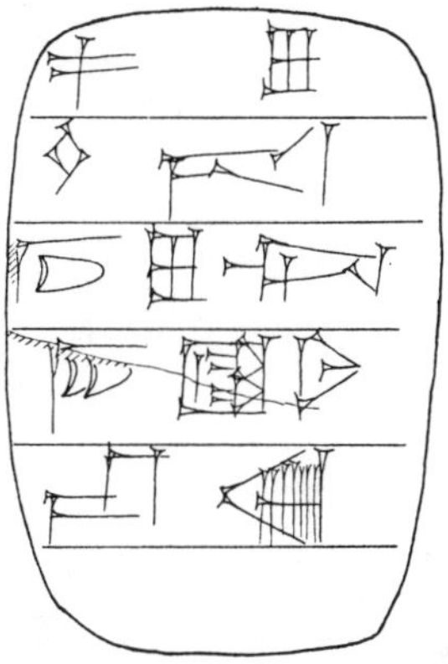

No. 48

Obverse *Reverse*

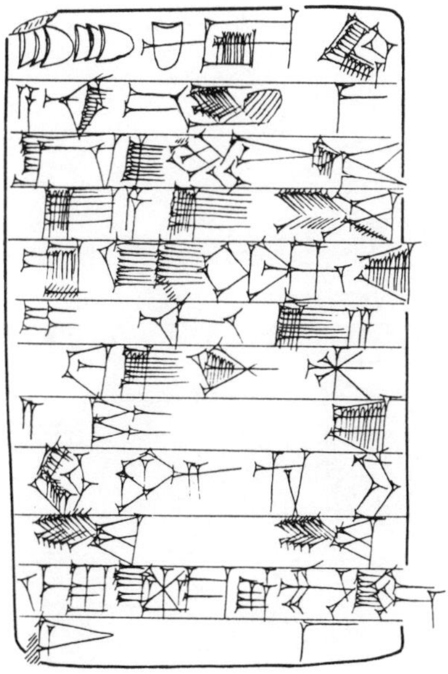

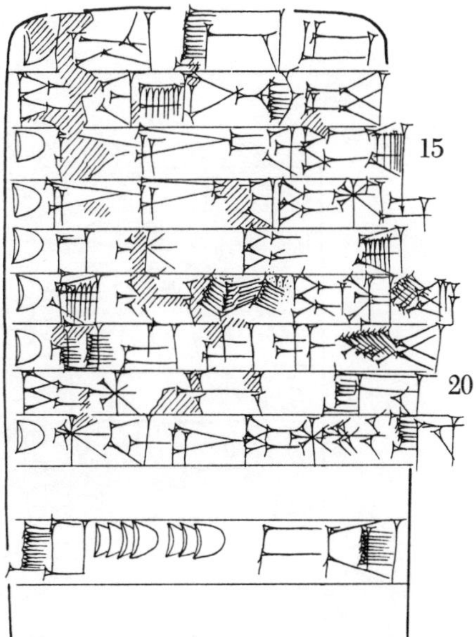

No. 49

Obverse

Reverse

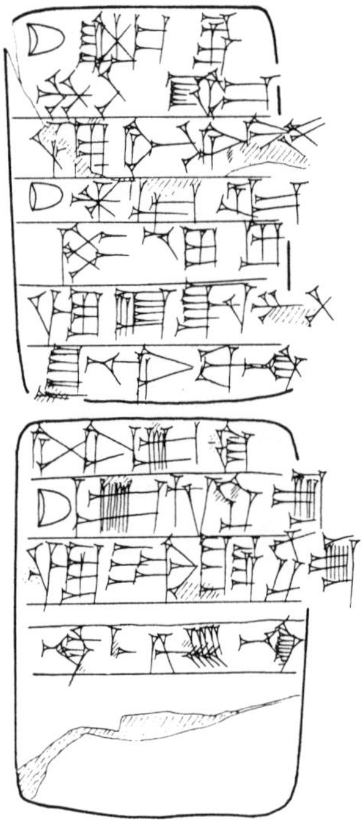

No. 50

Obverse

Lower Edge

Reverse

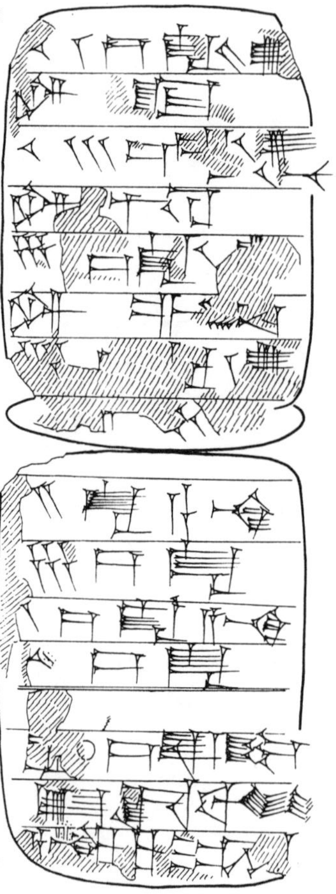

No. 51

Obverse

i ii

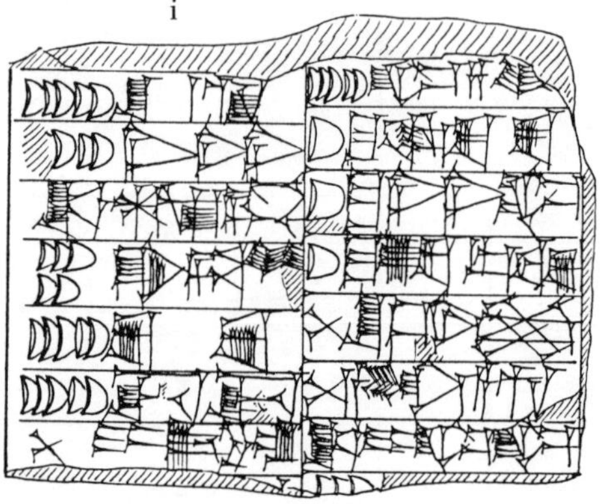

No. 52

Obverse

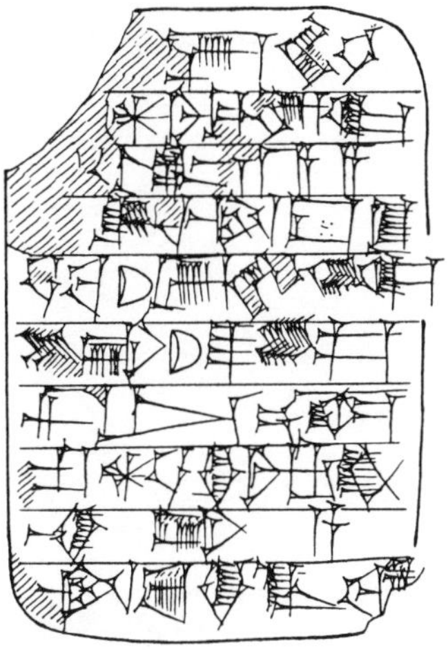

Reverse

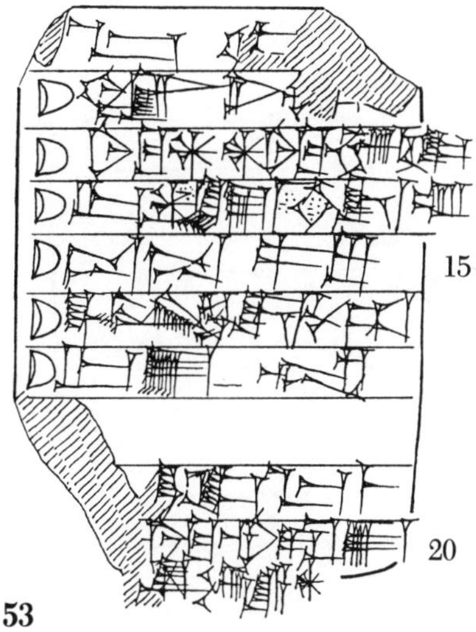

No. 53

Obverse

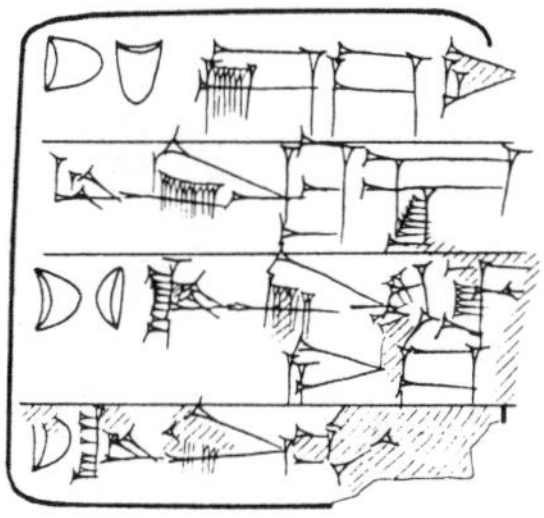

Reverse

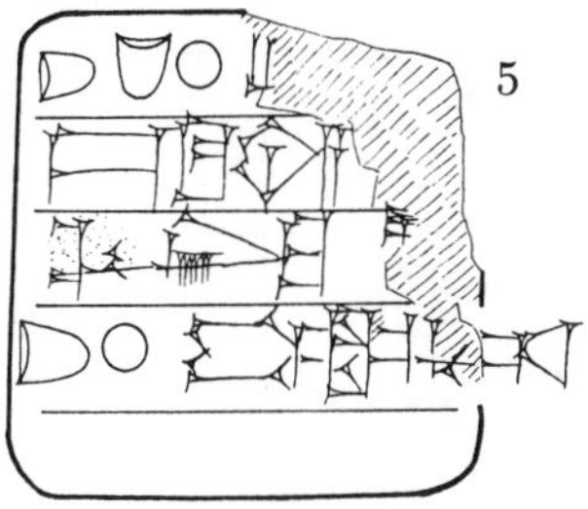

No. 54

Obverse

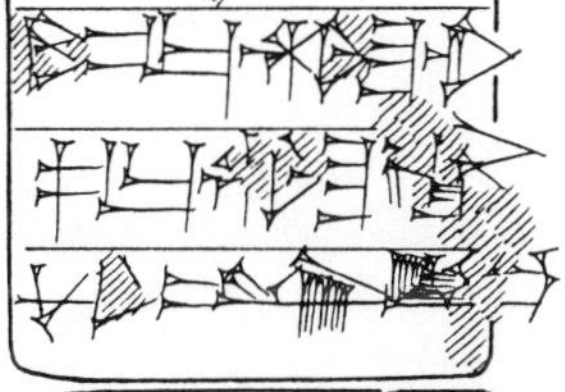

Reverse

No. 55

Obverse

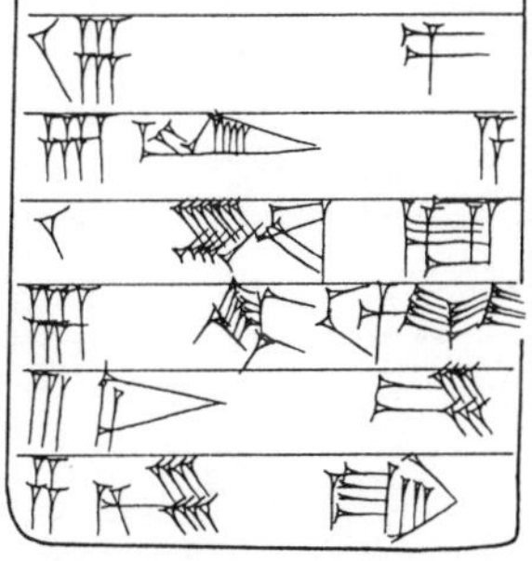

Reverse

No. 56

Obverse

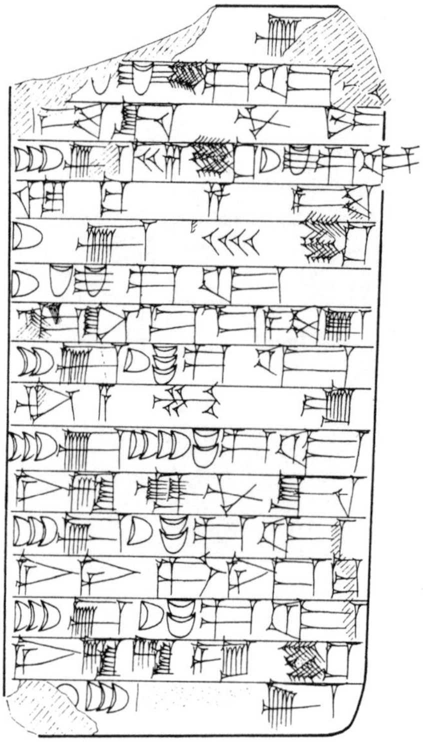

Reverse

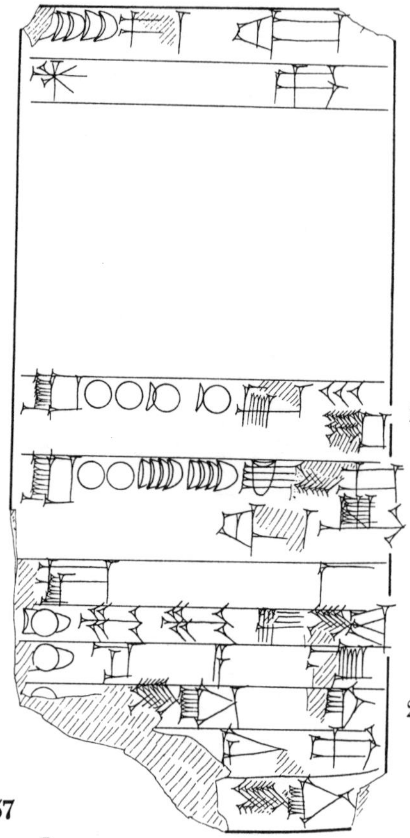

No. 57

Obverse

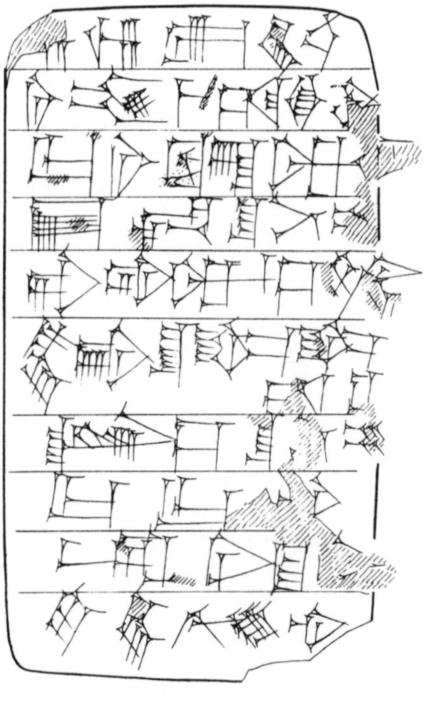

Reverse

No. 58

Obverse *Reverse*

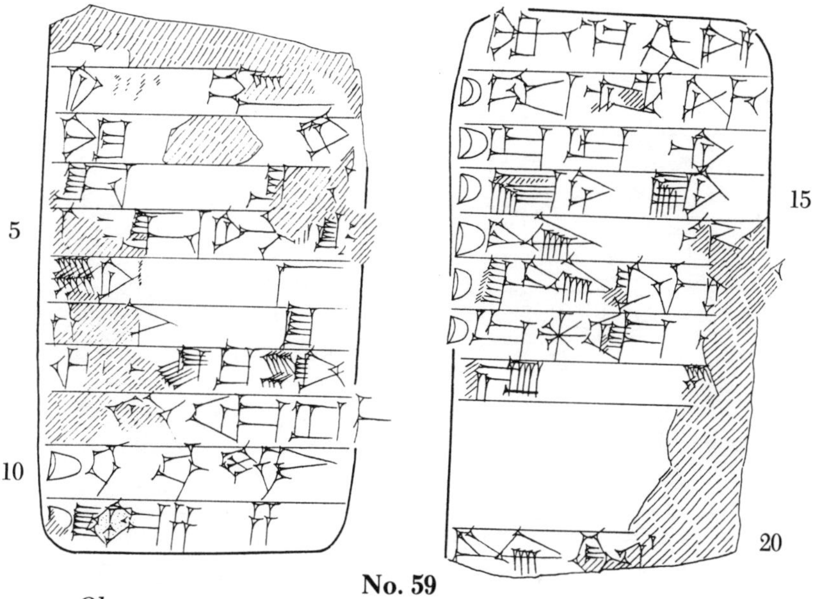

No. 59

Obverse *Reverse*

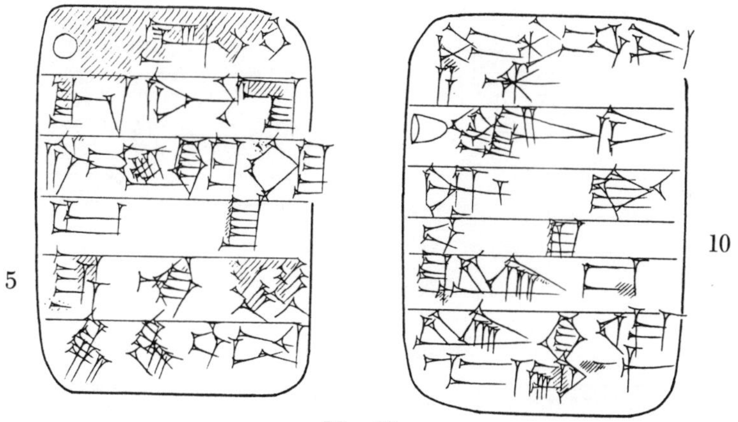

No. 60

Obverse *Reverse*

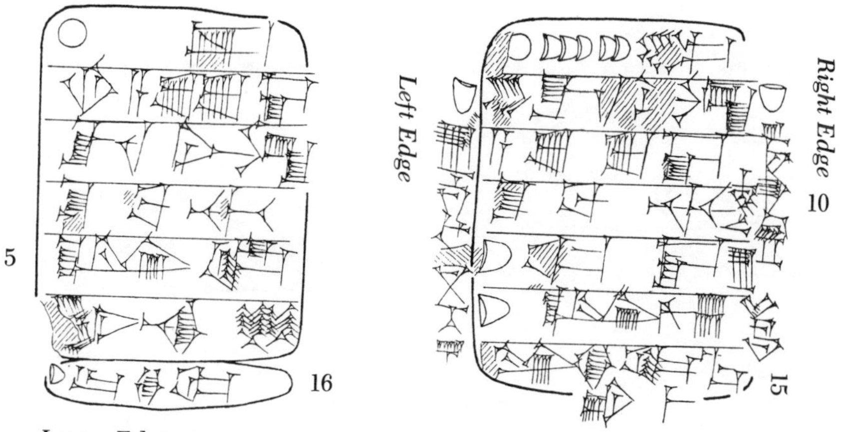

Lower Edge

No. 61

Obverse

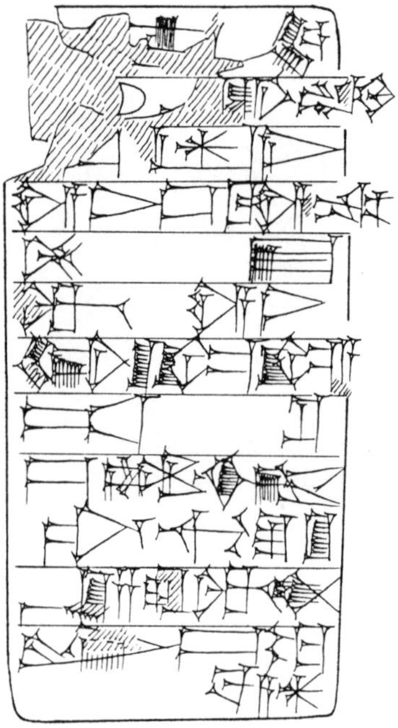

Reverse

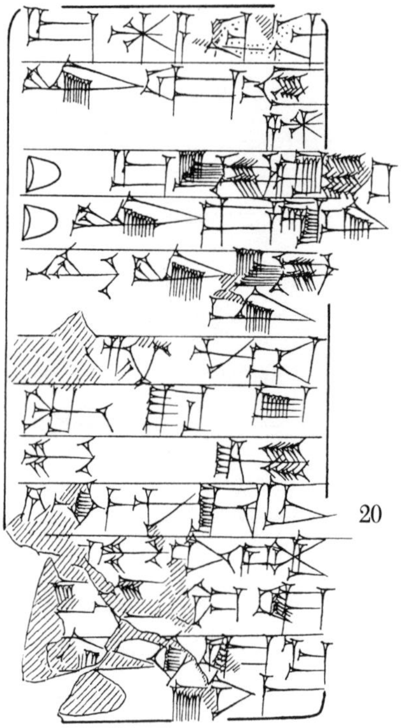

No. 63

Obverse

Reverse

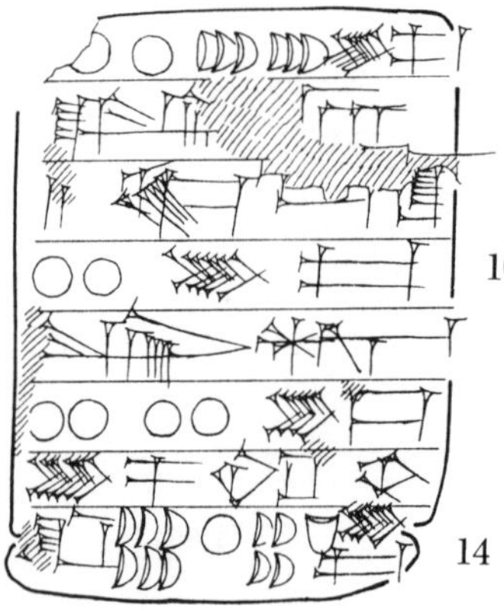

Upper Edge

No. 64

Obverse

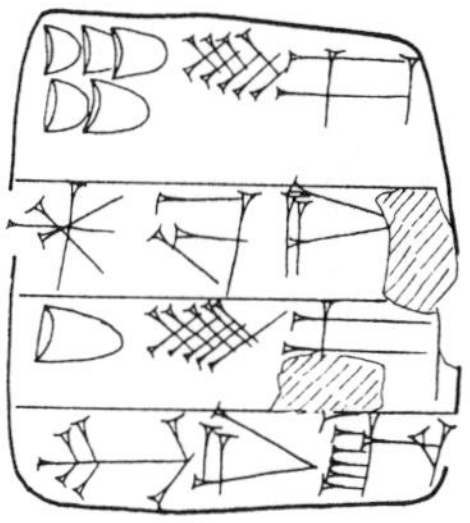

Reverse

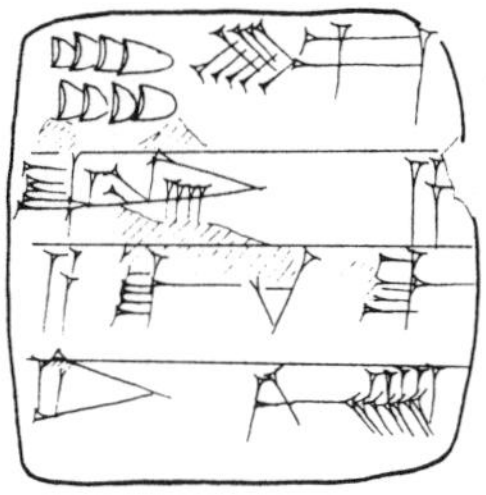

No. 65

Obverse

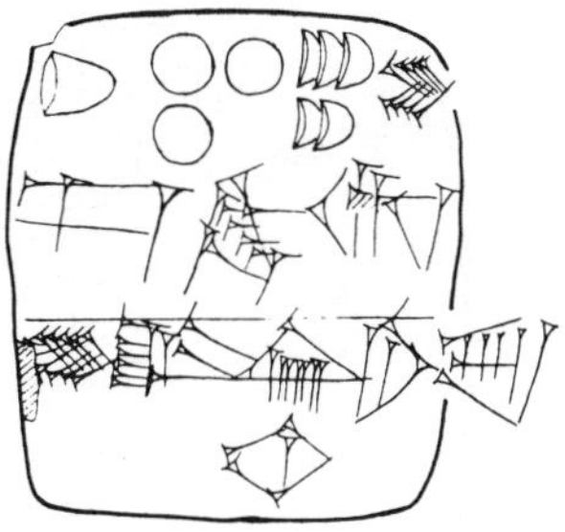

Reverse

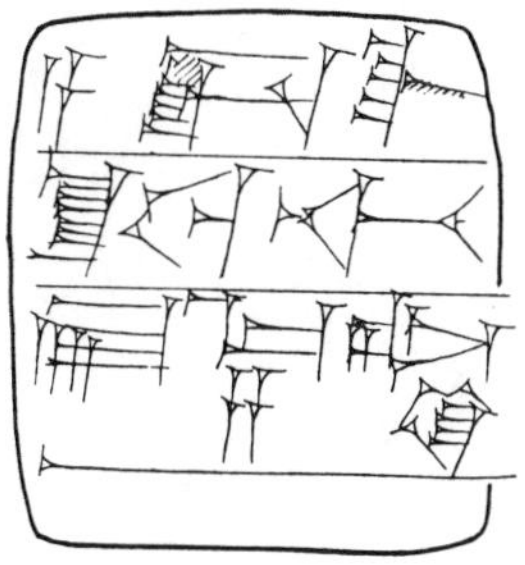

No. 66

Obverse

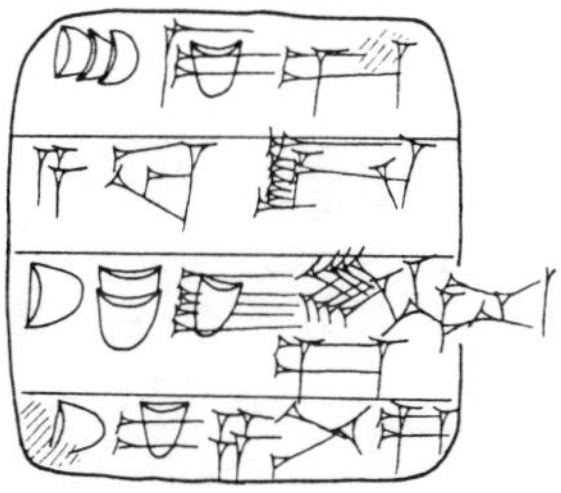

Reverse

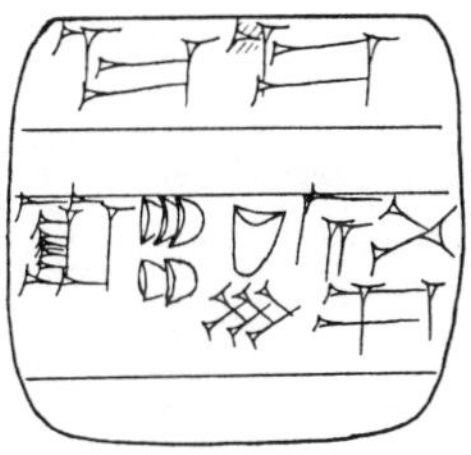

No. 67

Obverse

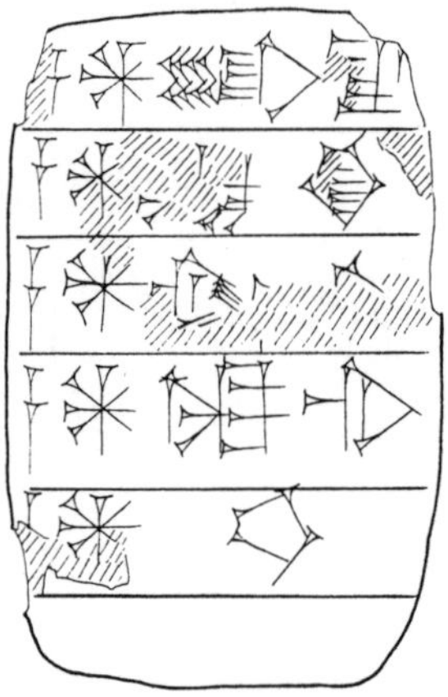

No. 68

Obverse

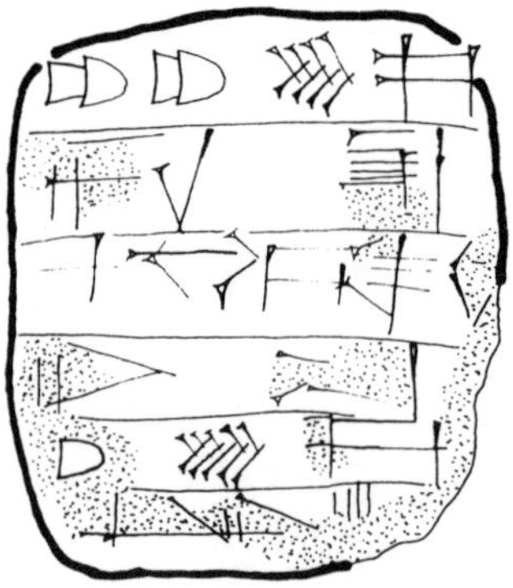

Reverse

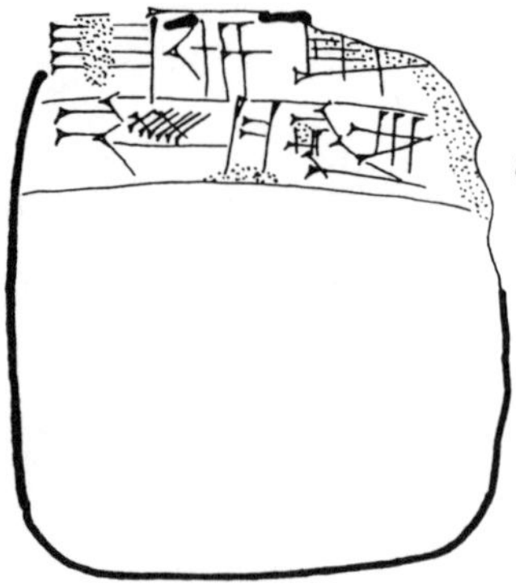

No. 69

Obverse

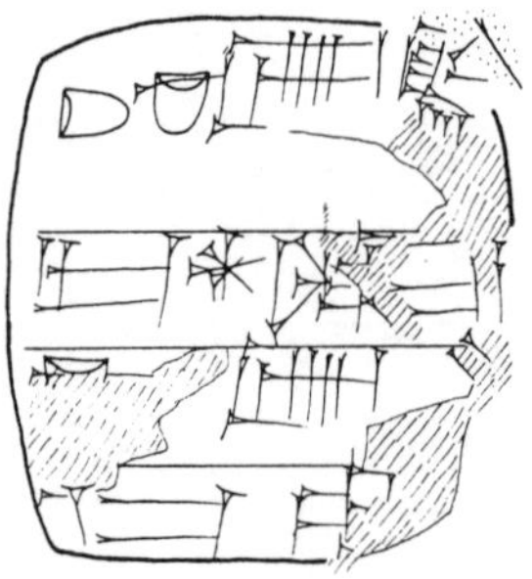

Reverse

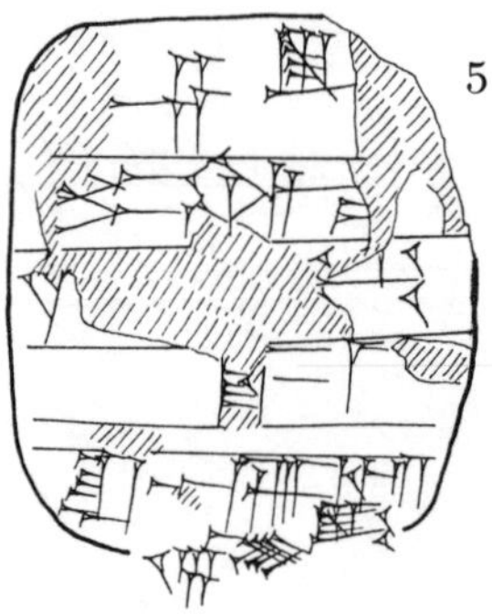

No. 70

Obverse

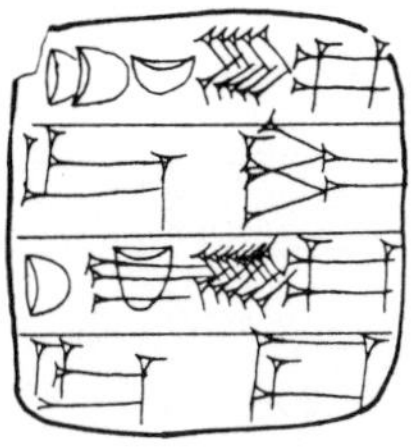

Reverse

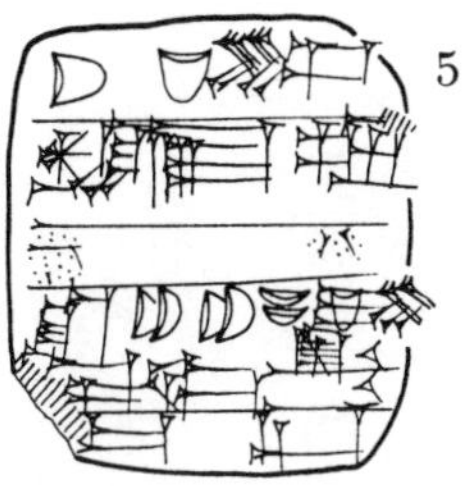

No. 71

Obverse

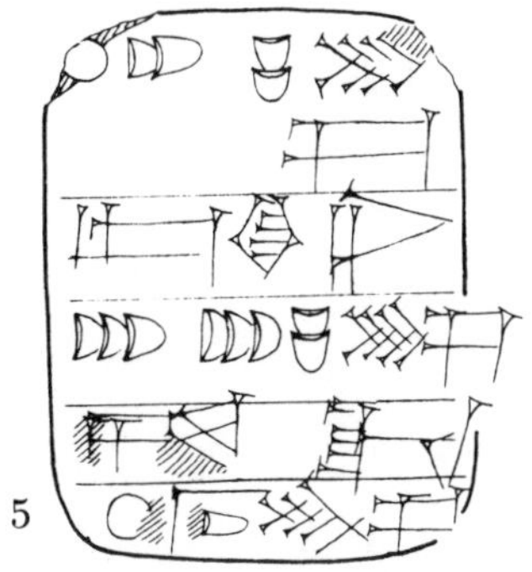

Reverse

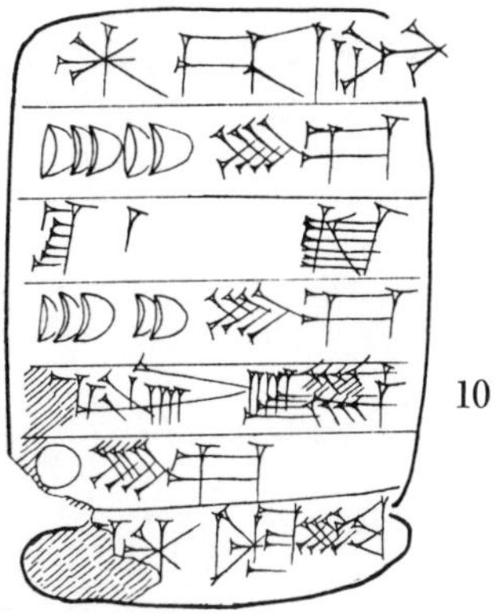

Upper Edge

No. 72

Obverse

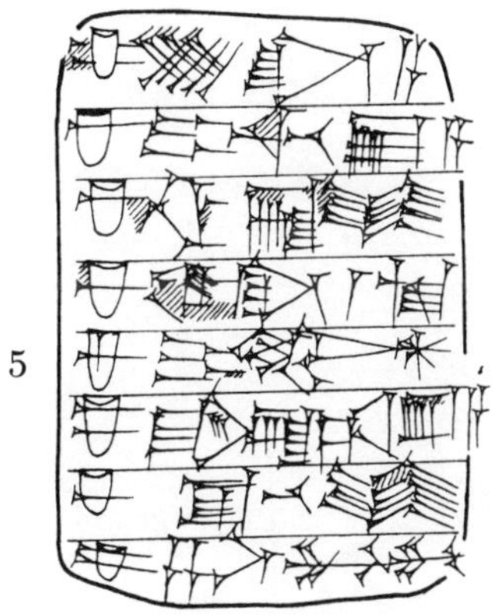

Left Edge

Reverse

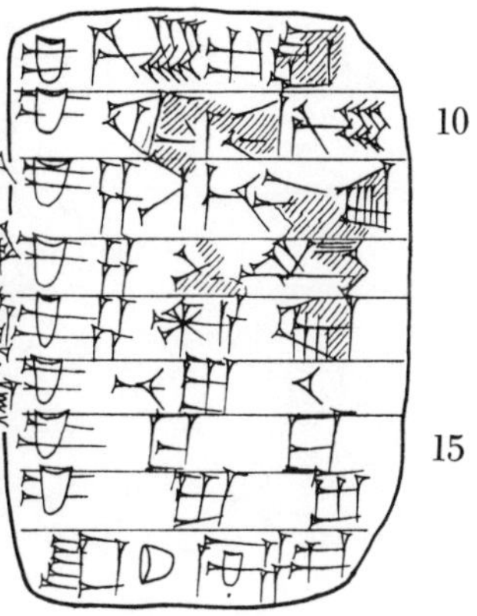

Plate 32

No. 73

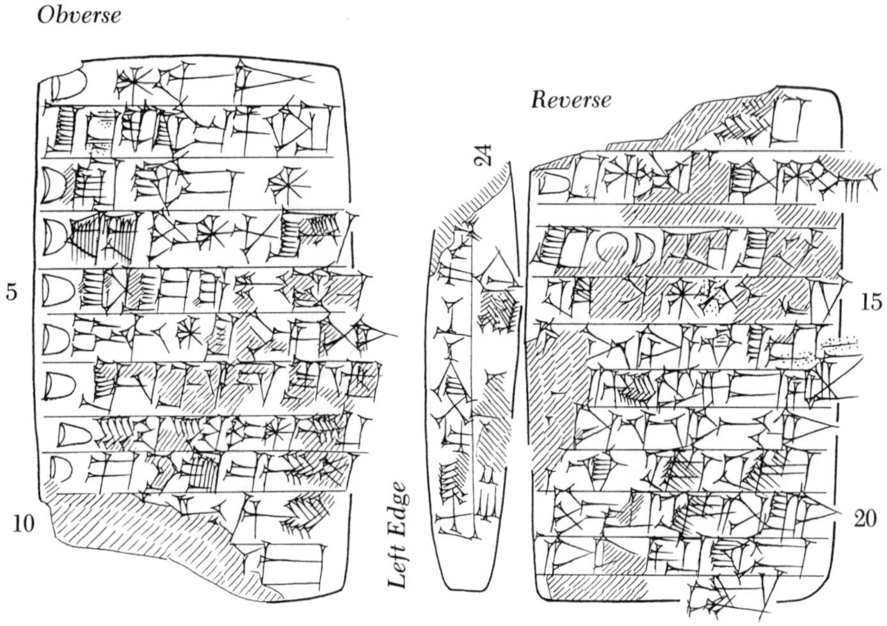

No. 74

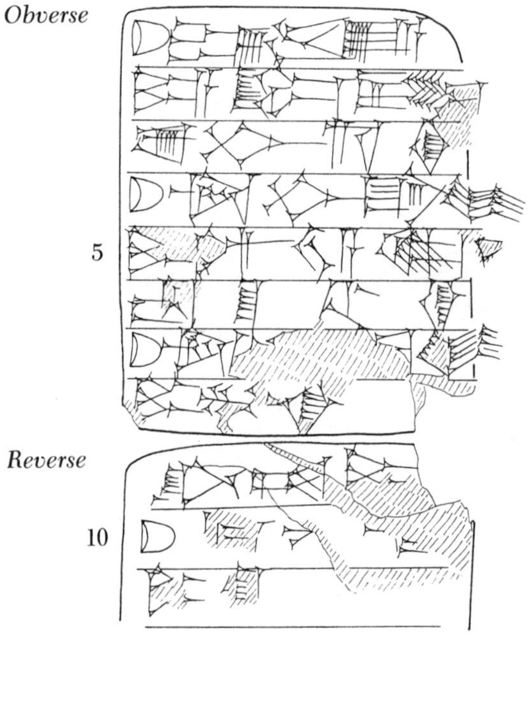